"I'm Not Gonna Die in This Damn Place"

"I'm Not Gonna Die in This Damn Place"

**MANLINESS, IDENTITY, AND SURVIVAL OF THE
MEXICAN AMERICAN VIETNAM PRISONERS OF WAR**

Juan David Coronado

Michigan State University Press • East Lansing

♾ The paper used in this publication meets the minimum requirements
of ANSI/NISO Z39.48–1992 (R 1997) (Permanence of Paper).

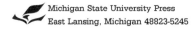 Michigan State University Press
East Lansing, Michigan 48823-5245

Printed and bound in the United States of America.

27 26 25 24 23 22 21 20 19 18   1 2 3 4 5 6 7 8 9 10

LIBRARY OF CONGRESS CATALOGING-IN-PUBLICATION DATA
Names: Coronado, Juan David, author.
Title: "I'm not gonna die in this damn place" : manliness, identity, and survival of the Mexican
American Vietnam prisoners of war / Juan David Coronado.
Description: East Lansing : Michigan State University Press, 2018.
| Series: Latinos in the United States series | Includes bibliographical references and index.
Identifiers: LCCN 2017017663| ISBN 9781611862720 (pbk. : alk. paper) | ISBN 9781609175542 (pdf) |
ISBN 9781628953213 (epub) | ISBN 9781628963212 (kindle)
Subjects: LCSH: Mexican American soldiers—History—20th century. | Vietnam War, 1961–1975—
Prisoners and prisons, North Vietnamese. | Vietnam War, 1961–1975—Prisoners and prisons, American.
| Prisoners of war—Vietnam. | Prisoners of war—United States. | Prisoners of war—Psychology.
| Vietnam War, 1961–1975—Veterans—United States.
Classification: LCC DS559.4 .C67 2018 | DDC 959.704/37—dc23 LC record available
at https://lccn.loc.gov/2017017663

Book and cover design by Charlie Sharp, Sharp Des!gns, East Lansing, Michigan
Cover image (first inset on the left) of Elias Espinoza is used with permission.
Other inset photos are used courtesy of Juan Coronado.

g green
press
INITIATIVE   Michigan State University Press is a member of the Green Press Initiative
and is committed to developing and encouraging ecologically responsible
publishing practices. For more information about the Green Press Initiative and the use of
recycled paper in book publishing, please visit www.greenpressinitiative.org.

Visit Michigan State University Press at www.msupress.org

Contents

Foreword

THE WAR IN VIETNAM AND THE CIVIL RIGHTS MOVEMENT OVERLAPPED in time and entangled the domestic social and political struggles of the period. The Chicano Movement had its roots in the post-World War II period, in the disenchantment among Chicano veterans who expected more for having served their country than a return to the subordinate status of a racial minority in the nation's Southwest. This disenchantment combined with an optimism about civil rights grounded in key court decisions that continued the "long march to freedom" in the struggle to dismantle the institutional features of American racism (e.g., *Mendez v. Westminster*, 1947). With the defeat of the Axis powers by the Allies, the nation experienced a surge in progressivism and economic expansion. The National Labor Relations Act empowered the rights and voice of labor, and the American working class embarked on a series of improvements in the terms and conditions of employment and in the quality of life. All of these social and political gains were part of a series of social democratic improvements across a broad range of life dimensions that occurred at midcentury.

At the same time, however, the roots of today's conservative movements were growing stronger, especially as White Americans resisted the Civil Rights Movement and the loss of a sense of psychological superiority or advantage grounded in racial ideology and practices. The period was characterized by domestic social tensions and struggles, and at the international level, the nation flexed its anti-Communist muscles, taking on the pro-Communist forces in Vietnam following the departure of the French in 1954. In 1955, through the Southeast Asia Treaty Organization (SEATO), the United States was instrumental in setting up the Government of the Republic of Vietnam (GVN or South Vietnam).

The anti-Communist government of South Vietnam set in motion repressive measures that engendered resistance by different sectors of society, including Buddhist monks and nuns, students, business people, intellectuals, and peasants. By the end of the decade the Communist Party of Vietnam, after having failed to unify the country by political means, accepted revolutionary violence to overthrow the corrupt puppet government. In 1961, President Kennedy received a report from a team he had sent to South Vietnam that assessed the scope of American aid requirements and called for increased military, technical, and economic aid, as well as advisers that would help South Vietnam achieve military success. President Kennedy responded with limited support in terms of equipment and advisors, but the anti-Communist government continued with repressive measures, especially against Buddhist monks. In 1963, the U.S. supported a military coup that changed the leadership in South Vietnam, setting in motion a series of regime changes over the next few years. Following the assassination of President Kennedy, his successor, President Lyndon Baines Johnson, began taking more aggressive military engagement in Vietnam's civil war.

In the United States the Civil Rights Movement was gaining momentum, with Rev. Martin Luther King Jr. leading the March on Washington in 1963, where he delivered the "I Have a Dream" speech, which inspired many Americans, including Chicanos. During this period, Rodolfo "Corky" Gonzales was organizing Chicanos in Denver against police brutality; César Chavez was organizing farmworkers in California; Reies Lopez Tijerina was organizing Chicano land grantees in New Mexico, and Albert Peña Jr. was leading the Political Association of Spanish Speaking Organizations in Texas. Chicano demands were growing across the Southwest and began to consolidate ideologically with the publication of *Yo Soy Joaquin*, an epic poem by Corky Gonzales that articulated the conquered status of Chicanos and the promise of liberation and self-determination. In 1968, several of the Chicano leaders were active participants at the Poor People's March in Washington, where Corky delivered the "Plan del Barrio" speech, which called for reforms in housing, education, law enforcement, land, agriculture, and the economy. In 1969, he led the first National Chicano Youth Liberation Conference in Denver, which furthered mobilized Chicanos across the Southwest. As these events were transpiring across the country, Chicano soldiers were being killed in the Vietnam war, while others were being taken as prisoners of war (POWs).

In this volume, Juan David Coronado presents the first major work on the experiences of these POWs. Although limited in numbers, these POWs tended to have similar backgrounds as members of an oppressed racial minority group, but they differed in their patriotism and in their political perspectives. Indeed, their experiences reflected the racial dynamics that characterized the United States as well as the political movements of the period, with family members, in some cases, taking anti-imperialist stances here on the mainland. Upon their return, the nation was deeply divided over the war, and White resistance to the Civil Rights Movement was increasing. During the 1970s, when former Chicano POWs were reintegrating into civil society, the social tensions and antiwar struggles had diminished, and the economic problem of stagflation created opportunities for political conservatives to gain footholds on political power. By 1980, when Ronald Reagan was elected to the presidency, conservatives were gaining power and the nation was moving in the direction of free market fundamentalism, which gained allies among anti-Communists, the Religious Right, and social conservatives. In short, this was the political context to which they returned.

The experiences of the Chicano POWs not only reveal their struggles to survive, they also provide a window into the racial and political dynamics of the period from a Chicano perspective, as well as into the Chicano world of *machismo* of that period. Today, with the Trump regime serving as the fullest expression of free market fundamentalism, along with its racist, sexist, homophobic, authoritarian, and fascist elements, readers should reflect on the political continuities and discontinuities between the period of the Chicano Vietnam POWs and the present antidemocratic features of America. We are in a period of neoliberal nationalism in which the democratic principles many Chicano soldiers believed they were fighting for in Vietnam are being threatened in an open and direct way by an American plutocracy.

Preface

THE INTENSE HANOI HEAT AND HIGH HUMIDITY OF JUNE OFFERED NO comfort to our shocked bodies, which were exhausted and suffering from jetlag.[1] I was serving as a graduate assistant with the Texas Tech University Vietnam Delegation, a study-abroad group that visited Southeast Asia in the summer of 2008. We had left LAX Friday at midnight and arrived at Nội Bài International Airport in Hanoi Sunday morning local time. Saturday was completely lost, and the effects from the twelve-hour time progression certainly did not ease the concerns some in the group had of going through Vietnamese customs, especially after having been cautioned of the strict laws, and more importantly of the authoritarian "Communist" officials. For a *fronterizo*/borderlander like myself who grew up crossing the U.S.-Mexico border frequently, often greasing a few palms (in Mexico) and dealing with abrasive customs officials (mostly in the United States) flexing their authority, this was nothing new to me.

Actually, entering Vietnam was fairly straightforward, as our visas were in order and perhaps customs officials were already expecting our arrival. I embarked on a research trip to Vietnam that not only submerged me in

Vietnamese culture and exposed me to the historical sites of the Vietnam War[2] (or American War as it is known there), but that took me to an enchanted world that played center stage in my studies. More importantly, this journey forever changed my life. It brought me face to face with a place several of my subjects would not dare return to "without a gun in hand." I knew I would not be exposed to the Vietnam of the Cold War era when Americans deeply invested blood, lives, capital, credibility, and time in the preservation of a Communist-free South Vietnam. But I would, however, experience as much of Vietnam as possible.

I quickly absorbed the atmosphere and familiarized myself with the surroundings of downtown Hanoi. The smells produced by the innumerable food vendors swamped the streets as locals inundated the sidewalks by early morning to eat at their favorite stands. It was a friendly atmosphere, and I was approached by several young people who were interested in knowing about me and even treated me to pastries being sold out of wheeled carts stationed on the side of the road. We conversed about a number of topics, but their main interest was about life in the United States, and they were noticeably enthralled about life on the U.S.-Mexico borderlands.

The crowded sidewalks paled in comparison to the congested streets. The traffic lights throughout Vietnam seem like a mere suggestion, and driving etiquette seemed to revolve around the very simple premise "Don't get hit." This concept was especially true when dealing with larger vehicles (buses and trucks) that regardless of the situation always seemed to have the right-of-way. Busy intersections lacked uniform lanes as dozens of motorbikes (the transportation of choice in Vietnam) erratically positioned themselves to continue on to their destinations. It was very clear to me that I was right in the middle of where I needed to be at that time.

By the second day "in-country," I was dealing with an obnoxious thirty-six-hour trial as I had trouble adjusting to the twelve-hour time difference from Texas time and was functioning without any sleep. The antimalarial medication kicked in, provoking a mild case of insomnia along with other side effects, including paranoia that allowed me to experience Vietnam through a totally different lens. Still, despite the circumstances while adjusting to the new scene, I was eager for our midafternoon visit to Hỏa Lò.

Americans primarily know it as the Hanoi Hilton, where American prison-ers of war (POWs) spent endless days waiting for the war to end. The cold two-story concrete compound had been constructed to hold Vietnamese political prisoners during the French occupation in the 1880s.

Today, Hỏa Lò is a museum, preserving pro-Vietnamese, socialist, and anti-imperialist sentiments, while at the same time charging visitors a cover fee. Like most indoor and outdoor war museums in Vietnam, Hỏa Lò showcases their long-embattled history with exceptional nationalist pride. Interestingly, the museum is not only dedicated to the time it was used to hold American POWs, but it also focuses on the Vietnamese political pris-oners who were imprisoned under French occupation. The once dreaded prison now stands as a tourist site with visitors flocking in droves, as they tend to do at prominent museums. A gift shop filled with books and souve-nirs is located at the entrance of the museum, and as you exit, Vietnamese children swarm around you with pirated American and Vietnamese books on the war in numerous languages along with all sorts of trinkets for sale. I wondered about the upheaval during the Cold War that prompted the forceful tension between Hanoi and Washington. After all, if this old prison now serves as a tourist attraction, then capitalism is obviously alive in this socialist society.

With the passing of time and reconciliation between both countries, the Vietnamese have moved beyond the war years and embrace Americans and their culture.[3] The exhibits at the Hanoi Hilton are representative of how the American War is remembered in Vietnam as nothing more than "just another war" in their tumultuous history. Among the artifacts on display at Hỏa Lò are a guillotine used by the French to execute Vietnamese political prisoners, a picture of Commander (Ret.) Everett Álvarez Jr. (the first American aviator shot down in North Vietnam and the first prisoner of war at Hỏa Lò), and Senator John McCain's flight suit from the day of his capture. The McCain display has even been updated to reflect the senator's 2008 candidacy for the presidency of the United States.

While Senator McCain arguably has become one of the most recog-nized former prisoners of war, Álvarez also shares a special status. On Au-gust 5, 1964, Álvarez became the first Hanoi (North Vietnamese) prisoner when the United States retaliated against the Gulf of Tonkin incident that had occurred days earlier. "I started the war," Álvarez proudly says of his role in Vietnam.[4] Yet, long before Tonkin, the United States had been militarily involved in Southeast Asia (SEA). Although Álvarez would become the longest-held POW in North Vietnam, he was not the longest-detained prisoner of the entire war. Major Floyd "Jim" Thompson served the longest term as a POW, surpassing Álvarez by over four months.[5] On March 26, 1964, Thompson fell into the hands of the National Liberation Front (NLF), also known as the Viet Cong (VC),[6] in South Vietnam. Still, neither Thompson nor Álvarez can claim to be the first American POW in Vietnam.

On November 22, 1963, the same day an assassin's bullet ended the life of President John F. Kennedy in Dallas, Texas, between two hundred and five hundred Viet Cong attacked a Special Forces camp at Hiep Hoa, located between Saigon and the Cambodian border.[7] Two days later, Captain Isaac "Ike" Camacho, a Green Beret from El Paso, Texas, fell captive to the Viet Cong. However, ten years prior to Tonkin, in June 1954 during the final days of the French Indochina War, a group of Viet Minh near South China Beach in Da Nang captured five U.S. troops who had been supporting French military air units, including Airman 2/C Ciro Salas Jr. of Los Angeles, California.[8] Within three months, the American government successfully negotiated the repatriation of the five Americans. Their experiences in the summer of 1954 foreshadowed the destinies of nearly seven hundred Americans in Southeast Asia who would fall captive during the Vietnam War.

These three Mexican Americans,[9] Salas, Camacho, and Álvarez, share a significant experience in the POW narrative. Ciro Salas and his group were the first Americans captured in Vietnam and have previously been excluded from most POW lists. Isaac Camacho was the first American in South Vietnam to successfully escape from captivity, while Everett Álvarez became a household name after being the first American pilot shot down and captured in North Vietnam. Due to the media coverage of his capture, he has been included in many historical accounts—both academic and nonacademic works. However, more can and should be said about Álvarez, who spent eight and a half years in captivity.

The experiences of these three Mexican American POWs were exceptional and distinctive. Yet, despite the uniqueness of their POW experiences, much has remained unsaid about them. The large majority of historical accounts have minimized the Mexican American POW experience. Even more has remained unwritten about the experiences of other Mexican American former POWs who, with two exceptions, were captured in South Vietnam, and their stories fall in the category of "jungle prisoners," whose experiences have been underemphasized and marginalized.

Acknowledgments

COMPLETING THIS MANUSCRIPT HAS BEEN A WILD JOURNEY THAT HAS taken me to Southeast Asia and all across the United States. With much support, push, and encouragement, *hemos llegado* (we have arrived)! I have been truly fortunate in having personal and professional backing from family, friends, colleagues, and former professors. This volume that inserts Mexican American prisoners of war into the historical narrative of the Vietnam War has been made possible through the help of many people. I will attempt to recognize as many people as I can possibly remember. If I miss someone, I truly apologize, but know that in these pages lies my gratitude to you.

The oral histories included here bring to life a rich history that had previously been underappreciated. Therefore, it is with tremendous gratitude that I thank the former Mexican American Vietnam prisoners of war included in this study. This work would not be what it is without their assistance, kindness, and more importantly their history. I want to thank José Astorga, Joe Anzaldúa Jr., Everett Álvarez Jr., Isaac Camacho, Ciro Salas Jr., Hector Acosta, José David Luna, Juan Jacques, Abel Larry Kavanaugh Sr., and Alfonso Ray Riate. While most of these men welcomed me into their homes and offices and treated me with utmost respect, others respectfully answered my calls and letters. I am also appreciative to their wives, who made me feel welcomed. I owe gratitude to Larry Kavanaugh Jr. and his wife Heather for opening up and filling a gap in the history of Larry Sr. I want to acknowledge former POWS Lew Meyer, Mike Benge, and Mike Mc-Grath for their determination in helping me find some of their old friends. No matter what any joker says, former Vietnam War POWS are *heroes*. I also want to thank Chuck and Mary Schantag and the P.O.W. Network for all their help.

I visited and requested materials from numerous archives, libraries, and repositories, and I would like to extend gratitude to the staffs at those locations, including the Southwest Collection and Vietnam Center at Texas Tech University, Richard Nixon Presidential Library and Museum, and the Special Collections & University Archives at Stanford University. A special thank you to Curtis Gibbens with the office of freedom of information in the Department of Defense at the Pentagon who provided great resources. I want to thank Grace Charles from the Special Collections at Texas A&M-Corpus Christi and Dr. Brian Robertson who provided great material from the Nixon library. Along the way, I also met friends of former POWS, and I would like to thank Juan Apodaca, Billy Waugh, Anthony Williams, Albert "Smiley" Cuéllar, and the rowdy bunch in Refugio, Texas. I want to thank Danelle L. Jimenez for her efforts in convincing her father Juan Jacques to meet me. I also want to thank Rosalío Munoz for granting me an interview and sharing his efforts to organize the Chicano Moratorium.

I want to thank Texas Tech University's Department of History for all their support. Dr. Jorge Iber played a key role in the early stages of the development of this project. I would like to thank Dr. Ron Milam for making the trip to Vietnam possible. It gave me the necessary perspective to start this project. I am also appreciative of Dr. Jeffrey Mosher's constructive feedback. Dr. Miguel Levario served beyond his duties and never lost faith in me, and I am humbled by his patience. Thank you to Dr. Jim Reckner, Congressman Sam Johnson, and Johnson's office staff for help. A special thanks to Dr. Gretchen Adams.

While researching and writing this manuscript, I moved multiple times, from West Texas to my home in South Texas to my current location in Michigan. Aside from Texas Tech University, I worked for several other institutions of higher education, including University of Texas–Pan American (UTPA), South Texas College, and Michigan State University. These jobs provided the financial resources to keep writing and allowed me to share my research with students and colleagues alike. I am grateful to each department that employed me and to the staff that assisted along the way. I am also appreciative of the many students I taught along the way; their perseverance motivated me to finish this manuscript.

This work would not be possible without the direction of my supervisor and mentor, Dr. Rubén Martinez, director of the Julian Samora Research Institute (JSRI) at Michigan State University. At a time when academia has shifted under a neoliberal order that has made mentorship seem almost as archaic as chivalry, Dr. Martinez, true to his Chicano principles, has shown me the ropes and has helped me survive and thrive as a developing scholar. Dr. Martinez, a veteran himself, took interest in this manuscript, and I am both fortunate and proud to have this work featured in his Latinos in the United States Series. His editing has made this a much stronger book. A special thanks goes to the staff at JSRI for their assistance, including Marcos Martinez, Devin Mazur, Barry Lewis, and Nabih Haddad. A note of appreciation goes to Ernesto Vigil and Dr. José Angel Gutiérrez, who spent June 2016 working on a collaborative project at JSRI. Their wisdom, knowledge, and constructive feedback aided the development of this manuscript. Likewise, the faculty, personnel, and staff at the Office of University of Outreach and Engagement (UOE) have been incredibly welcoming and helpful. Special thanks goes to Beth Prince, Debbie Stoddard, Nai Kuan Yang, Paul Phipps, Ghada Georgis, and Burt Bargerstcok, among others, who contribute to the healthy working environment at UOE. Morning coffee talks with Drs. Jean Kayitsinga, Miles McNall, and Marcelo Siles provided a much-needed environment to bounce around ideas and that got the mind going.

Moving to Michigan, away from my natural habitat in the Rio Grande Valley in South Texas, has not been easy. Fortunately, Dr. Rubén Martinez and his family and friends, including Marcos, Clara, and Lori Brown, have been beyond welcoming. Dr. Martinez has also connected me with the community throughout the state, including Dr. Nino Rodriguez, who has been supportive of my work. A childhood friend, Ruben and Brenda Martinez and their family from Wisconsin have served as part of my support system in the Midwest. They, along with Rosalinda Martinez and her family, have demonstrated that adaptability for Tejanos (Texans) in the Midwest is promising and I appreciate their friendship.

Like many Chicanos, family remains at the centerfold of my life. My parents David and Josefina, my sister Yesenia Coronado and her husband Leonel Pulido Jr., and Ana Satterfield have been instrumental in the realization of this work. If not for them, I would not have the opportunity to fulfill this study. From a very young age, my parents instilled in me a blue-collar work ethic, as they themselves worked long laborious hours to provide me with an education. My sister, like my parents, has been supportive, and she has provided more than a helping hand. Ana pushed me to accept the position at Michigan State University and sacrificed much. Thank you Ana and Sophia for the pictures for the cover. I share this publication with my family and am in indebted to the friends and family who have been supportive. A special acknowledgement to a dear friend, Mr. José Omar Rivera from Mission, Texas. Apart from his encouragement, Omar provided his knowledge on Mexican Americans in the military. Through his tireless efforts this work is saturated with ample primary sources. Thanks also goes to Mr. Fred Ramos, from the University of Texas Rio Grande Valley Library, from whom I received many of those sources digitally.

I also want to acknowledge the support from the Southwest Oral History Association, especially, Sarah Moorhead, Dr. Marcia Gallo, Claytee White, Dr. Caryll Dziedziak, and the rest of the SOHA board who made it possible for me to share my work with a wider audience. Their encouragement and backing has allowed me to grow as an oral historian. I want to also thank those who provided feedback on this manuscript, including Dr. Martinez, Dr. Craig Howes, Charley Trujillo, Dr. Rumaldo Z. Juárez, and Gregg Jones. Much gratitude to John McPherson and Hai Nguyen for the Vietnamese translations. Also, a special thanks goes to the staff at the Michigan State

University Press, including Anastasia Wraight, Bonnie Cobb, Kristine M. Blakeslee, Julie Loehr, Annette Tanner, and Elise Jajuga.

Finally, I would like to thank several of my former mentors and professors who paved the way for Mexican Americans in South Texas. These individuals had immense impact on me, both professionally and personally. Mrs. Juanita Elizondo Garza was an incredible individual and professor who served UTPA and the community in South Texas. My first mentor, Dean Rodolfo Rocha, showed me the doors to academia and, in his true Rochista manner, encouraged me until his death. Dr. José R. Hinojosa, a student of Dr. Julian Samora, had a rare style of integrating his scholarly pedagogy with a strong dose of realism, which he delivered in a manner that *raza* and others could adhere to. The most important lessons learned from these three professors was that we Chicanos have a place not only in this country but in academia and that the battle to improve our society is endless but worth fighting, regardless of appreciation.

Introduction

WHILE I WAS RESEARCHING THIS BOOK, MY CURIOSITY WAS SPARKED AS clear similarities and differences among the POWs became more and more evident. The most considerable difference in terms of their experiences stems from whether they were a jungle prisoner (typically infantry captured in South Vietnam) or a Hanoi prisoner (typically aviators shot down in North Vietnam, although a small fraction were shot down in Laos and South Vietnam). Those captured in South Vietnam and held in the jungle naturally faced more severe circumstances than their counterparts in North Vietnam. Illnesses such as malaria and dysentery, along with lack of nutrition and medicine, severely reduced the POW population in the South. While POWs in South Vietnam claimed that they "couldn't stop dying," Hanoi POWs declared, "they wouldn't let us die."[1] If the prisoners died in captivity, the North Vietnamese would be held accountable and would compromise their global standing and reputation. Therefore, for the most part, American prisoners that had been identified as POWs in the North had access to better health care than those captured in the South.

Throughout the conflict, the North Vietnamese government attempted to demonstrate to the world its resolve against what it perceived to be an American imperialist threat that divided their country and sustained a puppet regime in Saigon. The North Vietnamese would only harm their global image if they allowed U.S. prisoners to perish. Therefore, extra precautions were taken in the North to assure, perhaps not the well-being of prisoners, but at least their survival.

On the other hand, with a high mortality rate among U.S. prisoners of war in South Vietnam, the North Vietnamese and NLF did not immediately announce the capture of too many POWs in the South. Releasing those names would make the Vietnamese publicly accountable for those lives, and they did not want to compromise their "noble" image with the inhumane treatment of prisoners while having to explain such a high mortality rate. Consequently, it took months and in some cases years before the North Vietnamese announced the names of American POWs, who by this point had either been labeled missing in action (MIA) or in several extreme cases killed in action (KIA) by the U.S. military, which could not locate them or their remains.

Furthermore, making the POW situation far more complex in South Vietnam was the fact that guerrillas hid throughout South Vietnam, blending in with the civilian population. Holding American POWs would not have been practical for the Viet Cong. Instead, prisoners were simply executed rather than having to be moved through a network of camps to avoid detection by American and South Vietnamese forces. As one jungle prisoner of war put it, "We had subconsciously anticipated being wounded or killed, but never captured. It wasn't a war in which people were captured in the south. That was for pilots flying over the north."[2] Infantrymen in the South knew the fatal risks involved in being out on patrol, yet captivity hardly ever crossed their minds. Moreover, Army training was in conjunction with this mentality, as their drills had not emphasized the Survival, Evasion, Resistance, and Escape (SERE) protocol that the Air Force, Navy, and to a certain extent the Marine Corps had enforced.

Of the 629 Americans captured during the Vietnam War, 572 were shot down in North Vietnam, with the large majority of them being White aviators, while the remaining 57 were infantry or "grunts" captured in South Vietnam.[3] For what at the time had been America's longest war, approximately 600 POWs seemed awfully low—especially when comparing these figures to the POW populations in the three major wars the United States had fought earlier in the twentieth century. During World War I, nearly 4,000 American servicemen were taken captive. In World War II, with an overwhelming number of ground troops, the number of American POWs rose to 130,000, and then declined to around 7,000 during the Korean War.[4]

Several variables contributed to the low number of American POWs in Southeast Asia: (1) improved technologies in transportation and weapons that led to a relatively low number of American combat troops committed in Southeast Asia (boots on the ground), (2) the nature of the Vietnam War itself as it heavily relied on the air campaign, and (3) the reluctance of the Viet Cong to take prisoners in South Vietnam. Both American military strategy and technological advances during the war led to fewer American prisoners of war. The air campaign over North Vietnam did not require ground troops, reducing considerably the number of soldiers committed. The lessons learned in other Cold War conflicts such as Korea (after Chinese involvement) convinced Americans to search for alternatives to sending infantry to the North. In South Vietnam, the helicopter gave the U.S. military a great advantage, easing transportation in highly contested areas where they otherwise would have been forced to commit more troops. The National Liberation Front or Viet Cong seldom took captives; thus, many American soldiers who were taken captive in South Vietnam were fearful of simply being executed. An American prisoner of war would have only complicated the war effort of the Viet Cong, who throughout the war tried to pass as loyal South Vietnamese citizens.

The emphasis placed on strategic bombing led to aviators accounting for the vast majority of American POWs in Southeast Asia. Since a college degree was required to become a pilot, the majority of the POWs captured in North Vietnam were White officers. Far from being a heterogeneous group, all but seventy-nine of the prisoners were commissioned officers, and half of the POW population belonged to the Air Force.[5] The large majority of Vietnam POWs in the North were White career military personnel, or "lifers," and quite different from the common "grunts" and infantrymen in South Vietnam.

Both African Americans and Mexican Americans noted that their ethnic groups were overrepresented in ground combat and were not participating in the air raids. Rev. Dr. Martin Luther King Jr. and the Black Congressional Caucus took exception when they discovered that only sixteen POWs were African American.[6] African American activists acknowledged the limited opportunities that existed for them in the military and the discrimination that kept them from rising in rank.

Chicanos and African Americans were not equally represented in relation to Whites in the higher military ranks, thus exposing an obvious inequity that existed in society and in the military as well. As minorities did not contribute significantly to the prisoner-of-war population, it became clear that they were not transcending social and racial barriers that continued to plague the military and their respective communities. Chicano activist Raúl Ruiz argued, "The fact that there aren't too many POWs that are Chicanos does not signify lack of participation, but rather that most prisoners are pilots. Chicanos don't become pilots. You need a college education for that. Not too many Chicanos go to college."[7] On the home front, the young Chicano community protested the high unemployment rates of returning veterans who did not climb the ladder in the military ranks and did not benefit from having served in the military.

The Mexican American POW population was even lower than that of African Americans, as only ten prisoners identified as Mexican Americans. By contrast, sixteen were African American. The number of Mexican American POWs may seem insignificant, as they only accounted for a slight fraction of the total population. To understand the significance of Mexican American Vietnam War POWs, however, it is essential to acknowledge the tremendous differences between POWs in the Vietnam War and those previously involved in American wars in the twentieth century. The Mexican American POWs ranged from airmen to infantrymen, and therefore their experiences are diverse. Their accounts enrich both military and Mexican American history, while filling a void in regard to the historical narrative of all Vietnam War POWs. Making the POW experience more interesting is the conflictive Vietnam War era, which saw the rise of the counterculture, women's liberation, antiwar, and civil rights movements, including the Chicano Movement, that impacted the war and the POWs in distinct ways. These phenomena made the home that prisoners of war returned to in 1973 seem almost like a different place from the one that deployed them.

Despite the small sample size, the group of Mexican American POWs gives a fair representation of the total prisoner-of-war population and the mixed experiences of its members. These differences stemmed from a variety of factors, ranging from branch of service to race/ethnicity and social background. However, the leading contributing factor that led to disparities in the POW experience often was each man's individual character and how each related and or responded to his captors, thus making each experience distinctive.

When 591 prisoners of war returned from captivity during "Operation Homecoming" in 1973, the first to arrive were the senior ranking officers.[8] As the nation highly anticipated their arrival, media coverage also awaited them. This upper echelon of POWs included early Hanoi shoot-downs and has been identified as "the superpatriots who felt we should have been in there killing them [Communists] by the thousands."[9] Being the first group to return home, their accounts became accepted as "the official story" of American prisoners of war in Vietnam. These stories were recounted and perpetuated by late shoot-downs that deferred to the older faction. "It was the guys who had been there longer who really suffered," explained 1972 shoot-down William Angus. "I didn't want to detract from their story."[10] As late returnees stayed quiet, the senior ranking officers dictated their experiences and took control of the historical narrative.

Other returnees suggest that POWs "were not of one mind." Aside from "the superpatriots" was another group that did not believe the American bombing campaign of Hanoi was producing a favorable outcome for POWs. Some prisoners even denounced American intervention in Vietnam. A senior POW, Navy Commander Walter Wilber, who was accused of collaborating with the Vietnamese, insisted "that the whole [POW] story had yet to be heard," as "each person has to tell his own story."[11] Despite the allegations against him, Wilber makes a valid argument. Prisoners throughout North and South Vietnam were exposed to different conditions, environments, and treatments, which consequently led to varied experiences among them. Each POW's narrative is worthy of recognition.

Jungle prisoners who had been captured in the South received minimal attention upon their relatively late return home. This group was largely composed of enlisted men, including several Mexican Americans. Their stories became haphazardly lost in the popular narrative or in "the official story" of Hanoi POWs. The senior ranking officers took offense to the indirect criticism levied by the experiences of jungle POWs who faced tremendously different and usually more extreme circumstances. "Hanoi, compared to our jungle camp, was like a Holiday Inn," suggested jungle and Kushner Camp survivor Frank Anton. American POWs imprisoned in the infamous Kushner Camp in the dense jungles of South Vietnam suffered a death rate of 50 percent. For jungle POWs, the nickname Hanoi Hilton was fitting as it had "comforts" unimaginable in the makeshift camps in the jungles of Southeast Asia, including South Vietnam, Laos, and Cambodia. As jungle POWs suggested that Hỏa Lò prison mirrored *Hogan's Heroes* (a World War II POW sitcom), Hanoi prisoners defensively took exception and labeled this faction to be "incompetent, undisciplined, and leaderless." Even worse, jungle POWs were increasingly ignored as the experiences of the Hanoi prisoners became "the official story" while their own accounts received little to no attention.[12]

Walter Wilber's assessment rings true as the history of Vietnam prisoners of war is much more complex than "the official story" insinuates. There remain many perspectives still to be included in the historical narrative. In assessing more individual cases, a greater overview and understanding of the experiences of Vietnam POWs is gained. While some of the stories from Mexican American POWs expand and support "the official story," others provide a vastly different account of the POW experience. This study of Chicano POWs emphasizes the viewpoint that their experiences were not universal, but particularistic. Overall, this work provides a further understanding of Chicano Vietnam *veteranos*, and more importantly, it sheds light on the military contributions of Mexican Americans, a group historically overlooked and underrepresented.

This group of ten former POWs is symbolic of the diverse Mexican American community that faced several challenges during the war. At the time, the younger generations of Chicanos within the Mexican American community on the home front explicitly protested the war in Southeast Asia, while the older "Mexican American Generation" (a term historian Mario T. García uses to identify the politically inclined Mexican Americans in the post-World War II civil rights movement) remained more aligned with their military roots. Mexican Americans faced daily discrimination in their communities, workplaces, and lives. The World Wars exposed them to a world beyond their segregated *barrios*, while at the same time their participation in the service allowed them to dream beyond the *barrios*.

By the time of the Vietnam era, the "Mexican American Generation" had made a tremendous social and political leap; to young Chicanos it was no longer enough to accept second-class citizenship. Discrimination, social inequality, and most importantly a high Chicano mortality rate in Vietnam plagued Mexican Americans as a whole. As Chicano casualties in Southeast Asia increased, the members of the older faction came to share the opinions of their younger counterparts in regard to the conflict. Vietnam veterans brought a synthesis among the older Mexican American generation and the younger Chicano generation, as both groups, who were once divided, grew bitter over the high Chicano casualty rate.

Despite sharing similar backgrounds, Mexican American POWs, just like the Mexican American community, shared diverse opinions about the war. Chicano POWs had similar working-class backgrounds, with the majority rooted in farmworking communities. At a young age, these men worked outside the home to help provide their families with the everyday necessities. As the men grew, each found fulfillment or comfort in joining the military. They had various reasons for serving in Southeast Asia and would eventually have personal differences in regard to identity and notions of masculinity. Mexican American communities had different views of their own identity, and of the war as well. Naturally, following captivity some former POWs were able to piece their lives together and lead successful lives, while others never fully recovered from the experience.

The group of ten Mexican American POWs under study here consists of three each from the Air Force, Marines, and Army, and one from the Navy. All these men came from the Southwest. The airmen were Ciro Salas Jr., from Los Angeles, California; Hector Michael Acosta, from San Antonio, Texas; and José David Luna, from Orange, California. The Marines were José Jesús "Joe" Anzaldúa Jr., from Refugio, Texas; Alfonso Ray Riate, from Bell Gardens, California; and Abel Larry Kavanaugh, from Denver, Colorado. The Army men were Isaac "Ike" Camacho, from El Paso, Texas; José Manuel Astorga, from San Diego, California; and Juan L. Jacquez, from Santa Fe, New Mexico. The sole naval airman from the group, Everett "Ev" Álvarez Jr., was a native of Salinas, California. Regardless of their origins, the war in Southeast Asia brought them around the world, and their experiences in captivity would greatly impact the former POWs after their release.

A variety of reasons—personal, philosophical, and ideological—motivated these Mexican American POWs to serve the American cause in Vietnam. While three of the ten men joined the military inspired by adventure with aspirations to fly, the rest enlisted simply to improve their standard of living. Also, motivating the group of POWs to join the war effort was the tradition of military participation within their families. Many felt inclined to follow in their grandfathers', fathers', uncles', or brothers' footsteps. Contrary to previous accounts that claimed that none of the returning men during "Operation Homecoming" had been draftees, Juan Jacquez had been drafted into the Army and later reenlisted.[13]

Moreover, Mexican American POWs served to demonstrate their resolve against Communism during the reign of the Cold War, when the United States sought to contain the spread of Communism. These men widely believed it to be their patriotic duty to stand firm against Communism. Many Mexican Americans pursued military participation in order to demonstrate their loyalty while attempting to obtain inclusion as mainstream Americans and the attendant benefits of first-class citizenship. A fear of being drafted also motivated other Mexican Americans to join, as by volunteering they could perhaps influence to a certain extent their military assignment.

On the other hand, not everyone who served was an unquestionable patriot. At least three POWs held antiwar beliefs, yet they still served valiantly and endured horrific and unimaginable circumstances. The men had nuanced experiences, which demonstrates agency within the Mexican American community and the Vietnam War prisoner-of-war population. In this study, I contend that in spite of the complex ideologies that influenced Mexican American Vietnam prisoners of war, issues of class, masculinity, and ethnic identity compelled Mexican Americans to serve in Southeast Asia, and these same factors also helped them survive the brutal Vietnamese prison camps.

Those not familiar with the general plight of Mexican American veterans might take exception to this work. Some military historians at first may believe that the topic of Mexican American POWs is irrelevant; since all veterans are Americans, there is no need to create a subfield. Veterans may agree with José Astorga's assessment: "We had a saying in Vietnam: We all bleed red. We are all brothers."[14] Sadly, the notion of equality that existed out in the field did not translate into the historical literature produced on the war or to the home front.

While the experiences of White soldiers have been emphasized in the historical narratives of the Vietnam War, the role of Chicano veterans has been minimized. Furthermore, upon return to civilian life, Mexican American veterans in many places throughout the Southwest generally did not go drink a beer and hang out at the American Legion Posts or Veterans of Foreign Wars Posts (VFWs) because social barriers that had been ingrained still existed. Instead, if they wanted to share war stories, find camaraderie, or unwind, these veterans frequented the Catholic War Veterans Posts or local bars. In the historical narrative, the discrimination against Mexican American veterans even extends to the minimalization of their historical contributions. Eventually, social practices changed, and in many places throughout the Southwest, Chicano veterans now play important roles in their local VFWs.

This study centers on the narratives of Mexican American POWs in Southeast Asia and their reintegration into civilian society. Other than Everett Álvarez's autobiographies and the recent biography on Isaac Camacho, the Mexican American prisoner-of-war experience has been overlooked. Due to the anomalies surrounding Álvarez's and, to a lesser extent, Camacho's captivity, they have received more attention in POW literature than their Mexican American contemporaries. This study will contextualize the experiences of all Mexican American Vietnam War POWs and explore their place in U.S. history and in the history of the war itself. There also remains a limited understanding of Mexican American veterans who served in Vietnam.

Finally, mystery surrounds Alfonso Riate and Larry Kavanaugh and the role they played in the antiwar movement within the walls of the numerous prison camps in Vietnam and their untimely deaths following their return. Both men were accused of collaborating with the enemy, and their statements fueled the North Vietnamese propaganda machine. Senior ranking officers whom the pair disregarded during their captivity have dictated most of what has been said about them. In this work, I will fill in the gaps that exist in scholarly works on Chicano Vietnam veterans.

The importance and uniqueness of Mexican American POWs is demonstrated while emphasizing their importance in the broader historical narrative of the Vietnam War. Chapter 1, "ChicaNamization," depicts the atmosphere the war generated within the Chicano community. Clear divisions were created across generations; the old and the young had opposing views on the war. This chapter also addresses the significant military contributions of Mexican Americans during the era.

Chapter 2, "The Formative Years," is a biographical sketch that provides insight into the lives of the Mexican American prisoners of war. It focuses on the challenges the men dealt with growing up in the Southwest (the men grew up in Colorado, New Mexico, California, and Texas, representing four of the five states considered the Chicano homeland). Chapter 3, "The Manly Ideals of Machismo, Duty, and Patriotism," examines motivating factors that influenced the group to join the military. This chapter challenges stereotypical notions of *machismo* and expands the rationales for serving in the military beyond the beliefs of warmongering. An array of contributing factors brought Mexican Americans to serve in Vietnam, and these same factors propelled them to survive captivity.

Chapter 4, "Resisting, Enduring, and Surviving Captivity, the Early Years, 1954-1967," and chapter 5, "Resisting, Enduring, and Surviving Captivity, the Latter Years, 1967-1973," examine the experiences of the men and contextualize their unique accounts within the larger POW narrative. Due to the "natural discourse" of this study (which focuses on the experiences of prisoners of war), the occurrences during captivity make up a large bulk of this work, and thus these accounts are separated into two chapters. The year 1967 serves as a historical marker in the POW experience, since there were more American troops captured in 1967 than in any other year that Americans were engaged in the Vietnam War. Details are given on each man's distinctive capture and captivity, as each of their circumstances are one of a kind. These chapters contend that a working-class upbringing in Mexican American *barrios* and rural communities made them resilient in their struggle for survival in captivity in Southeast Asia. In the men's efforts to survive, we see remnants from their disadvantaged youths that taught them to deal with poverty.

Chapter 6, "Homecoming or Rude Awakening?," surveys the reintegration of the men into American society. The social changes that transpired in the United States during the 1960s and early 1970s transformed American society, and for many POWs, especially those who had spent significant time in captivity, these changes were unfathomable. Here, I argue that there was a mixed reaction to captivity among Mexican American POWs. Some of the men suffered gruesome injuries and had to live with the aches and pains for the remainder of their lives. Other injuries were not physical, but rather emotional and mental. Post-traumatic stress disorder, depression, and other psychological disorders took a toll on several of the men and led to painful experiences, including suicide, as in the case of Larry Kavanaugh. This chapter brings the conversation about the mental, physical, and emotional health of all returning veterans up to the present day, given the continuing wars in the Middle East. Today, the severity of the compromised health of veterans is of utmost importance given the current military conflicts in which the United States is engaged.

The conclusion serves as a critical and concise précis, while offering suggestions on further understanding former POWs and Mexican American veterans. I conclude that Mexican American POWs should serve as a historical symbolic unifier between the Chicano generation and the older Mexican American generation. On a greater scale, American captives in

Southeast Asia served as a symbolic unifier between doves and hawks alike, and in essence, they helped unify a divided country living in turmoil due to the revolutionary times and to the unpopularity of the Vietnam War. This chapter also looks at the legacy of the Vietnam War and gives the Mexican American POW his place within it. With the great number of Latinos in the military, the large part of them being of Mexican descent, it is important to acknowledge the impact military service has on this growing population. Lastly, I address the current participation of Mexican Americans in the latest military conflicts in Iraq and Afghanistan.

The fusion of American, Mexican, and in some cases Indigenous identities and cultures influenced Mexican Americans to serve in Southeast Asia. These three distinct cultures also contributed to the making of a Chicano identity. Although each of these men's lives varies substantially from the others, by examining their personal experiences one can tentatively conclude that their ethnic identity influenced their participation in the Vietnam War and aided them in surviving captivity. This group of former POWS reflects the nuances that separated the Mexican American generation, the Chicano generation, the broader prowar and antiwar communities. Thus, Mexican American Vietnam prisoners of war serve as a microcosm of the entire Mexican American community during the conflict. Much as the prisoners of war as a whole, upon being repatriated in 1973, helped unify a divided nation, this group of Mexican American POWS may serve as a unifier in studying the various Mexican American communities and generations that became divided by the Vietnam War. By understanding this group, a rich military lineage that has existed among Mexican Americans and Latinos can further be appreciated by mainstream historical accounts that enrich the American heritage.

This work expands Mexican American history, military history, and U.S. history as it fills gaps in all three fields. Observing and recording the experiences of Mexican American prisoners of war cements an appreciation of the Chicano Vietnam War experience. This is a topic forgotten and overlooked by many. Military studies and historians have seldom focused on Mexican American contributions, which have been significant throughout the many wars the United States has fought and continues to fight. This poor practice has allowed Mexican Americans and Latinos to be chastised and omitted from the American military experience, thus depriving many Latinos of their patriotic and heroic achievements. Given that Vietnam was an unpopular war within the Chicano and American communities, little attention has been given to Mexican American veterans by scholars and activists critical of the war. Finally, the narrative of Mexican American prisoners of war allows further understanding of the Vietnam prisoner of war, as many of the accounts remain untold.

Meanwhile, Mexican Americans and Latinos of various backgrounds continue to serve in the U.S. military valiantly. As of 2014, Hispanics compose 12 percent of active duty troops, while accounting for 16.9 percent of all new recruits, with Mexican Americans making up the bulk of both.[15] The history of Mexican American veterans has much relevance to the social and political history of this nation, and is deserving of inclusion. Perhaps in recognizing the history of Mexican American veterans, this work contributes to the greater inclusion of Mexican American history into the "mainstream" American heritage. The Vietnam veterans focused on in this study deservingly are not only Mexican American heroes, but also American heroes who deserve to have their stories told and preserved. These men certainly are not criminals, drug dealers, gang members, or rapists. However, on the battlefield they did serve valiantly and in POW camps gave their captors a difficult time, so by several standards they may qualify as bad *hombres*.

CHAPTER 1

ChicaNamization

Since the end of the war, the Department of Defense has estimated that 83,000 Latinos served in Vietnam, while other figures show as many as 170,000 (with Mexican Americans making up the great bulk of the figure).[1] It is difficult to give an accurate figure on the number of Mexican Americans who served in the Vietnam War, as most Latinos who served during the war were simply categorized as "White" by the Department of Defense. The term or label "Hispanic" was first introduced in the 1970 Census, and in the military it did not became common until after the war. Determining Latino veterans can become tedious and confusing, especially with those individuals with Caucasian surnames, or with non-Hispanics that have Spanish surnames in the case of veterans of Filipino descent.

What is firmly documented is that Chicanos served with distinction, as ultimately ten Mexican Americans were awarded the Congressional Medal of Honor for their gallantry, including two nationalized Mexicans, Alfred Velazquez Rascon and Jose Francisco Jimenez. Significantly, Mexican Americans were among the first and last to serve in Vietnam. As early as 1954, a Mexican American airman, Ciro Salas Jr., was with the first group of Americans to be detained and held as prisoners of war by the Vietnamese, while Master Sgt. Juan Valdez was the last American soldier to leave the rooftop of the American Embassy in Saigon when it fell to Communist forces on April 30, 1975.[2]

Despite the vast contributions of Mexican Americans in Southeast Asia, the scholarly historical literature does not accurately reflect their participation. Even the earlier works by Mexican American scholars, which resound with strong Chicano nationalism, completely ignore *veteranos*.[3] Given the unpopularity of the war amongst Chicano youth and scholars coming of age during that era, it is no surprise that the perspective of Mexican American veterans was overlooked.

Chicano/a antiwar activists during the Vietnam War era became educated on the historic plight of the Vietnamese people, which was comparable to the struggles for equality Chicanos faced in the United States as well as to the broad struggles that oppressed people grappled with globally. To a certain extent, Chicanos were more mindful about Vietnamese history than their government leadership was willing to seriously consider before committing significant troops and capital. The long struggles of the Vietnamese people should have been further evaluated in order to understand what Americans were to be involved in.

Vietnam, and Indochina in general, has had a long history of oppression. First, the Chinese in 111 B.C. conquered and subsequently colonized Vietnam until 939 A.D. For the next nine hundred years, Vietnam had self-rule—until the mid-1800s, when it was then colonized by the French. With the weakening of France during the Second World War, the Vietnamese saw a glimmer of hope for self-autonomy. Yet, Imperial Japan had its own interests. With Japan's expansion in the Pacific, Vietnam would fall to the Japanese, and while some Viet people saw them as liberators, others saw them as their next occupiers.[4]

Stepping into the forefront with the desire for Vietnamese independence was Ho Chi Minh, who in 1941 led the Viet Minh, or League for the Independence of Vietnam. By 1945, Ho and the Viet Minh were backed and supported by the United States, the Soviet Union, and China. In April 1945, the CIA's predecessor, the OSS, met with Ho and trained Viet Minh troops in what would lead to an Allied victory in the Pacific. That same month, President Franklin D. Roosevelt, who once declared support for a free Vietnam, also passed away. With Japan's unconditional surrender in August 1945, an elated Ho Chi Minh and Viet Minh felt they had contributed to the Allied victory and, consequently, appealed to President Harry Truman, who succeeded Roosevelt upon his death. Truman, however, was not receptive to Vietnamese independence.[5]

Nevertheless, On September 2, 1945, Ho Chi Minh again attempted to appeal to Americans with the Declaration of Independence of the Democratic Republic of Vietnam. In his proclamation, Ho began with borrowing almost verbatim from the U.S. Declaration of Independence: "All men are created equal. They are endowed by their Creator with certain inalienable rights, among them are Life, Liberty, and the pursuit of Happiness."[6] He also appealed to the French, citing the declaration of the French Revolution that "All men are born free and with equal rights, and must always remain free and have equal rights."[7] Neither the American nor the French governments were supportive of the Vietnamese independence movement. Instead, the French decided to restore their control of the colony, and the United States—whose mindset was now obsessed with checking the strength of the Soviet Union—decided that France's recovery and prosperity as an imperial nation was in their own best interest in fighting the Cold War.

The American support of France's imperial influence in Vietnam was such that the use of nuclear weapons was discussed between both countries during France's last stand at the battle of Dien Bien Phu during the French-Indochina War.[8] In a dialogue between President Dwight D. Eisenhower's hawkish U.S. secretary of state John Foster Dulles and French foreign minister Georges Bidault, the words "nuclear bomb" were allegedly uttered. Today, there is confusion about whether the weapons of mass destruction were offered, requested, or merely suggested in regard to what it would take for a French victory at Dien Bien Phu.[9]

In 1954, after the Vietnamese victory over the French in the French-Indochina War, the United States and China, at the Geneva Conference, divided the country at the 17th parallel into North Vietnam and South Vietnam instead of granting full Vietnamese independence. Led by Ho Chi

Minh, the North was Communist and kept close ties to the Soviet Union and China. Meanwhile, the South, with the support of the United States, embraced a capitalist, open-market state controlled by a quasi-democratic government. The United States backed and installed Ngo Dinh Diem as president in the South under the condition that free elections were to be held between the North and South in 1956.[10]

President Diem, however, never followed through with free elections; thus, in the eyes of the North Vietnamese and anti-imperialist critics, Diem and his government were considered a puppet regime of the United States.[11] The U.S. poured endless amounts of money into support of the Diem regime that was committed to the American agenda of a Communist-free South Vietnam. His disdain towards the Communists allowed Diem free range, as Americans overlooked his brutal practices and transgressions based on his solid commitment to the containment of Communism.

At the end of 1961, the year President John F. Kennedy came into office, the United States with 16,0000 troops was heavily involved militaristically in Vietnam. The growth in troops that year was exponentially higher than the 900 U.S. troops stationed in South Vietnam the previous year under President Eisenhower. Military advisors and Special Forces dedicated to the training of the military in South Vietnam made up the majority of the early military personnel. Journalists referred to the conflict as merely a quagmire in the midst of the Cold War.[12] Committed to the domino theory invoked by President Eisenhower, the United States was dedicated to preserving a Communist-free South Vietnam.

By 1963, it was clear to many in the South that Diem, a Catholic elite (just like Kennedy), did not reflect or share the common interests of the solidly Buddhist nation.[13] The Buddhist Crisis itself sparked international outrage when the situation climaxed with the self-immolation of Buddhist monks that summer.[14] To most South Vietnamese and to the Kennedy administration it was clear that President Diem was impertinent and impotent in leading South Vietnam. In communication with Henry Cabot Lodge Jr., ambassador to South Vietnam, President Kennedy gave the green light for Diem's removal. With the collaboration of the CIA and South Vietnamese operatives, President Diem and his brother were executed on

November 2, 1963. Almost three weeks later, on November 22, President Kennedy met a similar fate in Dallas.[15]

Vice President Lyndon B. Johnson would fill the presidency and confront the simmering situation in Vietnam. Without President Diem's iron fist to contest the Viet Cong's attempts to infiltrate and take over South Vietnam, President Johnson would have to commit American troops to do so. Even though Johnson publicly addressed the fears of escalation, American troop levels would soon increase drastically in the attempt to maintain South Vietnam. For American foreign-policy leaders during the Cold War era, the situation in Vietnam was of grave concern as it might lead to another proxy war that could have been avoided. To the Vietnamese, who had been disenfranchised, marginalized, and colonized for far too long, it was more than just a proxy war.

On two separate occasions on August 2 and 4, 1964, the USS *Maddox* and USS *Turner Joy* allegedly received enemy fire from North Vietnamese boats off the Gulf of Tonkin in North Vietnam. Today, it is questionable whether the Gulf of Tonkin Incident occurred at all. However, the confrontation provoked Americans, and President Lyndon Johnson quickly informed the nation of the North Vietnamese aggression and ordered military retaliation. Within days, the Gulf of Tonkin Resolution was overwhelmingly passed and Johnson was granted military authority in Vietnam.[16]

It was within this context that Americans went to war in Vietnam. The American public became enthralled by the first televised war and watched the nightly reports from their living rooms across the country. Notable American journalists and scholars—such as George C. Herring (*America's Longest War*), Neil Sheehan (*A Bright Shining Lie: John Paul Vann and America in Vietnam*), and David Halberstam (*The Best and the Brightest*)—made significant contributions to the literature on the Vietnam War.[17] However, the early works did not take into account the experiences of Chicanos.

It took the country almost a decade to heal from the discord that lingered from the war. By the 1980s, works and studies on the Vietnam War became more prevalent. Veterans themselves contributed significantly in expanding the literature, and soon almost all perspectives on the war were being covered. Still, the Latino perspective was slighted. Mexican American veterans, fueled by frustration from being snubbed, decided to write them-selves into the growing literature. Chicano veterans realized they now had to battle for inclusion in the historical narrative on the Vietnam War. These additions came with the challenge of overcoming the common belief that it was not necessary to have the Latino perspective if all soldiers were treated the same, and since discrimination or segregation during the Vietnam War era did not exist, therefore there was no need for the Latino perspective. The simple response is, if there was not and no longer is any discrimina-tion, what is keeping the experience of Chicano veterans from being told or recorded?

Throughout the research process, several people questioned the basis of this study. "Why are you picking on the Mexicans [Mexican American POWs]?," exclaimed Everett Álvarez.[18] Other people argued that there should not be a differentiation between POWs since they are all Americans. Rosalío Muñoz, cofounder of the Chicano Moratorium, wondered how I came upon such a topic.[19] Mexican American POWs and the Chicano community at large, however, experienced the war quite differently from middle-class White America; thus their perspective is needed to fully comprehend the era. Although the Chicano experience in the United States is comparable to that of impoverished Whites and African Americans, their situations re-main different. Regardless of class, there were unique obstacles that ethnic minorities and women confronted daily during the Vietnam War era.

By the mid-1960s, "The Mexican American Generation," as labeled by Mario T. García, addressed social inequality and began working with Presi-dent Lyndon B. Johnson's administration in attempting to bring improve-ments to their community. This older guard of Mexican Americans had been active in civil rights dating back to the 1930s and 1940s. However, at the same time, a younger faction within the community, Chicanos, gained attention for embracing a more vocal and demonstrative approach in what too many now saw as war on the home front.

The emerging Chicano activists addressed social, cultural, and racial concerns that had previously encouraged the Mexican American com-munity to assimilate to an American culture and shy away from their rich, diverse heritages. Chicanos thus embraced and defined their identity that was influenced by Indigenous and Spanish roots while at the same time impacted by American culture. By the late 1960s, the efforts of the older Mexican American faction became overshadowed by the changes brought about by this younger group of activists.

During the Vietnam War era, the United States, along with other countries around the world, was shaken by generational frustration, civil disobedience, and social protest, as the youth demonstrated their displeasure with the "Establishment." Throughout the Southwest, where all the Chicano POWs hailed from, several Mexican American groups were at odds with their unequal standing in society. By 1968, Rodolfo "Corky" Gonzalez, leader of the Crusade for Justice, showcased the struggles of Chicano inner-city youth nationwide. While Reies López Tijerina was at the brink of revolution in his quest for land reform in Tierra Amarilla, New Mexico, José Angel Gutiérrez worked to attain more political representation in Texas through the Mexican American Youth Organization (MAYO) and La Raza Unida Party (RUP). In California and leading a national charge, César Chavez, Dolores Huerta, and the United Farmworkers Union (UFW) organized farmworkers and advocated for their rights while challenging the systemic oppression that existed.

Also in California, Rosalío Muñoz led the Chicano Moratorium, an antiwar group that highlighted the concerns the Chicano community had in relation to the Vietnam War. The escalating war in Vietnam became a great concern for the Chicano community, which incurred significant burdens in the war, and consequently triggered a Chicano antiwar campaign throughout the Southwest. On August 29, 1970, the Los Angeles Police Department (LAPD) and Los Angeles County Sheriff's Department responded with brutality when the Chicano Moratorium led an antiwar rally.[20] This incident, which is referred to as Requiem 29, resulted in the death of native El Pasoan Rubén Salazar, who worked as a journalist for the *Los Angeles Times* and as a reporter for KMEX.

On August 29, twenty thousand antiwar demonstrators were attracted to East Los Angeles. Afterwards, Salazar, who participated in and covered the event, went into the Silver Dollar Cafe/Bar to cool off. Shortly after, Los Angeles sheriff's deputies arrived, claiming they were responding to an allegedly armed individual. Other accounts suggest that Salazar entered the bar with the intention of "shaking off" a suspicious pair of men who had been following him.[21] Without warning, the sheriff's deputies fired two tear-gas projectiles into the bar, one of which struck Salazar in the head, killing him. L.A. County sheriff's deputy Tom Wilson fired the tear-gas projectile that ended the life of Rubén Salazar.

During the Vietnam era, the Chicano community faced concerns about civil rights, police brutality, political representation, lack of economic opportunity, poor education, social inequality, and the overwhelming number of Chicano casualties in Vietnam. These concerns forced an outlet in the popular presses and music. Salazar, an Army veteran himself, had served the *Los Angeles Times* as a war correspondent in Saigon and knew firsthand the rising casualties among Mexican Americans. More importantly, Salazar showcased in the "mainstream" media the issues Chicanos faced, and exposed many community concerns. Salazar had previously traveled to Santo Domingo, where he served the *Los Angeles Times* as a foreign correspondent and covered the U.S. intervention in the Dominican Civil War. He also spent time in Mexico City during the protests over the 1968 Olympics that led to the Tlatelolco Massacre at the Plaza de las Tres Culturas.

According to Ernesto Vigil, former member of the Crusade for Justice and expert on FBI surveillance during the Chicano Movement, Salazar may have been targeted because of his critical reporting and his interaction with leftist movements and groups.[22] Salazar had grown sympathetic to the oppression of Chicanos and others who were subjugated globally, and he began reporting it at the national level. Those looking for an explanation of whether Salazar's death was a murder or a mere accident need look no further, as the motive to silence a Chicano journalist concerned with social justice was clear as day. A Los Angeles sheriff's deputy ended Salazar's life without even being prosecuted, and the pathetic and biased inquiry further convinced those within the Chicano Movement that their war was at home and not in Southeast Asia.[23] With the untimely "assassination" of Rubén Salazar, the Chicano Moratorium and Movement were dealt a tremendous blow, but would continue to be fueled by his status as martyr to the Chicano cause.

Chicanos through various groups, including the Crusade for Justice and the Brown Berets, rallied behind Salazar's death and addressed the longstanding issue of police brutality against the Mexican American community. Chicanos who protested at home could not identify with the war in Southeast Asia, nor could they vilify the Vietnamese, who instead Chicanos identified with as common victims of American imperialism. On the other hand, these youths saw their own government as the villains. Not only did they see their leaders as imperialists, but they also saw how their own people were dying needlessly in a war that did not make sense to Chicanos and would not bring improvements to their communities or country. Rosalío Muñoz and the Chicano Moratorium argued that as White middle-class males became experts in obtaining draft deferments, predominantly White draft boards filled their quotas by conscripting impoverished Mexican Americans. As the number of Mexican American casualties rose in Southeast Asia, Chicanos began making the assertion that this indeed was a type of genocide against their youth.[24]

Rosalío Muñoz, who had successfully challenged his induction into the Army, saw the importance of having a solely Chicano antiwar movement, as they faced unique challenges as a minority. "Historically, Chicanos have only been offered the dirtiest work of American society. Chicanos pick the crops, man the factories, sew the clothes, wash the dishes, and clean the mess of White America . . . This demonstration aims to expose the fact that second to Vietnamese, the heaviest burdens of the war have fallen on the Chicano community," pointed out Muñoz. "The Chicano people, through its moratorium, is now saying that the front line for Chicano youths is not Vietnam but is the struggle for social justice here in the United States."[25] With strong Chicano nationalist sentiment, Muñoz worked to move away from the national antiwar movement and strictly set a fitting Chicano agenda.

The Chicano Moratorium attracted *raza*[26] from across the Southwest who saw the conflict in Vietnam as secondary to their fight to obtain first-class citizenship. Both high-profile Chicanos and common folk rallied behind the cause. Chicanos took to the streets to vocalize their disapproval of the war and the draft. Witty slogans were chanted throughout the streets:

"*Chale* No, We Won't Go!," "*Chale con el* Draft!," and "Bring All Our *Carnales* Home . . . Alive!" Protestors even concluded with a chant praising Che Guevara: "Che, Che, Che Guevara."[27] Chicanos praised El Che and Fidel Castro for their recent victory in overthrowing a corrupt and tyrannical dictator who was supported by the United States in Cuba. Their determination to stand firm against "Yankee imperialism" and in defense of the Cuban people, who had been long exploited by foreign interests, were admirable to many Chicanos. Still, other Chicanos served in the U.S. military in efforts to topple the Castro regime during the Bay of Pigs Invasion and in the highly confrontational Cuban Missile Crisis that almost brought about a nuclear war between Cuban ally, the Soviet Union and the United States.

Highly concerned about the escalation of conflict on the home front and the social inequality suffered by impoverished inner-city youth, Chicano civil rights attorney, novelist, and activist Oscar Zeta Acosta, attracted to the moratorium, declared, "It's time we did more than march; your whole life has to be for the Chicano . . . So far as the Vietnam War is concerned, I have nothing to say about it; it doesn't exist; our fight is here."[28] Acosta—better known in popular culture through his pseudonym, Dr. Gonzo, as interpreted by his dear friend Hunter S. Thompson in the novel *Fear and Loathing in Las Vegas*—wrote his own novel based on the events of the Chicano Moratorium in 1970, *The Revolt of the Cockroach People.* The antiwar sentiments were immense, and Chicanos articulated the message through as many venues as possible as the feelings of oppression had been brewing long enough.

The controversy over the Vietnam War also reached the music industry. Vocalizing her displeasure with California's political leadership was Chicana singer/songwriter and activist Joan Baez. Baez performed "Drug Store Truck Driving Man" at Woodstock in 1969, a song she dedicated to then governor of California Ronald Reagan (pronounced as Ray-GUNS by Baez's band).[29] Reagan drew criticism from antiwar groups, including Chicanos, who felt that the administration was prompting draft boards to meet their quotas by drafting the poor, including a high number of Chicanos. Baez vocalized strong opposition to the war in Vietnam: "Browns and Blacks are the targets of the most vicious attacks by the state because minorities are the easiest to manipulate. They are the brunt because America needs them

... One of the tragedies of war is that poor people of every nationality are the ones who carry most of the guns, suffer, fight, and die."[30] Although the majority of the casualties in Vietnam were Caucasian soldiers, at certain points throughout the war, Chicano and African American casualties were disproportionate to their populations. Eventually in December 1972, Baez traveled to Hanoi and delivered mail to U.S. prisoners of war during Operation Linebacker II, also known as "the Christmas Bombings."

Not all Mexican Americans were critical of the war effort. Some artists sought to boost the morale of soldiers by traveling to Vietnam and performing for thousands of U.S. troops. Domingo Peña, host of Corpus Christi's KIII-TV's *Domingo Peña Show*, which aired on Sunday mornings over a sixteen-year period, led a twelve-artist tour of Vietnam in January 1968. Accompanying Peña were the popular Paulino Bernal y Conjunto Bernal from Kingsville, Texas; Las Rancheritas, a female *mariachi* from Alamo, Texas; and local Corpus Christi comedian José "Cantinflitas" Moreno. Domingo Peña called it "the most gratifying, tremendous experience of my life," as he reassured the public of the well-being of their soldiers in Southeast Asia.[31] "The most important thing for you to know is that your sons and husbands and nephews are being taken care of. They don't lack anything," stated Peña. "You should see the morale. It is just tremendous. Our men are 100 percent with our government. They don't mind being there. Some are back for their second and third times. We even talked to wounded ones who would gladly do it again."[32] Peña painted a very positive picture of the Chicano Vietnam War experience, and perhaps his close relationship with Dr. Héctor García, who remained a loyal ally to President Lyndon Johnson and to the war effort, had influence on his perspective.

Dr. Héctor García and the American G.I. Forum—also from Corpus Christi, Texas—sponsored this first "all-Latin American group" to perform for soldiers in Vietnam. Through collaboration with the United Service Organizations (USO) and President Lyndon Johnson, the all–Mexican American delegation went off to Vietnam on a seventeen-day tour.[33] Peña served as spokesperson for the twelve-person tour. "It's such a good feeling when boys run up to you crying for happiness to see someone from back home," said Peña about his Vietnam experience.[34] Peña recorded thousands of messages from soldiers, which he would broadcast on his radio show.[35] The public wanted to hear from their soldiers, and the soldiers plagued by the homesick blues were eager to send their greetings. Peña's assertion differed tremendously from the views expressed by Chicanos who spoke against the war. Peña's claim also contrasted drastically with the reported military activity in Vietnam. Coinciding with the all–Latin American group's visit in January 1968 was the siege of the Marine Base at Khe Sanh, which lasted five and a half months during the Tet Offensive that saw the intensification of combat throughout South Vietnam.

Ray Camacho and the Teardrops also supported the troops and performed in Vietnam on three separate occasions in 1970, 1971, and 1973.[36] Ray Camacho's experience was slightly different from Peña's account and reflective of the interpretations given by veterans in the historical literature. In describing the troops, Camacho stated, "They count the days and the hours till they come home. We played 'By The Time I Get to Phoenix' and some of them cried. It was hard for us too." In summarizing his experience Camacho concluded, "American GIs are the greatest audience in the world," however "[many] feel like they're forgotten at home."[37] Previously, Camacho had performed on USO tour events in Korea, where the band performed in thirty-five shows during a twenty-day period and many times they could hear gunfire nearby.

Luis Cacho, a *mariachi*, also performed at a USO-sponsored event in Vietnam, where his sound catered to the Latino active duty listener. At local venues and *bailes* in the Southwest, Little Joe y La Familia and other Mexican American *orquestas* and *conjuntos* attracted Chicano audiences and sang folk songs or *corridos* about the heroics of their men fighting in Vietnam. Many within the Mexican American community embraced the patriotic endeavors of their brothers and sisters who served in Vietnam.

Observing the war effort was the "Mexican American Generation," who had served in the military during World War II, along with the surviving few who had served in World War I. After coming home and continuing to experience inequality, they became politically active in the American G.I. Forum and the League of United Latin American Citizens (LULAC). The "Mexican American Generation" felt that by working within the system, they would soon obtain equality. By the 1940s and 1950s, the Mexican American generation became involved in mainstream issues regarding civil rights, including fighting for inclusion on juries (*Hernández v. Texas*, 1954) and ending school segregation (*Mendez v. Westminster*, 1947, and *Hernández v. Driscoll CISD*, 1948), while maintaining respect for, and loyalty to, the United States.

By the time of the Vietnam era, the Mexican American generation had demonstrated political mobilization and had significant voter turnout for both John F. Kennedy in 1960 and for Lyndon B. Johnson in 1964. Johnson rewarded Dr. García by appointing him alternate ambassador to the United Nations. Aside from Dr. García, numerous Mexican Americans were making an impact on the national political scene. In San Antonio, Texas, Henry B. González had been elected as a Democratic member of the United States House of Representatives; Edward Roybal occupied the same position in his home district in Boyle Heights, California; and Raymond Telles Jr. had successfully become the first Mexican American mayor of a major American city (El Paso) and moved on to garner significant appointments under three different U.S. presidents, including President Johnson.

Despite the working relationships between President Johnson and Mexican American politicians and statesmen, both sides bumped heads on a variety of issues, especially the overwhelming casualty rate of Mexican American soldiers in Vietnam. After a thorough analysis in 1967, Congressman González noted that the Spanish-surnamed constituted 41 percent of the population in his district yet accounted for 72 percent of Vietnam casualties.[38] Congressman Roybal made similar inquiries and concluded that while Mexican Americans were overrepresented in combat, there was a limited number of Mexican American officers. Eventually, "Johnson's anguish about the war was heightened by the unfairness of the draft. He saw it as another injustice visited on the less fortunate minorities."[39] The president's solution called for more token appointments of Mexican Americans and African Americans on draft boards.

In 1970, Dr. Ralph Guzmán, professor of political science at the University of California, Santa Cruz, produced a brow-raising study regarding Chicano casualties in Vietnam. Guzmán concluded that between January

1961 and February 1967, Spanish-surnamed soldiers from the Southwest (Arizona, California, Colorado, New Mexico, and Texas) accounted for 19.4 percent of all American troops killed in action (KIAs) in Vietnam. Likewise, Guzmán noted that from December 1967 to March 1969, Spanish-surnamed soldiers from the Southwest accounted for 19 percent of the KIAs in Vietnam. At the time, those Spanish surnames only tallied close to 12 percent of the population of the Southwest and 4.5 percent in the country. Guzmán showed that Mexican Americans carried a disproportionate burden in their sacrifice to the war effort. Not included in Guzmán's study were the many other additional Mexican American *veteranos* with English surnames.[40]

As entire Mexican American communities became aware of the staggering figure of Chicano KIAs, they not only became disillusioned with the war, but they began as well to focus more on the terrible inconsistencies that existed on the home front. The Guzmán study merely reinforced what Chicanos already knew: that they were overrepresented among the casualties in Southeast Asia. Meanwhile, Chicanos also saw a contradiction between their second-class citizenship and their high death rates in Vietnam. Chicano soldiers demonstrated tremendous valor; yet at the same time, their heroism accounted for an overwhelming number of casualties. Why should they die in greater numbers than other groups only to be discriminated against in their home country?

Chicanos who protested the war argued that casualties among Mexican Americans were disproportionate for several reasons. The draft that targeted them was the primary culprit. Also, social barriers remaining in the United States that hindered the life chances of many Mexican Americans were to blame. High school and college-age Chicanos were especially concerned about the high death rates since the draft directly threatened their futures. Given the circumstances, young Chicanos often supported and participated in the antiwar demonstrations. Still, the question remained as to why Chicanos were dying in such high proportions in Vietnam.

Poverty, patriotism, *machismo*,[41] along with the lack of educational opportunities all contributed to the high number of Mexican American casualties in Vietnam. Soldiers from Hidalgo County in the Rio Grande Valley located in deep South Texas, a predominantly Mexican American region along the U.S.-Mexico border, had a death rate almost double the national rate in 1968. In March 1968, figures showed that one American soldier had died per 9,170 people living in the United States; however, the deaths among soldiers from Hidalgo County equaled one per 4,739 Americans.[42]

Not coincidentally, Hidalgo County ranked as one of the most impoverished areas in the country. Lack of opportunity and the inability to obtain educational deferments pushed Chicanos to the frontlines in Vietnam. Poverty-stricken, marginalized, and motivated by *machismo*, they often took the more dangerous jobs in Vietnam as their families back home relied heavily on their service allotments for subsistence.[43] The Rio Grande Valley historically has demonstrated high levels of patriotism and has furnished a great number of soldiers in America's various conflicts, including those today in Iraq and Afghanistan.

The Mexican American generation, which was extremely patriotic, not only supported the war effort in Southeast Asia but also saw the high casualty rate as "a badge of honor."[44] The Mexican American generation, including Dr. Hector García of the American G.I. Forum, felt they had a patriotic duty to fight for their country and attain a sense of belonging in a nation that often saw them as second-class citizens. This group wanted to show the broader populace and the rest of the world that the Mexican American people were loyal and valuable citizens in the United States. Hence, during the Vietnam War they saw that young Mexican American soldiers were simply reinforcing their patriotism and loyalty. The Japanese American community demonstrated similar efforts during World War II. In order to prove their loyalty, Japanese American men and women overcompensated with their service to the American war effort and valiantly served in the Army, including with the 100th Infantry Battalion, 442nd Regimental Combat Team, WACs (Women's Army Corps), and the Military Intelligence Service.[45]

In a sense, the older generation was living vicariously and saw in the young (or at least hoped to see) the kind of effort and attitude that they had brought to an earlier war. Under Johnson's administration, Vicente Ximenes, a longtime member of the American G.I. Forum, became the United States commissioner of the Equal Employment Opportunity Commission and also headed the president's newly founded Inter-Agency Committee on Mexican American Affairs. Defending the war in Southeast Asia while criticizing draft dodgers, Ximenes, a proud World War II veteran, exaggeratedly boasted that "Mexican Americans don't burn draft cards because we have none to burn. We volunteer."[46]

Both the Mexican American and the Chicano generations wanted similar improvements to their society along with first-class citizenship. Their approaches differed, yet their resolve to attain equity cannot be denied. With the appointment of Vicente Ximenes, along with Dr. García's accomplishments and the activities of the American G.I. Forum and LULAC, betterment in the lives of Mexican Americans seemed to be gradually occurring.

To young Chicanos, progress did not come quickly enough. They saw the few appointments of Mexican Americans to political positions of authority as merely token in an otherwise civil rights agenda that targeted Black America. Criticisms of the Johnson administration simmered as Chicanos became convinced that their concerns were not a priority to the Texan. They also grew impatient with the older guard of Mexican Americans who supported Johnson. Consequently, young Chicanos branched out, launching grass-roots movements dealing with what they believed were more important issues, which included local and national concerns.

Chicanos rallied behind an array of concerns ranging from addressing social inequality, along with police brutality, to supporting *los pintos* (Chicanos in prison), to backing the struggles of farmworkers, to promoting cultural reaffirmation. Chicanos also were adamant in endorsing their Mexican culture and Indigenous roots, which to a certain extent had faded due to forced and voluntary acculturation. Cultural plurality became a key component as Chicanos embraced their heritage along with their identity as "Brown people" or "people of color." Chicanos took their pride to the streets during protest marches carrying signs that read "Brown Is Beautiful" and "Brown and Proud."

At the same time, Chicanos negotiated their American identity, that also had a tremendous influence on who they were. Living in the United States, American popular culture had a tremendous impact on Chicano youth; thus their American identity counted significantly in what it meant to be Chicano. Chicanos also addressed numerous concerns that impacted their daily lives in an impoverished America that saw them as second-tier citizens. Their fight for equality became quite broad. Due to the large number of problems that Chicanos sought to tackle, *el movimiento* became easily open to criticism and derailment. Just like several civil rights groups of the era, Chicanos faced accusations of being extreme radicals and of having Communist sympathies, which caused a loss of credibility during the Cold War.[47] In more extreme circumstances, Chicano organizations such as the Crusade for Justice and Brown Berets were infiltrated by police, federal agents, and informants.[48]

While protesting their status as second-class citizens, the younger, more leftist Chicanos sympathized not only with the Communists in North Vietnam but also with the recent victorious revolutionaries in Cuba, and also with other leftist groups seeking power throughout the globe. With a broader view of the fight against oppression and imperialism, young Chicanos embraced the figures of Fidel Castro and Ernesto "Che" Guevara, whom they identified as being symbolic of the struggle against global imperialistic oppression.

At the same time, in one of the many ironies of war, a Cuban interrogator simply known as "Fidel" tortured and interrogated Chicano POWs in Southeast Asia.[49] After his brutal assault led to the death of an American POW, "Fidel" became known for his ruthless treatment of POWs as well as for the iconic Che-like beret he wore. Yet, Chicanos protesting the high casualty rates of their brothers in Vietnam also embraced the symbolic figures of those who tormented their fellow Chicanos— an intricate paradox indeed that demonstrates the complexities that exist within Mexican American communities.

As the deaths took a toll among Mexican Americans from the Southwest, Chicanos who protested the war believed the conflict was generating a Chicano genocide.[50] The older Mexican American generation had closely aligned itself with President Johnson, and its members were now accused by the youth of being "*Tío Tacos*" (the Chicano equivalent to Uncle Tom). Moreover, Chicanos indicted the older generation for selling out and catering to the imperialistic purposes of those in power. Even though the Vietnam casualties were mounting in the Mexican American community, civic and social leaders such as Dr. García would not dare challenge President Johnson in public on the matter. No other American president had been as inclusive towards Mexican Americans, and in exchange they pledged their blind loyalty to President Johnson and the American military strategy in Vietnam.

Young Chicanos considered the war in Vietnam to be unjust and that it showcased American imperialistic goals while resulting in the needless deaths of people of color. Yet at the same time, young Chicanos themselves reflected American culture as their demonstrations coincided with the counterculture and antiwar movements popular on university campuses and throughout the world at the time. The younger generation protested, believing that they no longer had to affirm their Americanism by going to war. The older generation saw the actions of the young as a sign of weakness from what they considered to be a bunch of unpatriotic whiners.

Chicano civil rights leader and scholar José Angel Gutiérrez challenged the Mexican American generation: "The G.I. Forum, particularly Dr. García would admonish us for leafleting against the war. For marching and demonstrating against the war. And when we pointed-out the extreme casualties that we were being suffered as Mexican Americans. They felt [García and the G.I. Forum] that it was a badge of honor, that you should be willing to put your life up for your country. We thought that was ridiculous. We were already born here. We were already Americans. We don't have to be proving anything."[51] Dr. García and the Mexican American generation's struggle for political inclusion came at the time of the mounting casualties suffered by Chicanos in Vietnam.

The Vietnam War further divided a nation that was already divided. In a post-*Brown v. Board of Education* society dealing with problems of integration and with implementing the Civil Rights and Voting Rights Acts, the conflict in Vietnam curtailed social progress. The war almost served as the proverbial "wrench" by diverting the nation's attention away from civil rights and back to the Cold War. The nation became polarized by a war that showed no end in sight, while Johnson's War on Poverty took a back seat.

The Johnson administration engendered further opposition to the war by not being transparent about American military intervention and its aims.

During and after the war, however, American prisoners of war and soldiers missing in action (POW/MIAS) became unifying points for the country. In 1970, doves and hawks alike came together and demonstrated solidarity and support of POW/MIAS by wearing metal bracelets engraved with their names.[52] Even those against the war found compassion toward POWS and argued that the government used them as pawns to defend and extend the iniquitous and illegal war in Southeast Asia.[53] Still, some Chicanos critical of the war believed POW/MIAS created a diversion from the real issues.

Chicanos argued that the government's overt emphasis and focus on POW/MIAS shifted attention away from the unpopularity and controversy surrounding the war and brought attention to the "victimized" men who needed to be freed. Raúl Ruiz commented, "The U.S. government looks upon the POW as a tremendous propaganda issue. The government feeds and propagates the emotionalism around the POW, if only to detract attention from the real cause of the war in Indochina. Without American involvement, there would not be any POWS."[54] Ruiz held that by rallying behind POW/MIAS, the country was practically giving newly elected President Richard Nixon a free pass in continuing an unjust and illegal war. Chicanos accused President Nixon of hiding behind POW/MIAS to further expand the war in Southeast Asia. Ruiz, in supporting the antiwar movement, further stated, "We must prevent other American men from becoming POWS for the simple reason that we should not want them to participate in the killing of innocents."[55] Many Chicanos disagreed with the war as they saw needless amounts of death on both sides.

The National League of POW/MIA Families, a committee formed by families and relatives of POW/MIAS who organized in efforts to account for their men and obtain their release, could not disagree more with Ruiz's statements. The POW/MIA families and those who supported the Vietnam War criminalized the North Vietnamese for their inhumane treatment of American POWS and their lack of accountability.[56] These groups demanded answers and the return of their men. They supported POW/MIAS and at the same time fueled President Nixon's war effort.

From 1968, during Nixon's presidential campaign, until the end of the Vietnam War in 1973, POW/MIAS became a central focus to the Nixon administration and the American public. Antiwar proponents argued that President Nixon shifted the attention to POW/MIAS as he expanded American intervention in the surrounding countries of Laos and Cambodia. In a sense, prisoners of war became "a virtual cult as many people were persuaded that the U.S. was fighting in Vietnam in order to get its prisoners back. Following the president's lead, people began to speak as though the North Vietnamese had kidnapped four hundred Americans and the U.S. had gone to war to retrieve them."[57] As Nixon and his administration projected this illusion, groups such as the National League of American POW/MIA Families, who were emotionally tied to the matter, pledged their unquestionable loyalty to the war effort. Critics, including Ruiz, clearly saw through the façade and realized Nixon was utilizing POW/MIAS as leverage in furthering the war in Southeast Asia.

Not all POW families were in support of the war and of President Nixon. Delia Álvarez, Everett Álvarez's sister, sternly criticized the Nixon administration and protested very strongly against the war. Delia agreed with the North Vietnamese who referred to American aviators as "imperial air pirates" and considered them war criminals.[58] Despite criticizing her brother and the American war effort, Delia hoped for her brother's release and safe return. Delia participated in antiwar rallies and vigils both domestically and internationally. She traveled abroad and demonstrated against the war as an effort to see her brother's return sooner rather than later. Delia saw her brother as a political pawn, used in the killing of an oppressed people in what she believed to be a politicized war.

In 1971, Delia accompanied Jane Fonda on *The Merv Griffin Show*, where the pair criticized the war.[59] Much to the embarrassment of her brother, Everett, an audio version of the television program was later played to American POWs in captivity in North Vietnam. "It was embarrassing. I was embarrassed, I never told her that, when I first heard her over the camp speaker. You know the bullshit that comes out. The propaganda. Her and Jane Fonda! I was with my friends and it's like a team. [I was] Embarrassed in front of the team," recalled Everett on having to listen to his sister's antiwar speeches while in captivity.[60]

Delia went on to form the Antiwar POW Families, an organization that recruited POW families to pressure the Nixon administration to end the conflict in Vietnam and bring back their men. Influenced in great part by the Chicano Movement, Delia protested the high casualties of Mexican American soldiers along with the death and destruction brought upon the Vietnamese. "What he [Everett] did was wrong and it has taken me many years to say that publicly. This entire country is a war criminal in that sense. This entire country is responsible for that war. My brother cannot be singled out for what he did nor [can] the soldier out in the field be singled out for what he has done," argued Delia. "Or the pilots today for what they are doing. President Nixon is also called a war criminal. Everyone is guilty for this war and what crimes we have committed against the Vietnamese people."[61] As the fighting intensified, Delia became convinced that the United States was responsible for the devastation of Vietnam and she continued to protest the war.

By 1970, the antiwar movement had become pervasive throughout Chicano communities and overshadowed those Chicanos who served. Today, little is recognized and remembered about Chicano Vietnam prisoners of war, their service, and their experiences. Despite the sacrifice of Mexican American veterans in Vietnam, the era is best known for the Chicano generation of the 1960s and 1970s as it struggled for civil rights. The majority of the Mexican American prisoners of war are lesser known than Delia Álvarez and Rosalío Muoz, who led antiwar campaigns throughout most of the conflict in Southeast Asia. The antiwar views that young Chicanos vocalized in the streets of the Southwest also appeared prominently in the historical literature and have overshadowed the efforts of the older generation. The perspectives of the previous generation, "the Mexican American Generation," appeared to fade as the new Chicano generation rose in the era of resistance and revolution, and the efforts of the youth were well-documented by the rise of the Chicano scholars who had participated in the movement or admired it from a distance.

Yet, the Mexican American generation was not the only faction within the Mexican American population to appear to lose prominence during the Vietnam era. The real loser in the struggles during the 1960s and 1970s was the Chicano Vietnam veteran, who was completely forgotten and overshadowed and at times chastised by all sides of history. In all fairness, the history of the Mexican American generation has been told, and even though they appeared to fade away during the Chicano era, the numbers of American G.I. Forumeers and LULACers actually grew. On the other hand, Chicano Vietnam veterans have been overtly excluded from the historical narrative as if their role was insignificant in the war. This lack of inclusion goes hand in hand with the lack of appreciation Latinos face in American society, as even today they are associated with negativity. Chicano Vietnam veterans have received little attention, as the historical literature is more reflective of the activities and struggles on the home front. Despite their tremendous service and contribution, the recorded stories of Mexican American heroism and patriotism are few and far apart.

Prisoners of war became a central focus of the Vietnam War as President Nixon attempted to use the POW/MIA issue to defend the war. Upon the release of American POWs, Nixon again used them as pawns to divert attention from his escalating Watergate scandal. Despite the general public's interest in the POW experience, the Mexican American perspective received limited play. Apart from Álvarez and perhaps Camacho, most Americans would be surprised to learn that there were Mexican American prisoners of war in Vietnam. Their contributions and perspectives became overshadowed by the cries of the dominant faction who denounced the war from thousands of miles away, from a home front that, despite the turmoil, had many more comforts than the triple-canopy jungles of Southeast Asia and inner-city prisons in North Vietnam. The historical literature has minimized the role of Vietnam *veteranos*, especially those who became prisoners of war, and thus they have become an "omitted generation." The history of Mexican American Vietnam veterans and prisoners of war became lost between the civil rights struggles of the Mexican American generation and the more vocal Chicano generation, with the latter becoming the focal point of interest for many historians.

CHAPTER 2

The Formative Years

EVERETT ÁLVAREZ JR. EPITOMIZES VIETNAM WAR PRISONERS OF WAR AS his capture in August 1964 resulted from the Gulf of Tonkin Incident, which is considered by most Americans as the start of the war. The history of Mexican American Vietnam War prisoners of war begins long before Tonkin. Airman Ciro Salas Jr. found himself a captive in Vietnam in 1954 at the end of the French Indochina War. However, the saga of Mexican American POWs goes beyond the notable event in the summer of 1954 that resulted in Salas's capture. Álvarez summed it up best: "In a way, I grew up to be a POW."[1] The narrative of the ten Mexican American Vietnam War POWs begins in the *barrios* and farming communities of the Southwest between the 1930s and the 1960s. There, the men battled poverty, hunger, and discrimination, and in doing so gained the survival skills necessary to cope with their captivity in Vietnam.

In the 1930s, the Great Depression had a major impact on the American population in the sense that it taught them how to cope with severe economic challenges. For the vast majority of Mexican Americans, this "survival mode" had already been commonplace. Many Mexican Americans throughout the Southwest worked long hours as laborers in commercial agriculture to subsist. "With the triumph of commercial agriculture" came overt segregation of Mexican Americans, maintains David Montejano.[2] By controlling how and where Mexican Americans worked, White Americans could shift that dominance to most aspects of life and thereby completely subjugate Mexican Americans under a unique type of Jim Crow.

By the 1940s, Mexican Americans living in the rural Southwest were exposed to an institutionalized form of second-class citizenship where they served as the hired help and remained isolated in their *barrios*.[3] It was very much a segregated society, akin to the inequality that plagued the African American community. In urban areas throughout the Southwest, Mexican Americans faced open discrimination from law enforcement officials who saw them as nothing more than criminals.[4] Despite the contributions of Mexican Americans in World War II and to the war effort domestically, predominantly Anglo authorities saw Mexican American youth as un-American and targeted them for trivial matters such as clothing. Police persecution culminated in the well-documented "Zoot Suit Riots" that erupted throughout Los Angeles in 1943.[5]

During the war years, the second-generation Mexican American youth in Los Angeles had embraced a Mexican American identity, as noted by George J. Sánchez. Distinguishing themselves from their more traditional Mexican parents, the youth embraced American culture and were particularly influenced by Hollywood and the jazz culture of the 1930s. The symbolic influence came through the use of the zoot suit, "with a broad-brimmed hat, long jacket, and draped trousers tapered at the ankles."[6] During World War II, the War Production Board—in response to war rationing—limited the amount of cloth to be used in suits. The zoot suit, which required excess fabric, was seen as un-American and inconsiderate, as it ignored the wartime rationing necessities.

As American GIs prepared to be shipped out to the Pacific Theater, the Los Angeles area became inundated with military personnel. Pumped up and ready to go fight the Japanese, Anglo-American soldiers assaulted Mexican American youth wearing zoot suits, launching a ten-day riot that resulted in the countless and unwarranted beatings of innocent Mexican

Americans. The situation worsened when the Los Angeles Police Department turned a blind eye, allowing the brutality to continue and expand throughout the city. The emerging Mexican American youth who embraced a more American identity than their parents became discouraged by the racial and cultural intolerance that targeted them due to their bicultural identity and their appearance.[7]

The bitter treatment fueled many Mexican Americans to seek opportunities beyond the Southwest. Mexican Americans sought work outside of Texas, California, Arizona, and New Mexico, their traditional homes, and ventured to the Midwest, where they found work in agriculture and the automobile industry at higher wages.[8] Leaving the Southwest demonstrated the resolve Mexican Americans had in improving their social standing and overcoming poverty and discrimination.

In the post–World War II years, organizations such as LULAC and the American G.I. Forum raised the consciousness of Mexican Americans. For veterans such as Dr. Héctor P. García, founder of the American G.I. Forum, World War II created an awareness of the inequality experienced by Mexican Americans.[9] The efforts against Nazi Germany and Imperial Japan convinced Mexican Americans to fight against their own discrimination, while also challenging them to make their society more reflective of the democratic values that they attempted to restore and uphold globally. Moreover, Mexican Americans felt they deserved equality, since they had served in the military and many continued to serve in defense of the country. Aside from creating class awareness, military service provided a modest living, which also attracted the Mexican American veterans.

Chicano veterans were plagued with the same exclusionary issues and practices faced by the rest of the Mexican American population. Through military participation, these men sought to overcome the challenges and obstacles posed by poverty and prejudice in their larger communities. Furthermore, they attempted to prove a sense of civic belonging by adhering to military duty. The draft also convinced several men to enlist, as they believed military service to be inevitable. By enlisting, these men could decide and perhaps dictate to a certain extent their roles in the given military branch of service.

To be sure, while certainly some of the men attempted to overcome so-cial barriers through military participation, the majority simply attempted to provide for their families with a steady income. Working and living with limitations had been commonplace; thus the men learned to survive hard-ship early in life. Isaac Camacho grew up on the banks of the Rio Grande in the farming community of Fabens, Texas, near El Paso, when at a young age he lost his father in a tragic automobile accident.[10] At that point, Camacho began to help provide for his mother and two sisters. "I had performed one heck of a lot of muscle work as a youngster," recalls Camacho.[11] To make sure he saved the wages he earned, he placed them in a jar he kept hidden on the roof of his home. In his youth, Camacho learned how to economize and became a responsible contributor to his family.

Camacho's work ethic arose from the fact that as a boy he became the man of the house, but it was his mother who set high standards. During Isaac's junior year in high school, his mother, Mrs. Mary Elorreaga, took a job as a cafeteria manager in El Paso and took the family with her. To make ends meet, Isaac worked as a bag boy at Furr's Supermarket, yet never abandoned his education. At Thomas Jefferson High School, Camacho served in the Ju-nior Reserve Officers' Training Corps (JROTC), where he found a passion for the military. Just prior to graduation, an Army recruiter visited Camacho's school, convincing Isaac and three of his friends to enlist. On June 6, 1955, right after graduation and three days after his eighteenth birthday, Isaac along with his three friends Juan Chávez, Roberto Armendariz, and José Vásquez joined the U.S. Army.[12]

Everett Álvarez Jr. had a similar upbringing. During his childhood, Álvarez grew mindful of his family's financial needs. His maternal grand-mother and his parents had overcome adversity and poverty to provide him and his two sisters with a better life. Álvarez recalled, "All three [parents and grandmother] had missed out on so many joys of childhood due to the rig-ors of poverty. To make ends meet they had all been compelled prematurely to take on the responsibilities of adults. And yet they had pulled through and survived."[13] These economic challenges grounded Álvarez with a strong character and instilled in him a hard work ethic. "Family stories of the adversities they [his family] faced had shaped my character and given me backbone," remembered Álvarez.[14]

"We grew up poor. You grew up knowing what it was to be without in terms of luxuries. You grew up learning to scrimp and save. Anyone who knows what it is to work alongside *braceros* knows hard work,"[15] explained Álvarez, on what it was like growing up in poverty in Salinas, California. "It seems like those guys would make good POWs in a POW camp. They'd know how to survive on bare minimum food. Maybe emotionally you learn that life isn't easy. None used to live past fifty."[16] Ironically, growing up in poverty turned out to be a blessing in disguise for Álvarez. As he toughened at the edges, Álvarez learned to cope with difficult surroundings. By working with Mexican *braceros* and keeping up with their pace, he developed a high level of endurance. More importantly, Álvarez learned necessary survival skills in his youth and today realizes the importance of his limitations: "When you had to eat *nopales* (cactus) with egg and that was your dinner, mustard greens were ok. We learned to cope with those things. When you have *nopales* and beans, hey, it's a luxury!"[17] Eating cactus was not standard procedure in Álvarez's training at the Survival Evasion Resistance and Escape Program (SERE), which prepared pilots going to Vietnam; however, the eating habits from his youth trained him not to be a picky eater.

Like many Mexican American families, Álvarez's family had instilled in him a hard work ethic and pushed him to obtain an education as a means to escape the poverty that plagued so many Chicanos in the Southwest. "As Mexicans growing up in my family, my father and mother pushed education, even though they didn't have it. And number two, you work hard."[18] After gaining distinction in high school in academics and athletics, Álvarez attended Santa Clara University and obtained an electrical engineering degree.[19]

In 1960, Everett enlisted in the U.S. Navy through the Aviation Officer Candidate Program. With an ambition to fly jets, Álvarez sought to serve his country and challenge himself in a different direction.[20] He set aside a career as an engineer, brushing away and defying social and racial barriers, and transitioned himself into a naval officer. At the time, only a limited number of Chicanos became pilots in the military.

Much like Everett Álvarez, José David Luna aspired to fly. At age twenty, on January 25, 1961, the Orange, California, native enlisted in the U.S. Air Force. After finishing basic training at Lackland Air Force Base in San

Antonio, Texas, Luna entered the Aviation Cadet Program of the Air Force for navigator training. On March 20, 1962, Luna was commissioned a second lieutenant and received his flying wings at the now decommissioned Harlingen Air Force Base in South Texas. From April 1962 to March 1963, Luna continued his next phase of training at Mather Air Force Base near Sacramento, California, where he trained to become an electronic warfare officer (EWO).[21]

Luna was en route to a military career that would relocate him throughout the country and eventually into Southeast Asia. From April 1963 to October 1966, Utah became home for Luna and his wife Pearl, as he served as EWO with B Flight of the 4677th Defense Evaluation Squadron at Hill Air Force Base in Utah. In November 1966, Luna's service took him to Southeast Asia, where he was stationed in Thailand. There he acted as an F-105F Wild Weasel EWO with the 354th Tactical Fighter Squadron of the 355th Tactical Fighter Wing at Takhli Royal Thai Air Force Base. Luna left his wife Pearl and son Jimmy in Roy, Utah, with the hope of returning soon after his overseas combat duty. For Mexican Americans like Luna, the military introduced them to a world beyond the traditional *barrios* they had grown up in, while making it possible for them to coexist in a setting that had been limited for the most part to Anglos.

Abel Larry Kavanaugh also left a wife and daughter stateside as he served in Vietnam. Born in Denver, Colorado, Larry descended from an Irish American grandfather and Mexican American grandmother. He grew up in a housing project in inner-city Denver, where he lived with his parents, a sister, and three brothers. Larry's parents struggled to provide for the family, forcing Larry to work odd jobs in his youth. Like many Mexican families of the time, beans and tortillas were the staples in the diets of the Kavanaughs. Quite often Larry went to bed hungry as the family had no food.[22]

For Larry, work took priority over education as his attention shifted from high school to odd jobs that contributed to the family's limited funds. Larry did find time for basketball, his passion, and maintained a thin, slender, and very athletic body that helped him excel. Yet, the housing projects limited his opportunities and often posed challenges that toughened up

Larry, who made a name for himself by being a tough Chicano who never backed down from a street fight.[23]

In the same projects, Larry met his future wife, Sandra Padilla. They met during their childhood and their friendship eventually blossomed into romance. Mrs. Padilla, Sandra's mother, regularly invited Larry over for supper as she knew of his family's lack of resources. Nothing fancy, just beans and tortillas, yet they were enough to satisfy Larry's empty stomach. The young couple came to share significant time together.

Larry and Sandra married when they were still in their teenage years. In an attempt to move past poverty and secure a better future for his young bride, Larry enlisted in the Marine Corps in 1967. Knowing he would be sent to Vietnam, the tough Chicano, Kavanaugh, did not hesitate and volunteered at the age of eighteen. As he left for overseas, Sandra learned she was pregnant with their first child, Cindy, who would be born while Larry served in Vietnam in April of 1968.[24]

Juan L. Jacquez from Santa Fe, New Mexico, also left a young bride and mother-to-be stateside upon being drafted into the U.S. Army and ordered to Vietnam. "When I finished basic," remembers Jacquez, "I was going to get married. A captain gave me a five-day delay before I went on AIT (Advanced Individual Training). I took it [along with an extended leave without approval]. I went to the stockade thirty days for it. I was in there two weeks. I knew how to cut hair, [so] I became the barber at Ft. Bliss."[25] Even though his short hiatus had immediate consequences, Jacquez prioritized getting married, as he knew he eventually would find himself going to Vietnam.

In his youth, Jacquez worked numerous jobs and was prepared for a life of hard work and to endure with extreme limitations. At the age of ten, his father was killed in an accident, forcing Jacquez to take on the responsibility of providing for his family, which included three brothers and three sisters.[26] Living in rural Gallina, New Mexico, posed confines to finding work as Jacquez found himself constrained to working in agriculture. He migrated into neighboring Colorado and Utah where he found summer work. "I went to Colorado on my own at the age of seventeen," Jacquez related. "I worked in the potato fields. At seventeen, I lied about my age and went to Utah. I knew the guy knew that I was making up a story. I was operating heavy machinery with an uncle, turning soil over."[27] The future Vietnam veteran was prepared to go to the extreme in order to provide for his family.

Toward his late teenage years, Jacquez was distracted by what he describes as his "teenage years of hell," and he admits he does not know how he survived them.[28] Without having a strong disciplinarian at home and having to take on the role of breadwinner, Jacquez became swayed by negative influences that led him to self-destructive behavior. Working kept Jacquez from focusing on school as education became secondary to survival. Also, diverting him was his recklessness, which often led Jacquez to the verge of getting in trouble with the law.

By the time Jacquez was nineteen, he continued to find himself providing for his family with limited opportunities. In June 1967, two months after his nineteenth birthday, Juan received his draft notice from the U.S. Army. Jacquez recalled, "It was nothing new. In those days, during the Vietnam War, people were getting drafted left and right. They were just dumping them [Chicanos] in there. My next-door neighbor had just gotten back, and I'm like 'I guess I have to go replace you.'"[29] He did not hesitate, nor did he try to challenge his induction; Jacquez proudly answered his country's call to duty.

Hector Michael Acosta also shared a hardworking background as a youth in which he found employment in several areas in his native San Antonio. To help make ends meet, Acosta mowed lawns during his youth. At age sixteen, he worked as a groundskeeper at Fort Sam Houston. He then took a job in a factory that built air conditioners. Throughout his adolescence, work became an integral part of Hector's life, as it did with many of the Mexican American youth of the time.

Growing up in poverty in blue-collar San Antonio, Hector never backed down from his tough living situation. Instead he set goals and aspired to surpass his impoverished upbringing. Deeply moved by San Antonio's rich Catholic heritage, at a young age Hector dreamed of becoming a priest one day. After being impressed by the technology of the time, he later sought to become a jet pilot. While never losing sight of his initial dream of becoming a priest, Hector worked hard and spent five and a half years in the seminary.

From 1963–1968, Acosta attended St. John Minor Seminary, Assumption Seminary, and St. Mary's University in San Antonio.

As he continued his education, Hector worked a variety of odd jobs as a handyman, a stock boy at Sears, and as a seasonal worker at the post office to help pay for his schooling. "I think I lived a challenging enough life," recalled Acosta. "I worked long hours. Lived in a shack. No heat or hot water. I lived a rather austere college life. I had saved a coupon from some store for two pounds of hamburger meat, for when times got tough."[30] His working-class background prepared Acosta to cope with limitations while he strove for an education to obtain a brighter future and transcend social and racial barriers.

By 1968, Hector's interest in the priesthood had dwindled as he and his soon-to-be wife, Orphalinda, began a serious relationship. He quit the seminary and set his sights on Orphalinda and completing a degree in psychology from St. Mary's University. After graduating in May 1970, Acosta attempted to fulfill his second childhood dream. With the aspiration of learning to fly jets, he joined the Air Force, entering the Air Force Officer Training School at Lackland Air Force Base on May 22, 1970.[31] He went on to receive his wings at Mather Air Force Base and became trained as a certified tactical reconnaissance and weapons system operator. In the summer of 1972, Acosta reported for overseas combat duty at Udorn Royal Thai Air Force Base and joined the 14th Tactical Reconnaissance Squadron, 432nd Tactical Reconnaissance Wing.

Leaving their homes and families behind was a great concern for Mexican American soldiers. They did their best to acculturate in the military environment, but they were greatly concerned for their grieving parents who were home waiting helplessly. Ciro Salas Jr.'s situation is reminiscent of the popular World War II-era song "Soldado Raso" [Buck private], which describes a young buck private who fulfilling his patriotic duty serves in the frontlines.[32] The young soldier is confident he will return home a hero and even receive commendation. His only worry, however, is his mother, who he has left behind. Pedro Infante's interpretation of the song resonated in the lives of many Mexicans and Mexican Americans serving in the U.S. military. During the Vietnam War era, "Soldado Raso" was covered by several

Chicano musical groups, and the song's lyrics were even updated to reflect the current military conflict.

> I am going as a buck private,
> I am going to the frontlines
> with brave boys
> who leave beloved mothers,
> who leave sweethearts crying.
> Crying at their farewell.
>
> I am leaving for the war happily,
> I got my rifle and pistol,
> I'll return as a sergeant
> when this combat is over;
> The only thing I regret:
> leaving my mother alone.
>
> Brown Virgin,
> send me your blessing,
> never allow
> heaven to steal her from me.
>
> My lovely Guadalupe
> will protect my flag
> and when I find myself in combat,
> far away from my land,
> I will prove that my race
> knows how to die anywhere.
>
> I leave early tomorrow
> as the light of day shines
> here goes another Mexican
> who knows how to gamble his life, that gives his farewell singing:
> long live my country.

Brown Virgin,
I entrust my mother;
take care of her, she is so good,
take care of her until my return.

Even with their lives in immediate danger, as Mexican American soldiers faced the dangers of combat and captivity, they primarily worried about the well-being of their families back home. Shortly after his release in 1954, Salas—evoking the spirit of "Soldado Raso"—wrote to his father assuring him of his safety.

Family also played a prominent role in José Manuel Astorga's life. The Tijuana-born Astorga was one of six children living with his mother in San Diego. Limited economic opportunity pushed Astorga to look for work outside of San Diego. After a short stint in the Job Corps working in auto repair and welding to help support his brothers and sisters, Astorga enlisted in the U.S. Army at age seventeen.[33] Worried for her son's safety, Mrs. Astorga reluctantly signed the consent forms required for José, a minor, to enlist in the Army.

In the military, Astorga believed he could acquire the necessary skills to thrive once he ended his service. To a certain extent, he enlisted to escape the limited opportunities and the inequality he faced on a daily basis. José was eager to leave the streets of San Diego, where police frequently abused their power and maintained a strict watch over Mexican American youth. Astorga, who experienced prejudice in downtown San Diego, recalled his treatment by law enforcement: "Police were very strict. [I was] wearing a fishing hat, they didn't like it. Told us to tuck in our shirt."[34] Astorga's experience with discrimination is reminiscent of the anti-Mexican attitude in Los Angeles during the early 1940s, which culminated in the Zoot Suit Riots of 1943.[35]

Alfonso "Al" Riate's enlistment in the U.S. Marine Corps was also shaped by law enforcement. According to old friend and fellow Marine Anthony Williams, Riate had an eventful youth in Santa Rosa and Pico Rivera, California (near downtown Los Angeles). After several run-ins with the law, Williams claimed Riate was given an offer to "Get out of the streets of Pico Rivera and out of jail" by "volunteering" for combat duty in Vietnam.[36]

In many ways, the Marine Corps provided Riate with a way out of the *barrio*. Soon after Riate's birth, his father passed away, leaving Riate under the care of his mother, who he never got along with. According to fellow prisoner of war John Young, "[Riate had] been on his own since he could walk."[37] His rough upbringing instilled a very aggressive nature in him. Riate, who never shied away from a good fight or from his true beliefs, posed as much of a threat to his fellow prisoners of war as he did to his Vietnamese captors.

José Jesús "Joe" Anzaldúa Jr. also enlisted in the Marine Corps, but the future major had slightly different reasons for joining. Being Mexican American from rural and racially conscious Refugio, Texas, led Anzaldúa to mature at a very young age. In the 1960s, Refugio experienced racial segregation: "Across the tracks *es el barrio de los negros* [the Black neighborhood] in the middle by [Highway] 77 *es el barrio de los Mexicanos* [the Mexican neighborhood], and on this side *es el barrio de los gabachos* [the White neighborhood]," acknowledges Anzaldúa's longtime friend and fellow Marine Albert "Smiley" Cuéllar, who described the segregated areas that existed in Refugio.[38] In Texas, as in the rest of the Southwest, segregation was beyond the Black and White paradigm as a third community, the Mexican American community, also fell victim to Jim Crow.

In his youth, Anzaldúa came to accept the barriers that existed in South Texas, but never did he equate it to race. "There were the haves and the have-nots, not necessarily attributed to a race. There were social barriers, as I would refer to it, that prevented them from going out with us. We accepted them [the social barriers]. We didn't acknowledge it as a prejudice, more of a social-economic barrier," commented Anzaldúa. Life in socially conservative Texas has historically taken a severe toll on Mexican Americans who grew up facing such stark treatment that it became acceptable to them and desensitized them from the blatant racism that supported and defended these practices.

To overcome the barriers and to help his family manage, Joe began to work at the age of eleven. He worked odd jobs, such as grain operator, ranch hand, and farmworker. "We grew up together," claims Smiley Cuéllar. "We lived about four to five blocks from each other. We went to school together.

We worked after school and on the weekends. *Ibamos a la pisca* [We picked crops—primarily refers to cotton picking]."[39] Historically, agriculture has been the way to subsist in South Texas as the weather and environment have been favorable for excellent farming.

Smiley and Joe remained friends throughout high school and dreaded being drafted into the Army, so they decided to enlist and perhaps dictate their military occupational specialties (MOS). "About three weeks before we graduated *llego el pinche* Marine recruiter, *vato, ahi en la escuela* [the Marine recruiter arrived at our school]. We knew they were gonna call us for the draft. *Y como te digo*, we did not want to get drafted, man. *Pero* we don't want to be in the damn Army, *vato*. So, shit let's volunteer for the Marine Corps, man," recalled Cuellar. "What really got us, *vato*, was the uniform. We looked at the uniforms *de los* Marines, *del* Army, *del* Navy. *Cuando estaban hablando los vatos* [when the recruiters were speaking]. *Chingado!* [Damn!] That son-of-bitch looks sharp to the max," reminisced Cuéllar over their recruitment into the Marine Corps [and the dress attire of their recruiter].[40] Anzaldúa and Cuéllar knew that one way or another they would find themselves in Vietnam and they accepted their destiny. "We knew we were going to Vietnam. That's what we wanted to do," explains Cuéllar.[41] They simply wanted as much personal input in the situation as possible.

Anzaldúa's parents had to sign consent forms since Joe was still seventeen. "My dad felt it'd be good for me. My mom was supportive but hesitant [since] I had some cousins who had been killed over there. They both had to sign for me to go in because I was a minor."[42] Joe and Smiley went into the Marine Corps under the buddy system, which brought some comfort. Two weeks after graduating from high school, the pair were sent to boot camp in San Diego. "After we graduated from boot camp, Joe got sent to Vietnamese school and I got sent straight to Vietnam and that's where we broke up," clarified Cuéllar. In total, Anzaldúa along with four other friends and classmates from Refugio served in Vietnam.

Cuellar remained in contact with Anzaldúa during their first couple of months "in-country" (Vietnam). "He was down south somewhere and I was up north. I used to write him. *Y nada y nada y nada* [No response]. I didn't know what the hell happened. I thought he might have been killed.

When I got back I found out he was a prisoner," explains Cuéllar. It was not until after his tour and return to Refugio in 1969 that Cuéllar learned of Anzaldúa's fate. "*Estabamos en una cantina aqui y llego el jefito de aquel vato. Y se me quedo viendo* [We were at a bar and Joe Anzaldúa's dad walked in and stared at me]. 'Why did you come back and my son didn't?' 'What the hell, man? *Tu sabes que Joe y yo somos asi. Asi pasa* [You know that Joe and I are close friends. It's just one of those situations].'" Mr. Anzaldúa complained that Joe was "in jail." Smiley explained: "No, no, no man it's different. *No esta en el bote*, he's a fucking POW, man!"[43] Despite the cruel war experiences that took the men in opposite directions, their friendship continues today.

While some Mexican Americans, after being influenced by their friends, joined the military under the buddy system, others joined for personal reasons and aspirations. The men shared similar experiences growing up in the Southwest, where they endured poverty, prejudice, and inequality. Food was scarce, and all ten men began working at a young age to help provide for their families. Alfonso Riate, Isaac Camacho, Juan Jacquez, and José Astorga grew up without fathers and became significant contributors to their families. After obtaining college degrees, José David Luna, Everett Álvarez Jr., and Hector Acosta joined the service with the aspiration to fly. Three men enlisted in the Marine Corps, one enlisted in the Navy, three in the Air Force, two in the Army, and Jacquez was the sole draftee into the Army and later reenlisted.

The group also shares several anomalies. Ciro Salas was with the first group of Americans to get captured in Vietnam in 1954. Isaac Camacho became the first prisoner of war to successfully escape in South Vietnam in 1965. In 1964, Everett Álvarez was the first pilot shot down and captured in North Vietnam. Larry Kavanaugh and Alfonso Riate, after being extremely resistant during their captivity in the jungle, allegedly joined the Peace Committee and reportedly collaborated with the enemy. Consequently, upon their return Kavanaugh and Riate, along with the other six members of the Peace Committee, were charged with mutiny. The charges would lead to tragedy.

The war was as controversial to this group of men as it was to the entire Mexican American community. While initially all men served gallantly and without reservations, Alfonso Riate and Larry Kavanaugh, toward the end of their captivity, became extremely vocal about ending the conflict, which brought tremendous destruction to Vietnam and brutal treatment to American prisoners of war. The dissent Riate and Kavanaugh demonstrated is similar to the sentiment expressed by the Chicano youth throughout the Southwest that called for the end of U.S. intervention in Vietnam. Riate and Kavanaugh, within the prisoner-of-war camps, called for an end to the war and criticized American intervention in Vietnam and the rest of Southeast Asia. Similarly, young Chicanos saw the war impact them personally as the nation relied on them to answer the call of duty.

Older prisoners such as Álvarez and career-oriented personnel expressed blind loyalty to the United States' war effort that paralleled the attitudes of the older contingency within the Mexican American community. This older faction equated patriotism with military service, as they were proud of their own contributions during the World Wars and Korea. This group believed that their military participation and the current overrepresentation of Mexican Americans in Vietnam entitled them to first-class citizenship. The older generation used the military contributions of the young in Vietnam to demonstrate that Mexican Americans were loyal patriots and vital for the preservation of American democracy. As this older generation fought for the inclusion of Mexican Americans in the mainstream, they showcased the strong military culture in their communities, which emphasized their loyalty and commitment to the United States.

CHAPTER 3

The Manly Ideals of Machismo, Duty, and Patriotism

AS A GUNNER ON AN M-113 ARMORED PERSONNEL CARRIER IN THE VICIN-
ity of Pleiku, South Vietnam, twenty-year-old Juan L. Jacquez, manning a .50
caliber machine gun, radiated with *machismo*. He, of course, believed himself
at the time to be untouchable. Like many young Chicanos, Jacquez's manliness propelled him to take ill-advised risks. He knew he was an immense
target for the enemy, but because of the weapons at his disposal, Jacquez
also felt immortal. Drafted at the age of nineteen, Jacquez (the only Vietnam
War POW to be a draftee) did not back down from serving. At his young age,
he was eager to fulfill the masculine task of serving in warfare.

> I spent my time in the jungle. Shit! *Ahora* [Now], I look back, kind of a
> stupid thing to do. But then, I volunteered and I did it. I thought at the
> time I was all proud because I had a Cobra helicopter riding on each side
> of me—"*Muy chingón!*" [Real tough guy!] I'm kind of special, you know. Shit!
> Do you know what I was hauling on that SOB? In those tankers? Chopper
> fuel! Even the choppers on the sides of me would have been gone. *Pero*
> [but], you know—"*todo pendejo*" [very foolish].[1]

Manliness was not the only motivating factor that persuaded the Mexican American prisoners of war to serve in Vietnam. Mexican American veterans served in the military for various reasons, and different influences provoked them to partake in the service. The Cold War, patriotism, religion, heritage, prowar propaganda, camaraderie, the thrill of adventure, and also a dreadful draft motivated the men to serve. However complex the rationales that inspired Chicanos to serve, gender, masculinity, and their ethnicity played key roles in these various motivations.

Historically, Mexican Americans, along with *mestizos* before them and their Native American ancestors, have played significant roles throughout military campaigns in North America. Natives from Mexico along with *Tejanos* (Spanish settlers living in the early missions in present-day Texas) fought against the British for American independence between 1776 and 1781.[2] Before the emergence of Latin American republics, the Native ancestors of Chicanos fought against their European colonizers and against other warring tribes. At a young age, through the interactions with family, boys gained awareness of gender identity often connected with taking on the role of protector. Military service and combat have been part of the history of Mexican Americans,[3] who have engaged in patriotic duty since the American Civil War.

In the twentieth century, the predecessors of the Vietnam generation participated in various wars in both the United States and Mexico. In many instances, the grandparents of Chicano Vietnam veterans had served and died in the Mexican Revolution of 1910, while other relatives served in the World Wars, Korean conflict, Berlin Crisis, and Cuban Missile Crisis. For some Chicanos, a rich military family tradition proved enough motivation to volunteer to serve in Vietnam, and they merely answered their country's call to duty as their fathers, uncles, and brothers had done before them. Latina Women also valiantly answered the United States' call to duty during World War II and proudly donned the uniform in patriotic service to their country.

For Chicanos serving in Vietnam, *machismo* or the conceptualization of manly ideals played roles at various levels. *Machismo* is often simplistically translated as male chauvinism. Yet, the term goes beyond that pretentious realm and has numerous interpretations. In Spanish, the word *macho* simply translates as "male." The term has been used in the United States to describe types as varied as the sexist and sexually driven Latino to the relentless boxer who ignores pain and brings the fight to the opponent. To a certain extent, the term has been used to discredit or neutralize Latino males and is comparable to how the Black Legend was used to undermine the Spanish during colonial times.

Ironically, Mexican American or Mexican men rarely embrace the term *macho*, but rather use the term *chingón*, meaning "tough guy." Professor of literature Omar Castañeda put it best: "*Machismo* is complex and multifaceted and too often, in Anglo-American interpretations, reduced to self-aggrandizing male bravado that flirts with physical harm to be sexual, like some rutting for the rights to pass on genes."[4] Along with the association of sexual flare, *machismo* has come to represent male dominance.

Prior to Spanish arrival, the Indigenous population had their own conceptualization of masculinity or *machismo*. In Pre-Columbian America, many Native cultures, such as the Pueblo people who lived in the present-day Southwestern United States, defined the warrior and the hunter as solely masculine roles. Warfare and hunting became rites of passage for adolescent boys on their road to manhood. These tasks were essential for males in the Southwest and signified a transition in life and that they could now be responsible and capable of sustaining a wife and procreating.[5]

Once the Spanish arrived, concepts of masculinity and warfare changed. Spanish soldiers, reaping the spoils of conquest, felt sexually entitled to the subjugated Native women. Through their sexual degradation of Indian women, Spaniards introduced a different form of masculinity/*machismo*, hence, sexual gratification became the most identifiable form of showcasing masculinity. Soon, Pueblo warriors also began to exploit the sexual rewards from combat. For each Spaniard, a Native warrior killed, he became entitled to the sexual exploitation of an Indigenous female, thereby changing the concepts of warfare, sex, and, consequently, masculinity among the Pueblo people.[6] Perceptions of manliness and sexual relations changed as both became synonymous with dominance. As instilled by the European colonizers, males in the Americas thus turned to power to exhibit manly virtues.

The Anglo-American interpretation of *machismo* reflects how the American establishment perceived Mexican Americans during the 1940s and 1950s. Going back to the Zoot Suit Riots in Los Angeles, for example, police captain E. Duran Ayers tied the alleged criminal nature of Mexican American youth to their Native ancestry. When describing the young *pachucos* involved in the riots, Ayers explained, "His desire is to kill or at least let blood. That is why it is difficult for Anglo-Saxons to understand the psychology of the Indian or even the Latin."[7] Despite city officials denying race to be a factor in the riots, the subsequent investigation revealed that race was a central factor.

Understanding the emerging Mexican American identity of the World War II era was as difficult for Anglo-Americans as it was for other Latinos unconscious of the everyday struggles Chicanos faced in the United States. In describing the Mexican American youth involved in the riots, Mexican writer and diplomat Octavio Páz's account, as noted by Américo Paredes, paralleled Captain Ayers's. Páz referred to the young *pachucos* involved in the riots as "sinister clowns whose purpose is to cause terror instead of laughter."[8] The Mexican American youth seemed alien to Páz, who could not accept this new hybrid identity or subculture that combined both the Mexican and his adopted American culture. Consequently, in Mexico and the United States, those individuals critical of, or not familiar with, the rising Mexican American identity coined and used terms such as *pocho*, *vendido*, and *agringado* (assimilated Mexican, sellout, and Americanized). These terms remain relevant today as they are used to describe someone who has been influenced by American culture and experienced the various levels of acculturation.

Mexican American masculinity or *machismo* is more complex than the traits Ayers and Páz attributed to the youth. In the rural borderlands of the American Southwest during the 1940s and 1950s, despite the image of the noble and chivalrous *vaquero* (cowboy) fading in the distance, honor, stoicism, and courage remained the cornerstone of masculinity. Social changes during World War II deeply impacted traditional American society. The shifting gender roles that brought a great number of women into the workforce and war fronts transformed the nation. Despite the changing society, males maintained traditional domestic responsibilities on the borderlands as they continued their roles as providers. Similar to the Pueblo people, even though the times were clearly changing, Mexican Americans attempted to continue with the responsibilities of providing and protecting.

Dr. Américo Paredes, a Mexican American scholar from the Rio Grande Valley in South Texas, added a different perspective to the conversation on *machismo* that his Mexican counterparts Octavio Páz, Samuel Ramos, and Vicente Mendoza had started in the 1930s. "In the United States as in México," Paredes states, "*machismo* in spite of all its faults has been accompanied by an array of impulses conducive to the greater realization of man's potential."[9] Masculinity, in Paredes's perspective, had nothing to do with sexual prowess, but rather relied on challenging and reaching a man's potential. Paredes's focus, it should be emphasized, is focused on frontier life, where a code of honor or chivalry remained important.

Furthermore, Paredes challenges the idea that *machismo* is solely a Mexican phenomenon, born from a Mexican inferiority complex, but claims that *machismo* can be found in various cultures throughout history and globally. In explaining Mexican and Mexican American *machismo*, Paredes universalizes the term and finds notable similarities among numerous masculine behaviors worldwide. He uses various examples, such as the frontiersman and backwoodsman during the age of Andrew Jackson that challenged East Coast aristocrats. He even goes back to the Nordic people and demonstrates how strength and dominance were enacted in bloody duels.[10]

Mexican folklorist Vicente Mendoza points out two types of *machismo*. One is true *machismo*, which is "characterized by true courage, presence of mind, generosity, stoicism, heroism, bravery."[11] "The other" Mendoza sees as "nothing but a front, false at the bottom, hiding cowardice and fear covered up by exclamations, shouts, presumptuous boasts, bravado ... Supermanliness that conceals an inferiority complex."[12] The real *macho* in Mendoza's eyes was the courageous, hard-working individual who endured racial, cultural, and personal strife. Mendoza romanticizes the rural Mexican male figures described in the historic Mexican *décimas* and *corridos* (poems and folksongs) that championed the "true" *machismo*. Mendoza's assessment of "true" *machismo* is similar to Paredes's views, both agreeing that masculinity was tied up with responsibility and dependability.

In Mexican and Mexican American communities within the United States, being *macho*, as Gloria Anzaldúa examined, became associated with being "strong enough to feed and protect his family, an adaption to oppression, poverty, and low self-esteem."[13] The responsibilities of feeding and protecting the family traced to the ancestors of Mexican Americans in pre-Columbian societies were also consistent with White middle-class ideals in the United States during the Cold War. Being *macho*, as noted by Anzaldúa, also became connected with *aguantando* or enduring oppression. *Machos* did not complain about life; they simply tolerated oppression and pain, continuing to overcome whatever obstacles came their way. This last factor in regard to addressing racial oppression became a divisive issue between the Mexican American and Chicano generations.

Samuel Ramos, a Mexican philosopher, examined the *pelado* (the inner-city Mexican *macho*) who embraced the behaviors described by Vicente Mendoza as the "false" *machismo*. Ramos never labels these behaviors as the "false" *machismo*; thus he embraces and promotes the negative image of the Mexican *macho* without labeling it as such and not mentioning the more positive attributes associated with *machismo*. He argues that the Mexican *pelado* values ruggedness and looks to power and dominance to overcompensate for his lack of refinement, which has created an inferiority complex that resulted from a history of conquest.[14]

Thus, in general, overpowering women and society becomes a defense mechanism for the Mexican male as he adjusts to a changing society that at times made him impotent in dealing with the complexity brought by the European conquerors. Throughout the Southwest, the Native and then Mexican American communities exhibited similar changes, as first they were conquered by the Spanish and then by Anglo-Americans, who successively imposed their hegemony throughout the region.

Ironically, the "real" *machismo* that Mendoza and Paredes refer to may have been closer to Teddy Roosevelt's views on masculinity. No other modern American president has exhibited his sense of masculinity more than Roosevelt. This parallel is born from the fact that Roosevelt, like Mendoza and Paredes, admired rural or frontier life. The American West resembled life in Mexico's rural communities and those along the American-Mexican borderlands about which Paredes wrote. These rural folks dealt with similar challenges in their daily lives, from combatting Natives to overcoming the rough terrain and surroundings.

Roosevelt believed that as a man accepted, confronted, and overcame challenges—both physical and intellectual—he developed character concomitant with manliness.[15] Thus, Roosevelt's model of true manliness, an ideal born of the frontier and the rural West, is dependent on fulfilling one's potential. These behaviors were required to survive the frontier life. During times of hardship, Roosevelt demonstrated stoicism and believed that challenging oneself proved to be the ideal way males coped with grief.

Roosevelt's conversation about masculinity occurred at a time when Americans feared their society was becoming feminized. As women in the West were obtaining suffrage rights and more women in the East were entering the workforce, men felt a need to further reinforce masculine gender roles. Gail Bederman strongly asserts, "Americans fearful about the dwindling potency of Victorian manhood found Roosevelt's formulations of racially dominant manhood exhilarating. For many, Roosevelt himself came to embody the essence of powerful manhood."[16]

Those critical of Roosevelt argue that in flaunting his masculinity he was overcompensating for what many considered a strong effeminate character. A man of wealth and privilege, Roosevelt often faced ridicule for his extravagant attire and high-pitched voice. More like the "false" *machismo*, Roosevelt evoked power to mask his weaknesses. Through a strong sense of nationalism, his notion of White superiority, and military participation, Roosevelt transformed his identity and his manhood would not be challenged again. With his distinguished military service, he embraced his new manly identity of "Colonel Roosevelt."[17]

The Spanish American War of 1898 showcased Roosevelt's masculine ideals. When Roosevelt left his desk job as assistant secretary of the United States Navy and formed the Rough Riders, his volunteer cavalry resembled the fruition of the boyhood concepts of masculinity in regard to alliances and teamwork. Ranchers, cowboys, hunters, and miners from the

Southwest, including Mexican Americans and others of Spanish descent, formed the base of Roosevelt's Rough Riders.[18] One of these volunteers, for example, was Captain Maximiliano Luna from New Mexico, who led Troop F at Kettle Hill in the Battle of San Juan. The Rough Riders are best known for bringing men from various backgrounds (except African Americans) together and forging a strong group identity and bond in a combat zone.

Military participation in the United States is the fruition of boyhood concepts of masculine ideals. From a young age, American boys are socialized to embrace masculine behavior. Throughout the nation's neighborhoods/*barrios*, working-class boys create clubs, gangs, or alliances where masculine concepts such as courage, athleticism, loyalty, and stoicism are perpetuated.[19] Young boys come to esteem these values; however, no other value is admired more than courage. Protecting the neighborhood or turf becomes important to the group as the boys grow and become brothers-in-arms. On a much greater scale, the camaraderie formed in the military is a similar group phenomenon.[20]

The same is true for Mexican American youth who are influenced as toddlers on being "*macho*," and more importantly, what ideals and roles they should embrace. The military perpetuated the various masculine ideals that Mexican Americans often embraced. Through military participation, men enhanced their masculine roles in society and the *barrio*.

Patriotism and manliness was exhibited and perpetuated through military participation throughout Latino communities in the United States. A tradition of Chicano family military participation motivated families such as the Garcías from Omaha, Nebraska, to exemplify patriotism. The father, Charles Sr., served in the Army Air Corps in Europe during World War II; then five of his sons, Charles Jr., Albert, Joe, Alvin, and Jerry, went on to serve in the Vietnam War, where Jerry was killed in action.[21] Other Mexican American families shared similar burdens in America's defense, such as in the case of the Arrey family from Norwalk, California, which lost a son (Urbano) in World War II and another (Frank) in Vietnam. Each brother posthumously received a Silver Star.

The mother of one of the most service-minded families in America, Angelita Ochoa of Tucson, Arizona, had ten boys who served in the armed forces, including five who participated in World War II and one who was killed in action in Korea. In addition, ten of Ochoa's grandsons went to Vietnam and a great-granddaughter participated in Desert Storm.[22] Other Mexican American veterans, such as Lieutenant Colonel Miguel "Mike" de la Peña, fought in all three wars (World War II, Korea, and Vietnam). De la Peña was one of the first Latinos to join the Special Forces and went on to receive the Combat Infantryman's Badge three times.[23] To be sure, the Mexican American communities served their patriotic duty with clear distinction during wartime.

World War II brought tremendous changes to labor in the United States. Across the country, in the war industry and within the armed forces, women had taken jobs left behind by men at war.[24] The García sisters are a prime example, as Elsie, Tillie, Ercy, Doris, and Josephine all five went to work in the Cobusco Defense Plant in Denver, Colorado.[25] After World War II, however, Americans attempted to readjust and reclaim their former society. Women were expected to return to their domestic roles, while men embraced the new Cold War concept of "ideal family wages," where men were to once again take on the responsibilities of being the breadwinners and protectors while women returned to the domestic household duties. The shift in gender roles that occurred during World War II for women, and the rising conflict against Communism caused a stir in American society. Cold War conformity called for the return to manly ideals of the nineteenth century when women once again returned to the home and the men to the workforce. In many ways, these challenges to masculinity in society paralleled the feminization of the late Victorian era, which confronted Teddy Roosevelt half a century earlier.[26]

Natasha Zaretsky has argued that to best combat Communism on the home front during the Cold War, White middle-class America believed they must conform to the "ideal family wages," also known as the "national family ideal." Accordingly, men were to provide substantially for the family by providing the essentials to the household, while women enacted the role of maintaining the household. Women were expected to recapture ideals similar to those expressed as republican motherhood during the post-Revolution era and teach their children traditional American values, which would fortify the nation's policy of containment.[27]

While women were expected to return to their domestic roles, men continued to answer the call as the United States entered new international conflicts. Comparable to the ancient Pueblo Indian culture, masculinity became linked to the ability to provide for the family as well as to military service.[28] Throughout the Cold War, for example, conformity called upon men to combat Communism, and Airman Ciro Salas Jr. fulfilled his duty. During the French Indochina War, the United States supplied the French with necessary planes and supplies to maintain a Communist-free Vietnam. Salas worked as a mechanic servicing American planes flown by the French against Ho Chi Minh's Communist forces. Eventually, Salas and four other Americans became the first U.S. POWs in Vietnam.[29] Manliness/ *machismo* became synonymous with military duty as Cold War conformity called for men to make sacrifices in America's defense.

Many Mexican Americans accepted the notion of the ideal family wages while continuing to fulfill their patriotic duty. They felt entitled to first-class citizenship (due to their service in both World Wars) and harbored hopes of one day becoming mainstream Americans. White middle-class ideals were not always attainable, yet Chicanos frequently sought these despite the social barriers. Cultural pluralism or "pluralistic integration" often presented the best option in obtaining upward mobility for the Mexican American generation.[30] Military service opened the door for many Mexican Americans as their sacrifice "legitimized" their aspirations for a first-class citizenship that historically had been denied.

José Manuel Astorga grew up in poverty in San Diego and joined the military seeking the national family ideal. The streets of San Diego provided few opportunities for the Tijuana native. Astorga, who experienced prejudice during his childhood, recalls the police in downtown San Diego being authoritative to the point of abusing their power when addressing the Mexican American youth. For Astorga, with limited means and options, providing for his five siblings and mother took priority over completing an education. "I left at age seventeen, went to the Job Corps in Pleasanton and stayed three months. I was taking auto mechanics and welding, lasted three months, then Nixon ordered it to shut down because of a government thing and I decided to go into the Army," recalled Astorga about his decision to enlist.[31]

For Astorga the concept of the ideal family wage was attractive, and he joined the military hopeful that he would learn a skill he could apply in the workforce as a civilian. "I wanted good training; I wanted a good job when I got out [of the Army]," he explained. Even though the military allowed Astorga to fulfill his financial responsibilities, his mother, who had relatives serve in World War II, was not supportive of his decision. "Because I was seventeen, my mother had to sign a paper saying it was okay for me to go in. She wasn't okay with it, but she said, 'That's what you want, okay.' I enlisted. I was not afraid to get drafted," recalled Astorga.[32] He earned his GED and quickly found himself with the 196th Light Infantry Brigade, F Troop, 8th Calvary, in Vietnam.[33] His new path in life would have devastating repercussions, as his tour would take a turn as a result of his captivity.

When confronted by an antiwar group on why he was going to Vietnam, Astorga responded, "It's simple . . . it's simple . . . it's simple, if you don't want to go, don't go. I believe in love for country and God. That's why I am doing it." Today, Astorga remains confident about his decision to serve: "That's how I feel and I still feel that way. Let's just say that I believed that what we were doing over there was right. Now apparently a lot of people felt it was wrong. But everyone is entitled to their opinion, and they hate me for it. That is how I feel, love of country and God."[34]

This sense of responsibility and patriotic duty, fundamental statements of a traditional masculine ideal, animated Astorga's service in Vietnam. The Cold War propaganda that intertwined military service, patriotism, and a strong sense of Christianity influenced Astorga along with so many others who became convinced to stand firm against the spread of Communism.

Manliness served as a motivating factor for other Mexican American former POWs. Echoing manly ideals championed by Theodore Roosevelt more than half a century before, José Jesús Anzaldúa Jr., Alfonso Ray Riate, and Abel Larry Kavanaugh found in the Marine Corps the challenge they looked for in life. "I volunteered," explained Anzaldúa, the only surviving member of this group.[35] "The reason I joined, it was an opportunity to do something in life, outside the realm of what my family could afford. I felt it was something honorable to do."[36] During the Vietnam War, most American troops served tours consisting of 365 days, while Marines served an additional 30 days because of the simple fact that they were Marines. Many young men sought to be challenged by the high and rigorous standards of the Corps. This was especially true for young Chicanos coming in with a chip on their shoulder ready to showcase their *machismo*. "What I was looking for was something that would challenge me and instill a level of discipline that you could not acquire elsewhere. [When joining] I never talked to another recruiter," clarifies the retired major.[37] The Marine Corps provided the manly challenge Anzaldúa looked for as he was set and intrigued to fulfill his manly potential.

After finishing basic training, Anzaldúa learned Vietnamese at the Defense Language Institute Foreign Language Center and Presidio in Monterey, California. The training propelled Corporal (Cpl.) Anzaldúa to become an S-2 Scout with H Company, 2nd Battalion, 5th Marine Regiment, 1st Marine Division.[38] He benefited greatly from his command of the Vietnamese language and could grasp information that most American soldiers and POWs could not. Upon his release in 1973, Anzaldúa remained in the Marine Corps, where he served until his retirement in 1992. The Corps provided Anzaldúa with the means to provide for his family and lead a comfortable middle-class life.

Like Anzaldúa, Sgt. Abel Larry Kavanaugh also served in H Company, 2nd Battalion, 5th Marine Regiment, 1st Marine Division. Prior to enlisting, Kavanaugh had married his childhood sweetheart, Sandra. The pair had grown up in one of Denver's housing projects with a high concentration of Chicanos. As the young couple struggled financially, Larry enlisted in the Marine Corps at the age of eighteen. The young Marine opted for a better life than the limited opportunities that existed in Denver for Chicano youth. In 1967, Kavanaugh enlisted while Denver-based activist Corky Gonzales contemplated the identity of Chicanos with his poem "I Am Joaquín." Kavanaugh's life in many ways mirrored the struggles of Chicanos portrayed in Corky's poem.

Alfonso Ray Riate was a good friend of Kavanaugh and a fellow member of the suspected Peace Committee that allegedly broke the U.S. military's Code of Conduct in the POW camps in Vietnam. Kavanaugh and Riate, along with six other POWs, reportedly separated from the rest of the group in the camps and formed friendly relations with the North Vietnamese in the various prisons in North Vietnam. Like Kavanaugh, Riate also joined the Marine Corps because of the limited opportunities of his youth. Riate's story reflects a more "street tough" lifestyle. He enlisted in the military to avoid going to jail as well as to challenge his manliness. "Al volunteered. When you come off the streets you think you're tough. The Marine Corps is tougher. [Plus] Dress Blues get the girls."[39] Power and sex values associated with manliness formed part of the basis for Riate's enlistment in the Marines. Cpl. Riate embraced the challenges the Marine Corps posed and sought the sexual benefits of what it meant to be a Marine.

In the case of Specialist Fourth Class (SP4) Juan Jacquez, the only POW to have been drafted, toughness is what propelled him on the battlefield. "[I felt tough] *muy chingón*," reflects Jacquez regarding his mentality out in the battlefields in Vietnam.[40] Despite being a draftee, upon being released from captivity in 1973, Jacquez reenlisted in the Army. The self-identified Chicano took various odd jobs to assist his widowed mother to raise the family of seven in Gallina, New Mexico. Jacquez's father had been killed in a hunting accident on Christmas Day 1958, prompting him to leave home at an early age to work at anything and everything.[41]

After his father's death, Jacquez along with his three brothers, three sisters, and his mother moved to Santa Fe to be closer to extended family. Eager to provide financially, Jacquez once lied about his age and experience to land a construction job. Thus, when he received his draft notice, he welcomed the steady paycheck. "I didn't join, I was drafted. But then I extended when I came back. I didn't get out right away. Altogether I served eleven and a half years."[42] Jacquez accepted his induction and served proudly despite not knowing much about the conflict in Vietnam. "Actually, I really didn't know nothing about the war! I really didn't know anything about the war at the time. Me, myself, in my opinion, nobody wants to go to war," admits Jacquez. "But when it comes down to it, I did not hesitate. When it's time to go, you got to do what you got to do. Now there was quite a few who took off to Canada and places like that just to stay out of it, but after it was all over they come back. I think that is chicken-shit. Patriotic? I was proud of it and I am still proud of it."[43] Jacquez observed his manly obligation to serve after being called upon by his country and remains proud of having fulfilled his duty.

In 1967, at twenty, Jacquez was with the 41st Squadron, 10th Cavalry, 4th Infantry Division in Pleiku, South Vietnam. Motivated by *machismo* and his foolish youth, Jacquez took many ill-advised risks. The majority of the time he served as a machine-gunner, which made him a prime target for North Vietnamese and Viet Cong snipers. Yet, the youthful Chicano never flinched, nor did he ever back down.

Army Special Forces Sergeant Isaac "Ike" Camacho also grew up in a farming community in Fabens, Texas, near El Paso. Like Jacquez, Camacho had to provide for his mother and two sisters at a young age following his father's death.[44] During his senior year in high school, Camacho served in the Junior Reserve Officers' Training Corps (JROTC), as all male students at Thomas Jefferson High School did at the time. Prior to graduation, an Army recruiter/paratrooper visited the school and made quite an impression on the student body, including Camacho. "That paratrooper was as neat in his dress as I have ever seen a military man. His boots gleamed like his toes were afire. I knew right then, that very day, the very minute I saw him, I wanted to enlist as soon as possible to become a paratrooper," recalls Camacho.[45] A few weeks later, and only days after his eighteenth birthday, Camacho along with three close friends enlisted in the Army. Like other young men, for Camacho joining an airborne unit would provide an adrenaline rush as well as a challenge. Moreover, airborne units historically offered recruits financial bonuses, an attractive incentive for any boy fresh out of high school.

Chicano activist Raúl Ruiz alluded to the poor economic status of Chicanos who became attracted to military duty by the financial lures posed by serving. "The Chicano and his cultural and economic image of himself have been flagrantly exploited by the government. If he is poor (and 95% are) then the service offers interesting and economically appealing propaganda," states Ruiz, who goes on to say, "They play on his *machismo* and he becomes a gung-ho all American."[46] The financial bonuses along with *machismo* convinced and continue to entice young Mexican Americans to serve in the U.S. military.

To other young Mexican Americans, jumping out of planes did not supply enough excitement. They wanted to fly fighter jets instead. "I wanted to fly," explains Everett Álvarez Jr. on his enlistment in the Navy.[47] After obtaining an electrical engineering degree at Santa Clara University, Álvarez entered the Navy's flight training program, where he satisfied his aspirations for flying and adventure. The future naval officer turned down what would have been a higher salary in the engineering field for the thrill of flying a Douglas A-4C Skyhawk. Consequently, he was one of the first responders to the Gulf of Tonkin Incident and became the first aviator to be captured in the Vietnam War.

At an early age, Álvarez performed at the highest level possible in order to stay competitive in the racially conscious town of Salinas, California. His cousin Alex Zermeño recalls Álvarez's youth: "Everett was All-American. He was always the quieter, shy guy, methodical, controlled. He never questioned society or the institutions. He just went right through them and survived them."[48] Álvarez used academics and sports as a ladder to obtain social mobility and inclusion as he established himself with his Anglo classmates. Álvarez's sister Delia, a Chicana activist who protested the Vietnam War, explains how being accepted during their youth depended on acculturation and assimilation: "My brother and I, we had to be 'White' in order to make it. It was like growing up between two cultures. We were afraid to get too brown."[49] Álvarez could not disagree more with his sister: "My sister, she's so fucked up. We were mixed with all the poor people. She feels inferior. We were afraid to get too brown? That's my sister."[50] Social and racial barriers became irrelevant to Álvarez as he was driven to succeed and surpass any obstacle.

During the 1950s and 1960s, Salinas was a booming farming community (the United Farm Workers Union had a strong base there), not only occupied by Mexican Americans, but by the disenfranchised "Okies and Arkies" seeking a new beginning. Everett recalls working hard, side by side with the poor whites who struggled just like the Mexican American community.[51] Álvarez accepted the living conditions and worked hard to overcome his humble upbringing. His sister Delia, on the other hand, questioned and challenged their living conditions along with the inequality that persisted in society. She then became active in the farmworkers movement and eventually in the antiwar movement.

First Lieutenant Hector Acosta shares an upbringing similar to Álvarez's. After working a variety of low-end jobs and making the needed sacrifices in order to receive a college education, Acosta joined the Air Force with the aspiration to fly airplanes. The working-class city of San Antonio shaped Acosta in a rough and rugged, yet compassionate manner.[52] Yet, the future airman aspired to a higher standard of living than the poverty he had been exposed to as a youth.

The priesthood was Acosta's first career choice, but after the changes of Vatican II, he decided for a career in the military. Acosta traded in a life of celibacy for flying military airplanes by dropping out of Catholic seminary school and enlisting in the Air Force, then volunteering for overseas combat duty. He believed that he had a patriotic responsibility to his country and signed up. "But we were in a war and my feeling about it was that either you stand and take a place in the line or somebody else has to stand there for you. And nobody was going to stand in the line for me. You just do that. That's what you do. It's a duty," explains Acosta over his commitment. "It's about caring for your country. It's about being a patriot. You don't have to hate the enemy to be a patriot. You don't have to love war to be a patriot. You just have to recognize it's a duty and somebody has to do it and stand up and do it."[53] Although fulfilling patriotic duty served as a motivating factor for Acosta, he was also moved by the fact that he had a manly obligation to serve.

Although the former seminarian held intense humanitarian ideals, he had ambitions in life and fulfilled them as a navigator. Acosta's ideas are among the most complex, as he shared much antiwar sentiment and had even participated in a march against the conflict, years earlier. The airman, however, remained respectful of his North Vietnamese counterparts who remained human beings and had the ability to end his life.[54]

U.S. Air Force Captain José David Luna also enlisted for personal adventure and volunteered for overseas combat duty. His father, Floyd Luna, acknowledged, "It was his duty to keep us free. We didn't feel too good. We feared for his life."[55] Flying an F-105F plane in combat missions in North Vietnam satisfied Luna's urge for adventure. Like the other navigators mentioned, Luna, along with Captain Isaac Camacho and Marine Major Anzaldúa, was a career-oriented soldier (lifer) who saw his military service slightly differently. This is not to conclude that the rest of the Mexican American POWs did not take their soldiering seriously, because they certainly did and through their captivity served beyond the call of duty. The "lifers" merely had other reasons for serving and planned a career in the military.

Various forms of manliness/*machismo* propelled and motivated the group of former POWs to serve in the Vietnam War and excel on the battlefield. Through military participation, Americans of all walks of life, including Mexican Americans, filled the demanding roles created by the Cold War. Following the "Mexican American Generation" who had served in World War II, the Vietnam generation continued the patriotic tradition of serving in combat.

For other Mexican American former POWs, financial responsibility for their families played an important role and prompted them to join the service. Seldom have Mexican Americans joined the military due to admiration of combat, as it is commonly romanticized. Manliness in the sense of challenging oneself and instilling discipline motivated the group. Military family traditions also inspired Mexican Americans to serve, as they too wanted to do their part in bringing honor to their families.

Despite the role that *machismo*/manliness played in the lives of Mexican American former POWs, their manhood and morale were about to be challenged by their captors. The North Vietnamese soon would attempt to emasculate the American POWs through interrogation, indoctrination, and torture. Their North Vietnamese and Viet Cong captors attempted to break down their prisoners both mentally and physically. For the Mexican American POWs, along with the rest of the American POWs, their captivity launched a different war. Since they could no longer physically harm the enemy, American POWs waged a war of resistance and endurance. Their war and their manliness now revolved around how much torture or torment they could absorb from the enemy before being broken and forced to provide the North Vietnamese and their allies with information.

CHAPTER 4

Resisting, Enduring, and Surviving Captivity, the Early Years, 1954–1967

LARGELY BECAUSE OF THEIR BACKGROUNDS, MEXICAN AMERICAN POWS were readily able to adjust to or accommodate themselves to the POW camp surroundings. Everett Álvarez put it best: "In a way I grew up to be a POW."[1] This group of men all grew up in the Southwestern United States between the 1930s and 1960s, with most coming from impoverished farming communities where desolation and poverty were commonplace. Going to bed with an empty stomach during their youth may have taught the future POWs to strive for a higher rung in society. While in captivity, they did not forget the scarcity they and their families had lived with, and these limitations prepared the men for the torment they now faced. The foundation and determination that enabled Mexican American POWs to survive had been embedded in them in their communities, including border towns and *barrios* in the Southwest. Their tireless perseverance, established by a strong work ethic, generated a stamina that permitted them to overcome demanding situations.

Grief-stricken and battered POWs clung to their dignity and manhood as a means to psychologically endure captivity. POWs maintained mental toughness by attempting to follow the military's Code of Conduct, which states that POWs are only to release their name, rank, birth date, and service number. The code also states that a prisoner is to resist interrogation to their maximum ability, while not accepting special favors from his captors, and will continuously attempt to escape. Out in the jungle, strictly following the Code of Conduct became a challenge as the Vietnamese and their allies, through torture, fear, and intimidation, broke each man. However, each Mexican American prisoner of war in Vietnam attempted to follow the Code of Conduct to the best of their interpretation and ability.

On June 14, 1954, over a month after the French defeat at Dien Bien Phu that brought a halt to the French Indochina War, the Viet Minh captured five American servicemen, including Airman 2nd Class Ciro "Joe" Salas Jr.[2] In many ways this incident foreshadowed American involvement in Vietnam. Salas had spent the previous three and a half years overseas serving in the United States Air Force. In 1954, he was among the two hundred American mechanics working at the Tourane (Da Nang) Air Base servicing American-supplied planes used by the French against Ho Chi Minh's Viet Minh forces.[3]

Salas and the four other servicemen borrowed a French three-quarter-ton weapons carrier and took a trip to China Beach near the village of My Khe outside of Da Nang.[4] The group went down the coast past Marble Mountain and went for a swim at China Beach, where fifteen to twenty Vietnamese surrounded them. "Armed with knives and grenades," the Vietnamese ordered the Americans into a truck and drove them inland.[5] Salas and his fellow comrades became the first American POWs in Vietnam.

The group was transported across several villages before being taken to a prison camp populated by French POWs. The group was initially presumed to be French, but thanks to Salas they were properly identified. Salas communicated to his captors in Spanish that they were indeed Americans and not French. "We were separated from them," recalled Salas, as the Viet Minh recognized them to be Americans and placed them in separate housing away from the French prisoners.[6] Salas's Spanish-speaking skills paved the way to better treatment and eventually to their release.

On June 23, after the group arrived at their eventual holding facility, according to intelligence experts, the group was asked to fill out a "personal history form" that practically matched the ones used during the Korean War by the Chinese and North Koreans.[7] Under the pretense that the Viet Minh would be informing their government and families of their captivity, the questionnaires attempted to extract information regarding the men's personal, family, and military histories.[8] The information requested by their captors went beyond the standard information (name, rank, service number, and date of birth) that the U.S. military would soon adopt the following year as part of its new Code of Conduct.

The downside of the group's experience was the numerous attempts to "brainwash" them. The group faced indoctrination sessions in which they were exposed to socialist literature and philosophies. Again, borrowing from the North Korean and Chinese playbook on POWs, the treatment by the Viet Minh was comparable to the American POW experience just years previously in Korea.

Through a spokesman, the group issued a statement thanking the Vietnamese for their treatment: "Since our capture we slowly came to realize American intervention in the Indochina War was against peoples fighting resolutely for independence. Had we realized the truth beforehand we would not have agreed to come to this country."[9] As noted by Stuart Rochester and Frederick Kiley, the broadcast attributed to the group in 1954 (whether genuine or not) would be similar to the statements made by American POWs and transmitted through Radio Hanoi or the National Liberation Front Radio during the war with the United States.[10]

Other than the psychological torment unleashed, the Vietnamese treated Salas and the group fairly, and they were not exposed to the harsh treatment endured by French POWs or later by American POWs. "We slept in bamboo huts and were fed two meals a day of rice and some fish and a little chicken. Sometimes we had hot water and tea," recalled Salas days after his release.[11] Even though the diet very much resembled that of the Viet Minh, it took Salas some time to adjust.

Still, there are no records indicating the group complained over food. They did, however, instinctively daydream of hamburgers and hot dogs. Living conditions, according to Salas, were not bad: "We lived in a private home for a month, then were moved south to another barracks where we were held two weeks."[12] Salas and his companions were held prisoners for two and a half months, and almost half the time was spent in the private home.

After intense negotiations, the Americans were released. Major General John W. (Iron Mike) O'Daniel, chief of U.S. military missions in Indochina, along with other top Department of Defense and French officials, worked on the repatriation of the men.[13] Once freed, Salas reassured his father of his safety via a cablegram: "Don't worry Poppa. We are free. Will write soon."[14] Like many Mexican American POWs, Salas's main concern during his military service and time in captivity was his family.

Yet, the uncertainty American prisoners of war had while in captivity as well as their health were of great concern. The biggest frustration for a soldier was the inability to fight back. Once captured, POWs had to reassess their strategy in "fighting the enemy." Through passive-aggressive behaviors, including resisting interrogation, acting ignorant, breaking tools, and acting ill or injured, prisoners of war managed to frustrate their captors, while at the same time maintaining and boosting their own morale.

"I think what scared me most was when some Cubans came to talk to me," claimed Isaac "Ike" Camacho, who was among the first to participate in what at the time was an experimental pilot program that would eventually become known as "the Cuban Program."[15] Camacho continued, on his experience with the Cubans:

> They had on berets like Ché Guevara. What they did was sit me down on a stump, and they stood over me and looked down. I guess they were trying to make me feel low, while they were on top. This one asked me, "*Eres Latino?*" (Are you Latino?), and I answered, I don't know what you're talking about. Then he asked me, "What is your nationality?" and I told him I was Indian. He asked me if I knew Fidel Castro, and I said no. He got real mad and said, "You don't know Fidel Castro?" I told him, no, the only Castro I know is the Castro I went to school with in Fabens, Texas. Next he asked, "Do you like guitar music?" I answered, yes, I like guitar music. Then he asked, "Do you like Sabicas?" I don't know who Sabicas is,

I told him. "You like guitar music, but you don't know Sabicas?" I said, No. He asked, "How come you like guitar music?" and I responded, because Elvis Presley played the guitar. They got mad, and I heard them say, "*Este pendejo no sabe nada. Es un baboso bien hecho*" (This fool knows nothing. He's a natural blithering idiot). They didn't realize that I could understand what they were saying. One of them said to the other, "*Ya no voy' a hablar con este*" (I'm not speaking to him anymore). So he walked around and put his gun next to my temple. "*Hacete para ya!*" (Move over there!) he said. I told him, If you're going to shoot me, just shoot me. I don't know what you're talking about. I just kept speaking English all the time until they finally said, "*Dejalo, el no sabe nada. El es nada mas que un titere de los Estados Unidos*" (Leave him alone, he knows nothing. He's nothing more than a puppet of the United States). My questioner finally spoke in English and said, "Well, you know you're here as a prisoner of war and these people have been suffering many years. We'll talk to you later." I think they were trying to break us down mentally.[16]

Cuban interrogators assisted the North Vietnamese in the cross-examination of American POWs for a brief period, between 1966 and 1968. Cubans by the names of "Fidel" and "Chico," and a third Cuban national who became known as "Pancho," along with an unidentified woman, interrogated, indoctrinated, and tortured American prisoners in Southeast Asia. Through the accounts of former POWs along with the work of the Defense Intelligence Agency, CIA, FBI, Department of Defense, and other military intelligence, Fidel has been identified as Luis Perez Jaen, a captain in the Cuban Ministry of Interior.[17]

With limited means and inability to fight back against his captors, Camacho planned to annoy and frustrate his interrogators. By not acknowledging his Spanish-speaking interrogators, Camacho annoyed the Cubans and, in a POW's mentality, was "sticking it to" the enemy. He would not be the first or last POW to resist only to eventually succumb to the demands of the enemy. This is not to indicate that Camacho or the other POWs were weak. It is simply to point out the cruelty of warfare and the overwhelming tactics employed by the North Vietnamese and their allies.

Despite being among the first to be captured in Vietnam, Isaac Camacho and those captured with him were not included in John G. Hubbell's *P.O.W.: A Definitive History of the American Prisoner-of-War Experience in Vietnam, 1964–1973.* The voices of jungle prisoners, for that matter, became lesser heard than those from Hanoi POWs. *Voices of the Vietnam POWs: Witnesses to Their Fight* and the notable *Honor Bound: American Prisoners of War in Southeast Asia, 1961–1973* were more inclusive of jungle POWs. Still, little was added on Mexican American prisoners of war.[18] Craig Howes, in his work *Voices of the Vietnam POWs*, mentions that prisoners who returned during the war (escaped or received early release) have been treated as "second class citizens."[19] Yet, Camacho was not paroled early, as he was the first American to successfully escape and still has received little attention.

Among the most intense interrogations Camacho encountered were the grilling sessions from the Cubans who attempted to demoralize and oppress him. The Cubans questioned Camacho's heritage after he refused to acknowledge their questions in Spanish. His refusal to comprehend his interrogators was solely a defense tactic, as Camacho attempted to follow the military's Code of Conduct. Despite his strong linkage to his Mexican heritage, Camacho demonstrated obliviousness toward anything remotely Mexican as the Cubans would have surely used any knowledge of his background against him. Instead, he embraced a popular American icon, Elvis, and hid his Mexican heritage as he had been trained. Despite pretending to be an assimilated Indian, the questioning of his Mexican identity was degrading; still, the situation did not lend itself to pettiness as Camacho's ego was the least of his worries.

The insult from the Cubans was reminiscent of how younger Chicanos back home involved in the movement had accused many Mexican Americans, especially those within the "Mexican American Generation," of being "*Tío Tacos.*" Not only was this an insult to one's identity, but it also implied that one was not manly enough and therefore had sold out or succumbed to those in power.

As a member of the 5th Special Forces Group (Green Berets), Sergeant First Class (SFC) Camacho fell prisoner to the National Liberation Front for South Vietnam (NLF)—known to Americans as the Viet Cong (VC)—in

November 1963. Camacho and his group, which at the time of the attack consisted of five Americans (of whom four were captured), found their camp at Hiep Hoa run over by Viet Cong. The group's duty for several months had been to train South Vietnamese soldiers, who would become Special Forces at a Civilian Irregular Defense Group (CIDG) camp, and protect a sugar mill that belonged to President Ngo Dinh Diem's sister-in-law Madame Nhu. President Diem's brother and chief political advisor Ngo Dinh Nhu was Madame Nhu's late husband. The brothers had been executed just weeks earlier during a military coup. On November 22, 1963, between two and five hundred Viet Cong attacked the CIDG camp and ordered the CIDG not to fight, as they were simply out to kill the Americans.

The senior officer that night, Lieutenant John Colby, ran into the sugarcane field and ordered Camacho to do the same. Camacho would have evaded captivity; however, as he was running with Lt. Colby into the field he decided to return to the camp and save three fellow Americans. "Something dawned on me right there. I've got three guys in there that I have to go back and tell them we are leaving. I just didn't feel that it was in me to bug out, under orders. Something told me, you got to go back in the camp and get those guys out."[20] Under heavy fire, Camacho returned for his friends.

The once strategic military post had been overrun and was now a chaotic scene. The odds were too severe, and after receiving a blow from an AK-47 to the back of the head and losing consciousness, Camacho was taken prisoner.[21] Camacho had disobeyed his commander and consequently his head was busted open, leaving his fate and those of three of his men in the hands of the Viet Cong. Nevertheless, they remained alive. Facing a more horrifying fate were the South Vietnamese trainees at the CIDG camp who were simply executed on the spot by the National Liberation Front.

The next moments proved to be most critical. As the Viet Cong fled the camp with their captives, American bombers seeking to aid the Camacho group (named after the highest-ranking soldier) began assaulting the area. At this point, friendly fire posed as much a threat as the National Liberation Front. Clearly upset over the air raid, the Viet Cong lined up Camacho and his partner, Sergeant George Smith, setting up a firing squad. Both men said their goodbyes and awaited death: "Smitty, it looks like they're going to execute us, so it has been good knowing you."[22] Camacho recalls, "I didn't cry, scream, or beg for mercy, I just faced the fact that the time to die had come."[23] Camacho did not die that night; however, his will to survive was gravely tested. Through psychological and physical torture, the Viet Cong began what would develop into twenty months of agony for the young Green Beret.

Despite the challenging trek and the initial Viet Cong assault, Camacho's life was spared. In what seemed to be several days later to Camacho, at the second temporary prison camp, the *Bacsi*, a Vietnamese medic, treated Camacho's wounded head and stopped his bleeding.[24] Here the group was stripped of their clothing and given black pajamas identical to the ones worn by the Viet Cong. Only Camacho was allowed to keep his boots after he wittily convinced his captors that he suffered from a horrid case of athlete's foot and could jeopardize everyone's health if he did not keep a lid on his feet. He, along with the others, were given Ho Chi Minh style sandals, but oddly Camacho never let go of his boots, which he kept tied to his cage throughout his captivity. The sandals were made from old tires with straps that criss-crossed by the toes and wrapped at the ankles. These *huaraches* were popular among the Vietnamese during the war as they were cost-effective and more practical than boots in the intense humidity in Vietnam.

For the next twenty-seven or twenty-eight days, SFC Camacho, Sgt. Smith, along with SFC Kenneth Roraback and Specialist 5th Class (SP/5) Claude McClure were systematically transported through a Viet Cong network across the Plain of Reeds near Cambodia's Parrot's Beak.[25] The Plain of Reeds was located in III and IV Corps (military zones in South Vietnam), which included Dong Thap, Tien Giang, and Lang Sen Provinces in South Vietnam and also parts of Svay Reang in Cambodia. Due to American surveillance in the area, the Viet Cong took many precautions in moving the Camacho group. After traveling 150 kilometers, the group reached its permanent prison camp, Central Office South Vietnam (COSVN), which was a North Vietnamese headquarters situated north of Nui Ba Den (Black Virgin Mountain) in Tay Ninh Province, South Vietnam. The camp was methodically positioned near the Cambodian border and within months moved into Cambodia to discourage American forces from either bombing it or encountering this significant and strategic North Vietnamese head-quarters.

The group was fed a Vietnamese diet composed of primarily rice and a few sardines. To many Americans, including Camacho, this was a starvation diet. Rice and sardines differed greatly from the rations American soldiers typically ate, and consequently, Camacho and the rest of the group saw their bodies beginning to weaken. The Viet Cong kept the POWs minimally fed. Once weakened, POWs were broken more easily, easing their collaboration. Their captors planned to use the prisoners' own testimony to condemn American intervention in Vietnam and undermine what the North Vietnamese and their sympathizers considered to be an illegal puppet government in the South. If the POWs were simply starved or if they died in captivity, the Viet Cong would not help their own cause in the eyes of the international community (which was trying to make sense of the situation in Southeast Asia).

Camacho, known to his captors as "Gmascho" or "Macho," was confined with his men in an area inside POW Camp B-20, known as "Auschwitz." Among the many challenges they faced, the most significant was their debilitating bodies that were withering away. Weakened daily by the low caloric intake, Camacho and his compatriots lost significant weight. At the time of capture in November 1963, Camacho weighed 178 pounds. By January 1964, he had lost close to twenty pounds and realized that rice alone was not going to provide his nutritional needs.[26] Still, limited portions of rice were the only option, and Camacho depended upon the grain to survive.

For other POWs, such as Frank Anton, who also spent time in the jungle, rice was an option he refused to eat. "Any hunger I felt was of my doing because I refused to eat the rice," admits Anton.[27] On the other hand, Camacho and the rest of the Mexican American POWs who were raised in extreme poverty ate all that was given to them since they were not picky eaters.

Camacho complained about the food to Phong, the Viet Cong interpreter, and eventually to "the man with the crooked glasses," who was also known as "The Commissioner," a high-ranking Viet Cong officer cadre identified in 1995 as Truong Huynh Mao.[28] When confronting "The Commissioner,"

Camacho exclaimed, "Our food here is not food at all, but only rice. You and your men can't live on rice alone, so I would like to make an official complaint about the lack of decent food."[29] Camacho's outburst may have secured improvements for the group in the long run, as their meals gradually improved, but in the meantime "The Commissioner" ordered Camacho to be placed in "the hole" as punishment for insubordinate and disrespectful behavior. The hole was literally a hole in the earth, only a couple of meters wide and so deep it required the use of a ladder.

Throughout Camacho's imprisonment, the Viet Cong attempted to indoctrinate the Americans and convince them to write statements condemning their support of what the VC considered the "illegal puppet government" in Saigon. The Commissioner would lead the indoctrination sessions:

> He would tell us what a predicament we were in, that they were being bombed all the time and it was hard to provide us with food and medicine. He would say, I understand that you've been sick, but you have no business in this country and must pay for your sins. What we expect from you is that you join with your fellow Americans, and now there are many people your age protesting the war, and you should join your comrades in the struggle to let the Vietnamese people live the way they want to.[30]

Following the military Code of Conduct, Camacho resisted the indoctrination sessions. Often using facetious remarks in rebutting the man with the crooked glasses, Camacho found himself punished for his disregard for authority. What shocked Camacho was their knowledge of the antiwar movement in the United States. "It cracked me up because they had every bit of information about the antiwar movement," confesses Camacho.[31] Even today, most military museums in Vietnam dedicated to the American War include a section on the American antiwar movement.

The Viet Cong planned to extract confessions from the Camacho group to bolster their own image across the world while at the same time accentuate the United States as an imperialistic nation. Camacho recalls the grilling sessions:

The interrogation included efforts to extract a confession, which mainly had to do with burning and looting and killing innocent children, murder and rape and all this other stuff. That's what the context of the confession was. Finally, they wanted us to admit that we had invaded their sovereignty by coming in and doing all these things. I never did sign it. They would pressure me by asking me, "When are you going to see the light?" I told them the confession did not mean anything to me, and I asked, "What do you want me to do, lie?" "No, no," they said, "the confession must come from your heart."[32]

Despite the indoctrination sessions, while understanding the high morale and strength of the Viet Cong, Camacho did not speak against U.S. involvement in Vietnam. Prisoners Claude McClure and George Smith, after facing the same indoctrination sessions, became convinced that American intervention in Vietnam was not warranted and began to accept and identify with the efforts of the Viet Cong. Smith acknowledged that the Viet Cong had a clearer objective than Americans did. When recounting what Americans were doing out in Hiep Hoa, Smith did not believe they were preserving democracy or defending South Vietnam. Instead he explained, "Nothing would pretty much suffice."[33] Smith saw himself and the rest of the group as high-priced guards securing a sugar mill belonging to Madame Nhu, President Ngo Dinh Diem's sister-in-law. With time, his thinking intensified, and Smith came to believe that they were safeguarding personal and selfish interests of a corrupt regime that threatened their security while oppressing South Vietnam and its people.

The North Vietnamese used numerous psychological and physical techniques to appeal to and subdue American prisoners. Eventually, Camacho's resilience softened after his captors rewarded fellow POW McClure with a letter that had been sent by his wife as compensation for his decision to sharpen *punji* stakes. This was the first correspondence received by any of the men. The day before, the group had been asked to sharpen *punji* stakes, a pointy wood or bamboo stick used by the Viet Cong as booby traps. At first, the entire group decided not to follow their captors' orders, refusing to sharpen weapons that could be used against fellow Americans. After being pressured and persuaded, McClure agreed to sharpen stakes, causing an internal division among the group. As a consequence for refusing, the rest of the men received the worst treatment they had thus far experienced in the camp.

After being overworked, starved, and mistreated, along with seeing McClure elated with an emotional letter, the group began to rationalize accepting their captors' demands. As far as Camacho and the men were concerned, by doing the assigned work, they were practically freeing the Viet Cong and North Vietnamese to perform other tasks, including sharpening *punji* stakes. So they rationalized and figured they might as well sharpen stakes themselves. However, the possibility of directly harming their fellow American soldiers complicated their reasoning. The group justified their decision by believing that Americans were highly unlikely to find this remote camp and would not be hurt by the stakes. After further deliberation, Camacho gave the order to sharpen stakes.[34] The following day the Vietnamese distributed mail and each man received a letter from his family.

Psychological warfare became as prevalent as physical punishment or torture by the North Vietnamese, who used all means possible to emotionally and physically break down the American POWs. As time in captivity slowly passed, Camacho constantly tested his captors to see how much he could get away with. If lucky, the Vietnamese found Camacho amusing and he received sugar, food, cigarettes, or other treats. If Camacho overstepped his boundaries, he spent the night in the hole. Camacho's singing, however, often pleased the Viet Cong guards, who were also bored in an isolated camp far from society. One song in particular brought joy to the ears of the enemy: "*Giai Phong Mien Nam!*"[35] (To liberate the South, we march on), the Viet Cong national anthem.

According to Smith, neither the group nor Camacho knew what the song meant, "but Camacho said he felt it must be bad, because they liked it."[36] To Camacho or anyone starving, singing this song was acceptable as "the end justified the means." Camacho needed to survive, and in order to nourish his weakened body he required extra food; besides, he had no idea the song called for the death of the "American imperialists."

The prisoners' grim living conditions further served as justification for cooperation. Yet, this did not mean that Camacho was willing to cooperate with the enemy in exchange for special treatment. Despite the Viet Cong promising to liberate Camacho if he signed a written confession, he refused. Camacho was housed in a "tiger cage," a 6 × 8 foot bamboo cage where his ankles were tied down by shackles and chains.[37] Escape seemed like a mere fantasy in the triple-canopy jungle where sunlight was as dim as Camacho's future, but planning an escape was always in the back of his mind. With guards always at the ready, sticking the barrels of their AK-47s into the cage to press against Camacho's spine, it would not be long before he wished to be shot and no longer suffer in misery.

Despite not wanting anything more than to knock out a guard, Camacho could not physically harm his captors. Instead, he demonstrated resistance through passive-aggressive behaviors. In spite of his situation, Camacho destroyed tools and equipment. It really was one of the few ways he could frustrate the Vietnamese. Once a guard known as "Anus" brought a mandolin to play at the camp. Camacho demonstrated an interest in attempting or pretending to learn how to play and broke a string. An irate Anus bickered and yelled in anger, as mandolin strings surely were not a common commodity out in the jungle.[38] When working at a rice mill, Camacho, tired of the work, resorted to breaking equipment. He broke a wheel pin, which was a central part of the rice mill and caused it to shut down. Almost instantly Anus struck Camacho with a rifle in his back, bringing him to his knees. Anus quickly locked and loaded over Camacho, and at that given moment Camacho almost begged to be shot as he was overwhelmed by the physical and mental anguish.[39] Instead, he was thrown in the hole for the night.

Even with the cruel treatment inflicted, he received slightly better treatment than his fellow prisoners of war. If anything eased Camacho's captivity, it was his ability to develop a better rapport with the Vietnamese. "Of the four of us, Camacho got along best with the [North] Vietnamese. Not that he didn't complain—he did, especially about the food. But he was more familiar with their customs than the rest of us, and he joked with them in sign language and the few words of Vietnamese he knew. He had black hair, and he looked a little bit like them," explains Smith.[40] Camacho used his wits for the advantage of the group, often convincing the North Vietnamese to provide extra food. One guard provided Camacho with a sack of peppers after seeing that Camacho and Smith liked them.[41] To pass the time and to have extra food, Camacho went on to plant a garden of peppers.

After establishing communication with the guards and observing their behavior, Camacho learned that they did not have the authority to take any action without going through a chain of command. So, he often made the most trivial requests merely to see a guard reprimanded for relaying the frivolous messages or to see how far he could push the boundaries. According to Smith, Camacho went as far as convincing the Vietnamese to allow the group to celebrate Smith's birthday. "One day Camacho, up to his usual tricks, persuaded Prevaricator to ask Suave to give me a birthday party," exclaimed Smith. "He called Prevaricator over and told him in great detail that birthdays in the States were very important days, and they were usually celebrated with great style. With presents and a cake—he gave him the whole story."[42] The Viet Cong became impressed by Camacho's cunningness, and their birthdays from that day forward became holidays.

The Viet Cong fed Camacho and the group extra food during holiday celebrations. Tet, the Vietnamese Lunar New Year, was the biggest celebration in Vietnam, and the Viet Cong shared the celebration with the Camacho group. Food was plentiful throughout the several days of Tet. The celebrations made the POWs' experience relatively tolerable. A celebration would not be complete without alcohol and tobacco, which were also available during holiday celebrations. "At Hiep Hoa I had thought Tiger brand beer was the worst in the world, but in the jungle it tasted as good as vintage wine. If they could they'd give us a pack of ARAs [cigarettes], sometimes a pack for each of us," explained Smith about the holiday celebration.[43]

Holidays aside, the prisoner-of-war experience was not a walk in the park for the Camacho group. One can even argue that the celebrations took place under the guise of indoctrination and perhaps to convince American POWs to sympathize with the Viet Cong cause. Even with the extra food served during the seldom-held celebrations, the men began to experience health issues and illnesses. Camacho fell ill from malnutrition, malaria, hepatitis, and beriberi. Being ill in a foreign land did not provoke kind thoughts, and at times death seemed likely for Camacho. His religious beliefs kept Camacho's hope alive, and a remarkable and unexpected coincidence aided him during desperate times. Camacho, who was brought up Roman Catholic in a Mexican American community, genuflected prior to eating. The Vietnamese cook at Camp B-20, a man the group had nicknamed "Coburn," one day genuflected back to Camacho, revealing that he was also Catholic. When Camacho fell ill, Coburn kept on bringing food to him and made sure he received extra protein. "The cook, Coburn, assisted in keeping me alive as much as any man," recalls Camacho.[44] Camacho recovered from his bouts with severe illnesses and continued coping with his situation while always planning an escape.

What really impressed the North Vietnamese about Camacho was his work ethic. Perhaps Camacho's work effort is what allowed him to have better relations with the Viet Cong than did his fellow POWs. As a youth growing up in a farm community near El Paso, Camacho labored long hours, as many Mexican American youths did in those days.[45] Living with economic limitations had been a standard feature of Camacho's youth, as he had performed strenuous labor on the banks of the Rio Grande in order to help provide for his family. Even The Commissioner became aware of Camacho's determination and attempted to use his ethnicity in the indoctrination attempts. "Gmascho, I know you have said your family in your state of Texas was poor, and you are not a rich American. You have told me you are part Indian and part Mexican. I have read about the Indians in America and know the Indians were illegally removed from their own land," lectured The Commissioner.[46]

Consequently, Camacho was given more work responsibilities that familiarized him with the surrounding jungle. Throughout his captivity, Camacho kept exploring ideas on escaping and being exposed to the jungle acquainted him with possible routes. It was the work details such as cutting wood that showed him an exit from the POW camp. Camacho explains, "You see they don't cut the immediate wood in the camp. They go a few miles out because they don't want to spoil the foliage in the jungle. This gave me an opportunity to see the trails."[47] Camacho kept a clear mental map of the area, and as he won his captors' confidence, more responsibilities were given to him, exposing him to more trails.

Camacho also credits his survival partially to his ability to eat all that was given to him. Whether he found maggots or rat excrement in the rice, Camacho ate his meals. Being raised with hunger taught Camacho not to be overly picky, as a meal was a blessing. He acknowledged that eating led him to stay healthier than his colleagues and helped him to eventually escape. Camacho explains, "What made it good was that I used to maintain pretty good health in comparison to the other prisoners cause I used to eat everything they gave me and I ate things you would never think as being tasty."[48]

Twenty months after being captured, Camacho saw an opening and planned an escape. By July 1965, to make room for new prisoners, the Camacho group was moved to "Camp Dachau," a new location within Camp B-20. The atmosphere there was much more relaxed and the group quickly nicknamed it "Paradise." The men's ankle shackles were stripped and given to new POWs; thus the group, including Camacho, became more at ease physically and mentally. Leading the newcomers was Marine Captain Donald Cook, who eventually died in captivity and posthumously received the Congressional Medal of Honor. Camacho, following the military's chain of command, began to acknowledge Cook as his senior and quickly established a communication network using a dead letter drop, using a secret location to leave a note, which does not require both parties to meet in passing information. Camacho informed Cook of his plan to escape and the senior officer gave his approval.

Having key components in place, Camacho then went forward with his plan. He had mapped out the area from his time out in the work details. Camacho had also managed to store a bottle full of rice for his escape. The most important tools for the journey were the boots still in his possession. Without the footwear, the terrain in the dense jungle would have been impossible to overcome. Smith and Camacho were being held in the same cage, and after discussing the plan, Smith decided it would be best for Camacho to go forward on his own. The boots became the determining factor in Camacho escaping on his own, as Smith realized that not having boots would have been detrimental to the attempt. Also, forcing Smith to stay was the fact that each POW had to keep a lamp lit throughout the night.

This required the POWs to hand the unlit lamp to guards who made rounds from cage to cage to relight lamps. If both men left, the Viet Cong guards would have quickly discovered that Smith and Camacho were gone. With Smith staying behind, he could simply hand over Camacho's lamp and have it relit without the guards detecting anything unusual.[49]

On the night of July 9, 1965, Camacho went through with the escape. After loosening a bar in his cage, he grabbed his escape kit, which included his boots, the bottle of rice, a broken mirror, and a piece of black nylon. Camacho also carried with him the letters "PW" that he had made from smoking papers and with which he planned to signal American planes.[50] The monsoon rains aided Camacho's escape, as the rain was so heavy it hindered the guards' visibility. Camacho recalls the night: "Thank God! One night all hell broke loose. We had a rainstorm like you wouldn't believe. And ah! The guard was sitting only five to seven yards in front of the cage because I could see his cigarette. I slipped out."[51] With everything in readiness and in his favor, Camacho bolted from Camp B-20.

Camacho's escape and evasion lasted four days as he navigated the dense jungles and rigorous landscapes of Southeast Asia. On the first night of his trek, he did his best to get a head start before the guards discovered his empty cell. Traveling in the dark and rain posed several challenges, but the lightning provided some direction. His plan was to travel east and eventually find friendly Vietnamese. Camacho encountered leech-infested swamps along with dense triple-canopy jungle.[52] After a failed attempt to signal to what seemed to be an American aircraft and losing his sense of direction, Camacho found a good spot to spend the night. The severe rain that hindered his travels also further convinced him of the need to stop for the night.[53]

Camacho's escape and evasion benefited from his experiences of having grown up on the borderlands. At a crucial point, he was forced to swim across a river. The very skill he mastered playing in the Rio Grande during his youth now aided Camacho in a life-or-death situation.[54] Swimming posed two benefits: first, he did not leave behind a trail for the Viet Cong to follow, and secondly, the river took him downstream away from the POW camp, which distanced him from his captors.[55] Although his travels, if successful, would eventually lead him to safety, there was nothing safe in his evasion. One of Camacho's biggest fears aside from the frequent encounter with snakes was being mauled to death by a tiger.[56] The fear was especially intense when he traveled through the dense jungles to avoid the trails where unfriendly Vietnamese could easily detect him.

Camacho's motivation, training, and luck propelled his escape. There was no turning back. Camacho knew that if this attempt were unsuccessful he would be executed. Survival itself proved to be enough motivation to continue through the rough elements.[57] Jungle mangos provided Camacho with some nourishment. "The jungle was dotted with mango trees that provided food. I pulled off a few mangos, stuffing two into my scarf," recalled Camacho. "I ate one of the mangos right there to satisfy my empty stomach that was starving. The damn thing tasted wonderful, and reminded me of eating this fruit as a kid across the Mexican border from Fabens, Texas."[58] Camacho was determined to do all he could to survive and make it to friendly lines. With luck on his side he managed to evade anyone who could have impeded his freedom.

After four days and much effort, Camacho reached friendly lines. Traveling through a rubber plantation led Camacho to an Army of South Vietnam (ARVN) base near Minh Than.[59] Yet, he could not just walk in and expect to be welcomed with open arms, as the black pajamas he donned and his scruffy beard could very well make him appear to be a Viet Cong. Likewise, Camacho's *mestizo* features could liken him to the Vietnamese. Camacho approached what appeared to be a French Renault sedan with a Red Cross emblem driven by a Viet/French doctor.[60] Camacho in his best French pleaded with the doctor, stating, "*M'aidez, Je suis un prisonnier de guerre! Je suis un Americain. Oui monsieur, M'aidez s'il vous plait.*" ("Mayday, I am a prisoner of war! I am an American. Sir, please help me.")[61] The doctor ordered Camacho to get in the car and took him into the ARVN camp.

Camacho convinced the doctor he was an American; now he had to convince several Vietnamese guards and officers with high-powered automatic rifles that he was indeed an American. After failed attempts at convincing a South Vietnamese captain of his situation, Camacho saw a fellow member of the American Special Forces.[62] The man came in and quickly recognized

Camacho. "My God Ike is that you?"[63] Camacho realized he was free: "It was then, right that minute—at that second—I knew—I was back with my own kind: An A-Detachment of the US Army Special Forces. I was free ... I was alive ... and almost well! I said silently, 'Thank you God. Thank you.'"[64]

By the summer of 1965 when Camacho successfully escaped, the war in Vietnam was at full throttle. With over 120,000 combat troops on the ground in South Vietnam and a continuous air raid over North Vietnam, the number of prisoners of war grew.[65] By this point in the war, Lieutenant junior grade (LTJG) Everett Álvarez had been shot down on August 5, 1964, in retaliation for the Gulf of Tonkin Incident.

Everett Álvarez Jr., along with two other pilots, was ordered to counter the North Vietnamese aggression. "As we were doing this, the realization struck me. My knees were shaking. I said holy smokes we are going into war. And what is the rest of the world going to think about this. They were fully waiting for us. The world was just black. By this time, I realize they are all shooting me. As we were just leaving I was hit. I said I got to get out, I'll see you guys later," recalled Álvarez.[66] His naval fighter jet, an A4C Skyhawk, was hit in Ha Long Bay near Hon Gai in Quang Ninh Province. Forced to eject, Álvarez suffered several injuries. North Vietnamese fishermen quickly surrounded Álvarez and began to question him. Álvarez attempted to hide his identity by responding in Spanish, "*Que? No entiendo. No entiendo.*" (What? I do not understand. I do not understand.)[67] Álvarez was the first U.S. pilot shot down over North Vietnam making him the first American inmate at the Hanoi Hilton.

Apart from a few Vietnamese prisoners, Álvarez was held on his own during the first ten months of captivity. "The initial days were a learning experience for me and for the North Vietnamese," explained Álvarez. "It was the first time they had somebody. I don't feel they really knew what to do, how to handle me."[68] The first couple of weeks proved to be the most debilitating as Álvarez was all but starved. Being fed disgusting meals, which included animal hoofs, chicken heads, and birds still covered in feathers, Álvarez weakened severely.[69] Further debilitating him was the uncertainty provoked by his captors, who referred to him not as a prisoner of war but as a war criminal.

Álvarez would be the first of a string of "Yankee air pirates," as the North Vietnamese referred to pilots they considered to be war criminals. He abided by the military Code of Conduct for those captured by the enemy. "My name is Everett Álvarez. I was born December 23rd 1937. My service number is 664124," answered Álvarez during his interrogation.[70] "As a POW you are not supposed to give anything but name, rank, service number, and date of birth. So I wasn't answering anything else," stated Álvarez. "So they said, 'Why aren't you answering?' I said according to the Geneva Convention I don't have to. Why not? Because, I'm a prisoner of war. 'You're not a prisoner of war. There's no war.' There are no diplomatic relations between your country and my country."[71] Technically the North Vietnamese were right since the U.S. Congress had not officially declared war on them.

Since the North Vietnamese considered American intervention in Vietnam to be undeclared, they attempted to convince Álvarez along with other Americans held in captivity that they were unlawful enemy combatants instead of POWs. The North Vietnamese made a valid enough point that provoked Álvarez to ponder his situation. "You don't think there is someone here who is going to come and represent you. You are in our hands now. We consider you a criminal. A war criminal," warned a North Vietnamese official.[72] Álvarez now feared for his life after being convinced that he could be tried as a war criminal and possibly face execution.

Fueling Álvarez in these darkest of times was his Mexican American ethnicity and the core values passed on by his family.[73] Again, Álvarez thought of his maternal grandmother, who had immigrated from Mexico, and his parents, who had overcome adversity and poverty to provide him and his two sisters with a better life. His family had worked hard and overcome overwhelming conditions as migrant-seasonal farmworkers. Now it was his time to rise to the occasion and endure his own overwhelming situation. Álvarez fueled himself with his family's experiences. "Family stories of the adversities they [his family] faced had shaped my character and given me backbone," remembered Álvarez.[74]

Like many Mexican American families, Álvarez's family had instilled in him a hard work ethic and pushed for him to obtain an education to escape the poverty that plagued many Chicanos in the Southwest. "As Mexicans growing up in my family, my father and mother pushed education. Even though they didn't have it. And number two you worked hard."[75] All his life, the junior commissioned officer had overcome immense social and racial obstacles, and this was not the time to abandon this course of action. The POW experience would indeed be his greatest challenge.

In several ways the humble upbringing prepared Álvarez to survive his situation. Within almost a year of Álvarez's capture, a string of American POWs made their way to the infamous prison in the capital, Hanoi. The large majority of these Americans were White, senior aviators. The story of these men has become what is known as "the official story" in Vietnam War POW literature as it has been told and retold in numerous works. Álvarez and some of these men had been together at Hòa Lò, but did not realize it until September 1965, as they had been purposely isolated from one another. These newcomers had been aware of Álvarez's capture and had started asking the Vietnamese guards of his whereabouts. On one occasion these men showed a guard a magazine with Álvarez's picture and made swimming gestures, asking the guard if he had seen the "wetback."[76] Most Chicanos would have been offended by the derogatory remark, but Álvarez (who the group of White officers also had confused as being a Vietnamese prisoner) was happy to know he was no longer alone, but among his fellow American aviators.

Following the military's Code of Conduct, the senior group that Álvarez was imprisoned with at Hòa Lò, and later at the Zoo (also located in Hanoi), set up a well-coordinated communication system. Similar to the Camacho group but on a much larger scale, the Hanoi POWs followed the military's chain-of-command structure where the most senior ranking officer gave orders that were to be followed by the rest of the cadre. A rank-at-shoot-down formula was created to determine the hierarchy of prisoners. After being integrated with higher-ranking officers, Álvarez joked, "This is the weirdest organization I've ever been in. The longer I stay here, the further down the ladder I go in the chain of command."[77] The group set up various communication systems. Aside from using the traditional dead letter drop, the group also developed a Morse-type tap code to communicate through the prison walls.[78] Orders along with news were communicated effectively through this sophisticated tap code.

Having a chain of command and communication brought cohesiveness and served as a support system for the prisoners, who now faced brutal interrogations and torture in the Hanoi prison system. One by one, prisoners, including Álvarez, were interrogated and through torture or threats of torture were manipulated to provide information and/or provide statements detrimental to the American war effort. The POWs felt distraught after succumbing to interrogations, as they felt powerless in a war in which they had been sidelined and now were powerless.

Between 1967 and 1968, nearly two thousand Cubans came to North Vietnam in support of their ally and representing global anti-imperialism.[79] Similar efforts were later seen by the Cubans in other parts of the world such as South Africa, where they supported Nelson Mandela's struggle to end apartheid. In August 1967, during Alvarez's imprisonment at the Zoo [POW camp just outside of Hanoi], Cubans assisting the North Vietnamese under the Cuban Program interrogated him and other American POWs. Through his brutal tactics and treatment of American POWs, "Fidel," the lead Cuban interrogator, quickly made a name for himself. He is believed to be responsible for the eventual death of Earl Cobeil, a POW from Pontiac, Michigan, who was beaten extensively at the hands of "Fidel."[80]

Fidel attempted to embarrass the Americans with anti-imperialist rhetoric comparable to what was vocalized by the real Fidel Castro. "You guys really think you're hot, don't you! Hot Yanks! But all you sons-of-bitches do is take the best from everyone else and give them your crap in return. You're all full of shit! Look what you did in Cuba! You bastards took sugar! And what do you give back? You sell them Coca-Cola!," bemoaned Fidel. "You take bananas from other countries! And what do you teach them? You teach them how to make milk shakes! Yanks, eh! And what do you do when you move into foreign countries? You screw their women! Their girls! Yankees make whores out of everyone's women—wherever you go! You screw up every place you move into! Then you wonder why they shout 'Yankee, go home!'"[81] Although short-lived, the Cuban Program had straightforward anti-imperialist agendas and brought a systemic change of pace to the dreadful POW experience, while continuing to unleash physical and psychological torment on American POWs.

Fidel played upon Álvarez's Mexican ancestry in attempts to persuade him with anti-American sentiment for the treatment of Chicanos in the United States. When dealing with minorities, Communist interrogators going back to the Korean War attempted to indoctrinate POWs by stressing the unequal treatment of minorities in the United States. "They tried to use it against me, the Cuban did. It didn't work. He didn't push it. He interviewed me for his [propaganda] programs and I flunked the interview. He decided not to put me in. The other guys he put in, he was pretty hard on them. He killed one of them. That's bullshit! That wasn't going to work," recalls Álvarez.[82] After not being selected for the program, Álvarez returned to the rest of the group.

Álvarez may have saved himself from the Cuban Program, but he did not fare much better from regular interrogations, which became routine during his captivity. "You come back [from an interrogation/torture session] and you're full of bruises. My arms turned black and hands turned black. You are starved. You come back with your roommate and he has gone through hell and you have gone through hell," explained Álvarez over the brutality unleashed upon him. Álvarez continued, "When you go through this [torture] and you have to finally say I have had enough pain. I'll write. You feel so low because you gave in. Something you never thought you could do. They can make you do things you don't want to do."[83] Through their persistent, meticulous, and agonizing interrogation sessions, the North Vietnamese and their allies broke American POWs, squeezing them of their dignity to carry on.

By interrogating Americans and pressing them to speak, the enemy in a sense emasculated and forced them out of their wills. POWs in Hanoi established counseling sessions to boost prisoners' lowered self-esteem. "Every day you thought you did something [that showed weakness] we talked about it," notes Álvarez, as the group rallied behind each other.[84] This support system served as therapy for the group and it allowed the men to address their gravest feelings. At the same time, it brought cohesion amongst the men as the severe reality they lived in, bound them to one another.

One of Álvarez's heartrending challenges was coping with the news of his wife's abandonment. The group showed Álvarez support after he was informed that his wife had decided to leave him. On December 25, 1971, Álvarez was called to headquarters where the Vietnamese guard gave him a letter. "Álvarez you have a letter from your mother. Your wife has decided not to wait for you. She has probably gone off with another man," the guard cruelly notified Álvarez.[85] The coldly delivered and heartbreaking news destroyed Álvarez, sending him into a deep depression on that Christmas morning. Throughout captivity he had remained motivated by the thought that one day he would be reunited with his wife and they would renew their love.

The young pilot, who had married five months prior to being shot down, longed for his wife. Daydreaming of their future reunion had motivated Álvarez to survive during dark times. He had not received mail from his wife, Tangee, in over a year, and this had certainly alarmed him, but he never considered Tangee leaving him. Instead, Álvarez worried for her well-being. So naturally, the heartbroken romantic lost hope, as he could not have learned of his divorce in a worse place and on, of all days, Christmas.[86] News of his wife leaving him further emasculated Álvarez. He could do nothing to win back his wife's love, and he became haunted by the idea that she was in the arms of another man.

For months an inconsolable Álvarez isolated himself from the group. His friends, though, never abandoned him and continued encouraging him. "God, Ev (Everett), it's tough, but hey, man, we're still alive"—such rallying comments were commonly directed at Álvarez by his friends who grew concerned about his mental state.[87] Through the camaraderie and bond with the "team" (as Álvarez identified the group), Álvarez eventually rose from his state of despair. He also began to occupy himself with activities such as dramatic storytelling and teaching Spanish.[88] To keep busy and productive, the prisoners set up a school as they sought to learn or at least keep their minds active. The bilingual Álvarez, logically, was a candidate to teach Spanish.

Air Force Captain José David Luna also taught Spanish in North Vietnamese prison camps. On March 10, 1967, Luna and his front-seater, Major David Everson, were shot down from their F-105F Wild Weasel at Thai Nguyen in Bac Thai Province, located about twenty miles north of Hanoi. Luna took part in the Air Battle of Thai Nguyen that had been ordered by

President Lyndon Johnson during Operation Rolling Thunder. Thai Nguyen housed one of the more important targets in the war, an iron and steel mill believed to be "Ho Chi Minh's pride and joy."[89]

North Vietnamese newspapers *Nhan Dan* (The People) and *Quan-doi Nhan-dan* (People's Army) boasted over the news of the captured "U.S. air pirates."[90] The government of North Vietnam used Luna's capture, like Álvarez's, for propaganda and political purposes, which lifted North Vietnamese morale and attempted to boost its global image. The North Vietnamese Army (NVA) regulars, along with militia, captured Luna at the steel plant and him by foot to a nearby village. Then they trucked him to another village and eventually by jeep to Hanoi.[91]

Luna would spend the next six years between Hòa Lò, the Zoo, and the Dogpatch (one hundred miles northeast of Hanoi). "For the first thirty months or better, we received no correspondence," stated Luna's father, Floyd Luna.[92] Eventually, his North Vietnamese captors would allow Luna to write his family. The future lieutenant colonel found himself isolated from his wife and family. Solitude took a toll on him and the other men and was possibly the toughest obstacle they dealt with on a daily basis. With the POWs physically, emotionally, and mentally depleted, the North Vietnamese expected indoctrination to be smooth. At the Zoo, Luna also became familiar with the Cubans, and resisted induction into their indoctrination program.[93] The production of propaganda statements by American prisoners of war became a key strategy for the North Vietnamese and their allies as they attempted to have Americans themselves condemn U.S. intervention.

In the spring of 1967, the North Vietnamese opened a third prisoner-of-war camp in the outskirts of downtown Hanoi. This new camp, "Plantation" or "Plantation Gardens," was opened with the primary intention of producing and circulating antiwar propaganda.[94] Plantation never had more than fifty-three inmates, as the North Vietnamese had special plans for these prisoners. Similar to the United States' military campaign "to win the hearts and minds" of the Vietnamese people, the North Vietnamese planned to use statements produced by prisoners of war to convince the American public to demand an end to the war. Prisoners of war served as a tool to motivate American withdrawal from a war that the North Vietnamese portrayed as being inhumane and imperialistic. Ironically, Plantation Gardens, which had been a French film studio, would now be the center for the production of antiwar propaganda.

(Ret.) Vice Admiral James Bond Stockdale, the highest-ranking Navy POW, recalls his meeting with the North Vietnamese top propaganda expert:

> They walked me into a room, with senior officers on both sides. Now the man in question was in civilian clothes. I knew who he probably was. Vin Quak Vin. I'd heard that name at Stanford. He was the propaganda expert of North Vietnam. He was totally fluent in English and we, we talked. And he was not hostile. He was picking my brains and I was picking his. But here was the punch line. And there was nothing dramatic or irate, he said "you know about the war as a matter of weapons." He said "the Vietnamese people know that we cannot compete with you on the battlefield." But he said "it's not that that wins wars anyway. It's national will. And when the American people get the idea of what this war is all about, they will lose interest in pursuing it." He said, "we are going to win this war on the streets of New York. And when the American people understand the war and you and your fellow prisoners are going to help them understand it, you will be their teachers. Then the war will go away." We [POWS] were a major factor in the strategy of the Vietnamese and we would be sort of a branch of the American antiwar movement. That's what they had in mind.[95]

The North Vietnamese knew they could not compete with the weapons of war that the United States possessed, so they attempted to use not only those weapons that were used against them, but also the voices of American POWS who had previously waged war.

Through their propaganda machine, the North Vietnamese demonstrated the effects of the war on the population and country. With pictures of dead and badly burnt women and children, along with images of destroyed villages and infrastructure, the North Vietnamese won public and global sentiment. The vivid, graphic films and photos—such as the depiction of the execution of Nguyễn Văn Lém, a Viet Cong prisoner, in the streets of Saigon by South Vietnamese General Nguyễn Ngọc—had overwhelming impact as well.

The American prisoners of war now served as pawns to convince the world, including the United States, of the deplorable war that wrought remarkable brutality upon Vietnam and its people. The prisoner-of-war experience took a dramatic shift at Plantation Gardens as the North Vietnamese intensified their indoctrination efforts and planned to use them to end the war. American captives would continue to suffer as a result of these efforts and solidly stood resisting, enduring, and surviving.

CHAPTER 5

Resisting, Enduring, and Surviving Captivity, the Latter Years, 1967–1973

IN 1967, ONE HUNDRED AND SIXTY AMERICAN PRISONERS OF WAR WERE captured, including "95 Air Force, 50 Navy, 5 Marine, and 10 Army."[1] This was the highest single-year total during the Vietnam War. One hundred and six POWs were captured the following year, 1968. However, due to the escalation of the war during the Tet Offensive requiring an increase of ground troops, it marked the highest year for Army and Marine captives, with 34 and 11 respectively. Also, with President Johnson's restrictions on the air campaign in March and October, the number of Air Force and Navy POWs dropped to 28 and 15, the lowest since 1964. The remaining 18 POWs unaccounted for were civilians captured within a six-day span, January 31 to February 5, 1968, during the Tet Offensive.[2] The group of civilians included Michael Benge, a consultant with the Agency for International Development, and humanitarian workers such as Betty Ann Olsen, who served as a missionary nurse and consequently died during her march into North Vietnam.[3]

By 1967, the American war effort in Vietnam was in full bloom, with the number of ground troops peaking at 536,100 the following year. It was also in 1968 that the United States suffered the most deaths in the campaign, laying to rest 16,899 soldiers in that calendar year (almost 30 percent of American deaths in Vietnam).[4] The escalation of the war distracted President Lyndon Johnson from his domestic programs, such as the War on Poverty, and after feeling the pressure within his own Democratic Party, he decided not to seek the party's nomination for the presidency, ending any quest for reelection.

In 1967, the 90th U.S. Congress in its first session passed a bill appropriating to the Johnson administration over $4.5 billion in military aid it had requested, while also including a clause preventing the expansion of the war in Vietnam. To the naked eye the bill's details, like many occurrences during the war, would be contradictory. Yet, convinced the funds would contribute significantly and bring Americans closer to victory, President Johnson signed the bill into law on March 16, 1967.[5] On the home front, the tide was clearly shifting as more and more Americans were growing disheartened with the war in Southeast Asia as images of the flag-draped caskets reached living rooms across the country through the evening news.

Domestically, the situation only worsened throughout 1968 as civil unrest grew; the antiwar movement was fueled by outrage provoked by the gruesome exposure to the intensification of the war resulting from the televised coverage of the Tet Offensive. With the assassinations of Rev. Dr. Martin Luther King in April and presidential candidate Senator Robert F. Kennedy in June, the country found itself in deep turmoil. By 1967, and more so by 1968, the American public's opinion on the war had certainly changed. Dr. King and Senator Kennedy both had been vocal about ending the conflict in Vietnam. They now joined with the likes of Congressman Eugene McCarthy (who also sought the Democratic presidential nomination in 1968) and Senators Wayne Morse and Ernest Gruening, who all vocalized their opposition to the war. The antiwar demonstrations at the 1968 Democratic National Convention in Chicago were marred by what became a full-fledged antiwar riot.[6]

A month after Luna's capture, on April 26, 1967, the Viet Cong seized Marine Corporal Alfonso "Al" Ray Riate on Hill 861 near Khe Sanh in Quang Tri Province during the Battle of Hill 881, also known as the Hill Fights (Americans gave generic names to hills to distinguish them). As squad leader of the

1st Squad, 1st Platoon, Kilo Company, 3rd Battalion, 3rd Marine Regiment, 3rd Marine Division, Riate commanded his troops over Hill 861 when they began to receive a substantial amount of small-arms fire from Viet Cong forces.[7] Riate and four other Marines were last seen lying face down and presumed to be wounded if not dead. It took American forces two days along with "hundreds of tons of heavy bombs and thousands of rounds of artillery" to take control of the hill.[8] As the battleground cleared, the repugnant stench of rotting flesh hovered over the devastated hill. The decomposing remains of the four other Marines were found and later identified. Riate, however, could not be located, nor did Americans find a trace of his body.

At first, there remained a glimmer of hope that Riate had survived, but by July 1967, the Marine's status changed from missing in action to killed in action.[9] Although improbable, Riate's survival could not be ruled out, as a body or remains were never located. Riate's family also could not accept his death, but became somewhat convinced after being given the details of the Battle on Hill 861. Eventually, his family reluctantly held a Catholic funeral service at the Sunnyside Mausoleum in Long Beach, California, and even placed a gravestone in his honor.[10]

In August 1967, it is believed that Riate, along with fellow Marine corporal Richard Burgess, were moved across the Demilitarized Zone (DMZ) and into North Vietnam. The pair are believed to have been only the second and third Americans moved by foot into North Vietnam, both after Floyd Jim Thompson, the longest-held POW in Vietnam.[11] The march took six weeks, and although it was backbreaking, his captors provided sufficient food and water. Riate thus became convinced the Viet Cong definitely did not want him to die.[12]

More than four years would pass before the Department of Defense would receive information on Riate. On June 3, 1971, a North Vietnamese Army (NVA) returnee told of an American POW he observed being moved north on Highway 9 near VC Hill 832, roughly two kilometers west of Khe Sanh, on April 24 or 26, 1967.[13] The description of the prisoner fit Riate, and according to the testimony, he seemed to be in good health and showed no signs of being wounded. In July, further evidence of Riate's survival surfaced. A message credited to Riate broadcast on Liberation Radio detailed an account of Americans committing war crimes in Vietnam.[14] Riate's survival still could not be confirmed.

On December 22, 1971, the North Vietnamese and Viet Cong released 1,001 letters from American POWs. Among the letters were eighteen from prisoners in South Vietnam, including one written by Riate. Two days later, Riate's brother received a letter from Alfonso on Christmas Eve.[15] Around the same time, Liberation Radio broadcast another message attributed to Riate wishing his brother Merry Christmas.

Riate was accused of violating the military Code of Conduct after he allegedly was allowed to contact his family in exchange for producing messages condemning American intervention in Vietnam. Nevertheless, he was anxious to notify his grieving family of his survival. Those critical of Riate argue that he violated Article 3 of the Code of Conduct by receiving special favors, in this case broadcasting messages and writing to his family. With his military status unclear for over four years and his family subsequently having had a funeral service for him, perhaps Riate's actions were understandable as he attempted to communicate that he was still alive.

In Riate's eyes, while Americans rained heavy artillery and bombs in his proximity, the Viet Cong had kept him alive. In order to receive better treatment and more food, which would enable an escape, Riate provided the Viet Cong with propaganda statements. Still, Riate did not grow complacent about the treatment afforded, and on two separate occasions attempted to escape. Each time, he was caught, shackled, and placed in a tiger cage. Article 3 of the Code of Conduct also states that a prisoner of war will do all he/she can to escape. While he violated one part of Article 3, it can be argued that the special favors he received were to prepare him for escape, which Article 3 also calls for: "I will make every effort to escape and aid others to escape."[16]

Once in North Vietnam, Riate continued to have mixed feelings about the war. He was accused of joining the Peace Committee (PC), an organization formed by American POWs that allegedly collaborated with the enemy.[17] Prisoners being moved north from South Vietnam along the Ho Chi Minh Trail were conveniently, methodically, and strategically placed at a prison named Portholes, but commonly referred to as Bao Cao, meaning, "your attention please or bow." Bao Cao was a phrase every POW came to be familiar with, as the North Vietnamese would not answer to them unless properly addressed. At Bao Cao, the North Vietnamese appointed Riate "room commander" before tactically moving him to Plantation Gardens.[18]

The cruel but methodical treatment Riate received at Bao Cao and in prison camps in South Vietnam had been deliberate, as the North Vietnamese wore him down physically, mentally, and morally. He became a new man. Riate became proficient in socialism and adopted the Vietnamese name Tran Van Te, becoming known as "The Teacher."[19] He allegedly furnished propaganda statements and even performed an antiwar song, "Play Your Guitars American Friends!," in Vietnamese and later recorded it after being released. Riate's song demonstrated strong resentment toward the war:

Introduction: My Name is Alfonso Ray Riate and I served six years as an American prisoner of war in Vietnam. During my time in captivity I learned to sing several songs in Vietnamese. I am going to sing a song made for the American People in the year 1971 about the American people who are working for peace and to resolve the war in Vietnam.

Washington tonight is brightening flame of fighting.
Hearing your singing is far resounding everywhere like the truth is
    shining.
Your beautiful image reflected day and night in the Potomac River.
You both play guitar and sing for protecting the life!
Dear friends! Play your guitars!
It makes the singing resound further, the blood boil to take hold the
    spring, and people demonstrate into the song of solidarity.
Are you hearing the whole of America is boiling?
How sorrowful bell of church is urging people to go on!
Are you hearing in Vietnam where there so many footsteps rush forward
    together to prevent killers, saving peace!
Dear friends! Play your guitars!
Following the gunshot in the South [Vietnam]. Forward! American people!

We go hand in hand to fight for peace, stopping aggressive war!
Singing together the ballad of Ho Chi Minh!
Singing enthusiastically the song of the fight![20]

Although he antagonized many prisoners, Riate also made friends with men who shared similar beliefs. Fellow Marine Private First Class Abel Larry Kavanaugh became good friends with Riate. Kavanaugh was last seen in Trung Phuong in Thua Thien-Hue Province located in I Corps, South Vietnam, on April 24, 1968.[21] Kavanaugh's platoon had been ordered to relocate, and shortly after, he was reported missing—a label he would carry for three and a half years until he was recategorized as a POW. Fellow Marine Robert Ray Helle, who was captured with Kavanaugh, recalls the incident: "They [American forces] figured out they left us behind. Sixty seconds after we were captured, a helicopter came over looking for us. But by that time we were under a treeline."[22] A firefight erupted. As Viet Cong forces closed in on Kavanaugh and Helle, Helle's weapon jammed as Kavanaugh shot a Vietnamese in the neck. After Kavanaugh was shot in the hand and Helle in the shoulder, the pair were subdued.

Kavanaugh received brutal treatment from the onset of his captivity. Like Riate before them, Kavanaugh and Helle were marched across the DMZ and into North Vietnam. Kavanaugh was placed at Farnsworth Camp, also known as "D-1," located twenty-five miles southwest of Hanoi. At Farnsworth, a guard attempting to break Kavanaugh cut-off part of his ear.[23] Another time, Kavanaugh tore down a wall to reach fellow American prisoners held in solitary confinement and was reprimanded by being beaten for several days. The young Marine frustrated his North Vietnamese captors and willingly absorbed the brutal punishment unleashed by ruthless prison guards. Fellow POWs recalled how tough Kavanaugh was and admired his resistance. "For two years, he was one of the best prisoners," recalls Army Chief Warrant Officer (CWO) Roy Ziegler. "He was one of the best prisoners. He resisted. He was strong. We admired Larry Kavanaugh."[24]

At D-1, Kavanaugh shared a cell with his old friend Helle. The rowdy pair caused great disturbance as they sang loudly, banged on the walls, and violated camp rules. As a consequence, after New Year's Day 1970, Kavanaugh and Helle were given solitary confinement for five months.[25] By the spring of 1970, after two years in captivity, Helle noticed what he called an "overnight" change in Kavanaugh. He began to act differently, noted Helle. "He started telling everybody that he was the 13th Disciple and that he was going to start straightening out all the problems of the world. God sent him …that's what he told us. He was extremely serious of this," said Helle.[26] The mental and physical duress may very well have taken a toll on Kavanaugh and disturbed his mental state.

At Farnsworth (just southwest of Hanoi), then later at Plantation Gardens in Northeast Hanoi, Kavanaugh and Riate along with six other Americans allegedly created the Peace Committee of Southeast Asia (PCS) and were accused of collaborating with the enemy, disobeying senior command, and making antiwar statements. "They had been labeled the 'Ducks' for seemingly following guards around the camp meekly in tow," concluded Rochester and Kiley, authors of *Honor Bound*.[27] After his stint at Farnsworth, Kavanaugh was moved to Plantation Gardens in 1971, where a clear division between officers and enlisted men existed. Kavanaugh and Riate, along with many enlisted men, came to oppose the war.[28]

The majority of the prisoners at Plantation Gardens were enlisted men (Army and Marines) who had been captured in Laos, Cambodia, and South Vietnam.[29] Plantation Gardens had a capacity of fifty-three prisoners, and Mexican Americans and African Americans accounted for a sizable segment of the foot-soldier population. The North Vietnamese convinced prisoners such as Riate and Kavanaugh along with others, some who were African Americans, to turn against the American war effort. Against the orders of senior POWs, the Peace Committee embraced antiwar and pro-Communist ideals as they called for an end to the war.

Historians have utilized what senior ranking officers (SROs) have deemed "the official story" to recount the American POW experience. However, further investigation suggests that various factors such as rank and branch of service may have been among the major reasons for dissension amongst the POWs.[30] Far from being a democratic order, military directives, to the frustration of lower-ranking POWs coming from the field, came top down. The sharp contrast that existed in the Hanoi prisons between officers and enlisted men, who now had been moved north and were housed with the Hanoi POWs, often led to a tense atmosphere. "Hanoi compared to our jungle camp, was like a Holiday Inn," stated Frank Anton, a jungle POW. "Nobody starved, nobody had to work themselves to death."[31] Coming from the jungle prisons, enlisted men found the Hanoi prisons to be softer and cushier. Officers in Hanoi prisons took exception to the indirect insult that suggested enlisted men had suffered more than they did.

Even after release, jungle POWs remained adamant about the harsher conditions sustained in the South. "I've heard about solitary confinement and I've heard about being put in cells and I've heard about poor food," commented Floyd Kushner. "I want to tell you I was damned glad to get to North Vietnam. I thought it was splendid ... it was so easy being in jail and getting a couple of meals of bread and soup a day ... I could have survived there for fifty years but in South Vietnam I couldn't."[32] The divisions between jungle and Hanoi POWs continued even after repatriation.

Air Force Colonel Ted Guy, the senior ranking officer at Plantation Gardens, set up strict command of the camp and ordered everyone not to accept early parole. For the Peace Committee and numerous jungle POWs this could not be a more absurd command. Among those who rejected this notion were survivors of the Kushner Camp that had endured some of the most cruel and torturous conditions. The Kushner Camp between 1968 and 1969 "lost more POWs to malnutrition and disease than Hanoi lost during the entire war."[33] Ike McMillan, who like José Anzaldúa had been invited to join the Peace Committee and rejected the offer, responded, "Man, you're crazy. If these people call me and tell me I can go home—I'm going home." Others notified Guy through "commo" (communication): "We respected his opinion but not his judgment and if offered unconditional release we would take it."[34]

Jungle POWs had seen far worse treatment than Hanoi POWs; thus early release seemed by many to be the only form of survival. When Guy pressed upon them what they believed to be ill-advised commands, jungle POWs and Peace Committee members alike rejected them. Having been shot down in Laos, Guy had spent time in jungle camps. Still, in comparison to the Kushner Camp, which had a mortality rate of nearly 50 percent, the camps that Guy had been imprisoned in had not been as severe.[35]

It may, however, be possible that inherent differences between the air campaign and ground combat, along with interservice rivalries, were partly responsible for the dissension. Combat troops argued that the pilots had it much easier than they did on the ground. "Colonel Guy was a flier who had never seen the war on the ground as we had; a career officer who went by the book whereas we were young enlisted men who still hadn't been influenced that much by the military and were still able to think for ourselves," commented an enlisted Army POW.[36] Another enlisted POW remarked that the senior POWs "have been subjected to the military mentality for a long time and if there's such a thing as brainwashing, the military does the best job."[37] In their opinion, a pilot merely bombed targets and flew back to a secured base and never got a good grasp of the day-to-day ground operations.

Combat troops, on the other hand, lived the war up close and personal. They often stayed out in the field for months at a time, and having seen firsthand the determination of the enemy caused many grunts (infantry soldiers) to grow disillusioned about the war effort.[38] For later POWs—those captured after 1968—the antiwar movement back home also plagued their thoughts. By this time, congressmen in both houses had issued strong statements condemning the war. The earlier captives, unaware of the unpopularity of the war back home, were sheltered from the American public's dissension over the war.

Naval and Air Force officers also had issues with enlisted men from the Army and Marine Corps, who they felt did not resist "as well" as they did and did not follow the military Code of Conduct due to their lack of training and discipline.[39] Still, by the time jungle POWs were fortunate enough to reach Hanoi, both their mental and physical health had been severely tested. Through torture sustained in the jungle camps, the North Vietnamese were able to control their American resisters and convince them to make antiwar statements that condemned American intervention in Vietnam, including their own participation.

Jungle POWs who had been captured in South Vietnam had issues with the chain of command set up in prison camps in North Vietnam. Since most POWs from the South blamed their commanding officers for their situation, they naturally resisted taking orders from a senior officer from another branch who had been in relatively less challenging combat settings. One jungle POW, an enlisted man, commented that the officer in charge in the mission that led to his capture "had no business leading a few men across the river in the first place. That's what got him killed. He was too goddamn gung ho." So "when a senior officer attempted to pull rank on the enlisted men," members of the Peace Committee and other jungle POWs had a difficult time following their orders.[40]

Complicating matters even more were the blurred lines regarding rank. "What Naval rank was higher than Air Force rank? Should rank at capture plus prison seniority outweigh a new shootdown's higher rank? Should the senior officer take command? Should the other POWs obey him?"[41] Left out of the command structure were enlisted men that made up the core of jungle POWs. The concerns raised by enlisted men, including the Peace Committee, were reasonable to some Army and Marine officials. In 1973, Army Secretary Howard "Bo" Callaway, upon dropping the charges against the Peace Committee, stated, "Army enlisted men had no legal obligation to obey orders from Air Force officers in North Vietnamese prison camps."[42] He, however, later recanted his position; nevertheless his initial statement was in line with those of the enlisted men who challenged the command structure. Much to the dismay of SROs among the Vietnam prisoner-of-war population, the Army also declared that the Code of Conduct was not a legally binding contract. The ruling by the Army brought the conflicts in the command structure to light and forced the military to establish clearer guidelines for prisoners of war.

What irked SROs the most was the Peace Committee's rejection of the POW command structure.[43] Riate and Kavanaugh, along with the other six Peace Committee members, allegedly furnished antiwar statements and informed on other POWs in exchange for better food, sugar, candy, beer, extra liberties, and even field trips. On August 3, 1971, the Peace Committee allegedly responded with contempt when confronted by the senior commanding officer. Air Force Captain Edward W. Leonard confronted the group: "Kavanaugh, you and your men are to stop all forms of cooperation and collaboration with the enemy. 'We'll do what we want,' Kavanaugh replied. 'Fuck you, Captain Leonard,' shouted one of the others, whom Leonard would later identify as Alfonso Riate." He then muttered he would protest the war in Vietnam until his death.[44] Shortly after the exchange with Captain Leonard, the group held a discussion over who was the real enemy, the North Vietnamese or Americans.

This dissident faction clearly had different views of the war and was influenced by the antiwar movement, to which the North Vietnamese had cleverly exposed them through Liberation Radio. The North Vietnamese used all statements made by prisoners of war to feed their propaganda machine in condemning American intervention in Southeast Asia. According to the North Vietnamese, these statements indicated that POWs had "seen the light" and renounced the American war effort. In July 1972, members of the Peace Committee and senior POWs Walter Eugene Wilber and Edison Wainwright Miller, who were also accused of collaborating with the enemy, allegedly met with antiwar activist Jane Fonda during her visit to Hanoi.[45]

Race also played a role in the rise and consequently in the persecution of the Peace Committee. Borrowing from the North Koreans, who used the racial conflict that existed in the United States to create divisions amongst POWs to facilitate indoctrination, the North Vietnamese also created a racial divide. The Peace Committee condemned the command structure and believed that it often was racist and senseless, as senior officers used it to establish conformity and control.[46]

In the case of African Americans and Chicanos, the North Vietnamese and Viet Cong attempted to create a wedge by showcasing a history of racism in the United States against their people.[47] Newspaper articles about the rise of the Black Panthers were disseminated to African American POWs. Kushner, a nonmember, also criticized the arrogance of "Hanoi POWs' belief that as well-educated, well-trained, and virtually all-White career aviators, they must have performed better than the young, usually enlisted, and often Black or Hispanic jungle POWs."[48] The Peace Committee members were targeted because they were young and antiwar, and as one POW suggested, "none of them [were] officers and some of them [were] Black."[49] They were easy targets, and by not following the chain of command they further complicated their situation.

The North Vietnamese observed White soldiers closely as well. In appealing to White POWs, the North Vietnamese used the antiwar movement in the United States to demonstrate the unpopularity of the war. Having tremendous influence over POWs were antiwar speeches from U.S. congressmen who condemned the war, consequently "providing the enemy with all kinds of moral support—and for free, without suffering any torture!"[50] For members of the Peace Committee it was disheartening to sustain brutal physical and mental suffering at the hands of the enemy until they produced antiwar statements, and here elected officials were openly criticizing the American war effort. Thus, they became convinced that their best option was simply to collaborate with the enemy and live slightly more comfortably.

Although the major clash between the Peace Committee and the rest of the POW population was their stance on the war, race, political ideologies, and age also created uneasiness. The members of the Peace Committee became well versed in Marxist literature and were granted access to a library with extensive socialist materials where they studied. After the incident with Captain Leonard, the Peace Committee became isolated from the rest of the prisoners at Plantation Gardens and were given their own area in the facility in northeastern Hanoi. The seclusion further alienated the Peace Committee members, and from a distance it became apparent that they received special treatment. "But, there were few that were getting special treatments," explained Juan Jacquez.[51] Joe Anzaldúa concurred: "We saw a group that was outside all the time that had more liberties."[52] This group, which consisted of members of the Peace Committee, received plenty of food and received extra time for exercise. They even received beer and candy in exchange for the collaboration.

It is debatable how Riate and Kavanaugh became part of the Peace Committee. According to a fellow POW, Riate and Kavanaugh saw themselves as "brown-skinned minorities who had an inferiority complex from what happened to them in the states."[53] Yet, the proud Chicanos could have been just a couple of renegades who disobeyed the command structure. The pair fell victim to extreme duress due to torture and the overwhelming atmosphere in the jungle camps. Being exposed to the realities of combat by experiencing the war "up close and personal" out in the field made an impact on Kavanaugh and Riate.

The duo sought an end to the war after they came to identify with the enemy who, like them, were a "brown-skinned" minority. Kavanaugh and members of the Peace Committee, much like fellow Mexican American veteran Charley Trujillo, began identifying with the Vietnamese: "Being from a rural area, after a while I started thinking; I said 'What are we doing out here?' They have certain physical characteristics that are very similar. They would come up to you and put their arm and they would compare arms and say 'same-same.' It seems as if they took our farmworkers to go fight their farmworkers."[54] Just like Trujillo, Kavanaugh and Riate began to question the purpose of the war.

Despite the controversy surrounding his actions, several fellow prisoners acknowledged Larry Kavanaugh's determination. Roy Ziegler, who was imprisoned with Kavanaugh, saw him as a victim. "He might have believed he was doing the morally right thing. But then we were getting worse treatment because we didn't do what he did. He was a victim of the war," Ziegler said somberly, "just like a lot of people."[55] Another Army officer who spoke on condition of anonymity described Kavanaugh as someone who would not do things half-heartedly and that "he felt guilty for the war and he overcompensated for it."[56] Whether Kavanaugh purposely collaborated with the enemy or not, he did remain loyal to his personal beliefs.

The same could be said about Al Riate, who also embraced his personal convictions. An old Marine friend, Major Anthony Williams, attests to Riate's commitment to the Marine Corps and does not believe Riate to have been a turncoat. "Al was a Marine's Marine. He was dedicated to the Marine Corps," stated Major Williams, who remains skeptical of the accusations against Riate.[57] Williams described Riate as a "brainiac" committed to his job and suggests that perhaps interservice rivalries were to blame for the accusations against Riate.

Fellow prisoners were very critical of enlisted men such as Riate and Kavanaugh when they provided their captors with propaganda statements. At the same time, officers who provided propaganda statements on Hanoi's behalf were given a pass by this same contingent of POWs: "When POW

Steve Leopold heard Robert Risner on Radio Hanoi sounding 'gung ho' on Hanoi's behalf he gave it no credence: officers' statements must have been extorted. When, however, he heard two enlisted POWs making similar remarks, Leopold 'was disappointed and depressed': these statements must have resulted from weakness."[58] There was a double standard when it came to officers and enlisted men who furnished propaganda statements, as often these same double standards remained prevalent in civilian society. All prisoners were forced against their will and provided the Vietnamese with more information than the Code of Conduct allowed. Either the contempt toward enlisted men by officers led to this double standard, or perhaps the factors of race, age, insubordination, interservice rivalries, or opinions on the war created this inequality.

The Peace Committee quickly made enemies with the senior ranking officers who attempted to establish structure. Colonel Ted Guy grew critical of the enlisted men, whom he described as "Some of the most disgustingly obsequious Americans. Men who could not seem to snap to attention fast enough when a Vietnamese approached, who bowed and scraped to their captors in the most servile fashion."[59] Not surprisingly, upon returning to the United States, Guy charged the group, including Riate and Kavanaugh, with mutiny.

Marine Corporal José Jesús "Joe" Anzaldúa Jr. attested to the treatment of the Peace Committee. "Riate and Kavanaugh, some people believed that they did what they did to get better treatment. And yes, they drank beer while we drank well water. But still in my mind I couldn't rationalize that someone could do that for a beer or to be out there [in recreation] five minutes longer," recalls Anzaldúa.[60] A North Vietnamese guard known as "The Cheese" and the Peace Committee openly recruited the Marine by playing the race card in attempts to convince him. When the Peace Committee was courting Anzaldúa and an African American POW by the name of Ike McMillan, one of the members of the Peace Committee said, "If my kid was a communist I'd respect his opinion." They responded, "Not us. We're imperialists."[61] Soon after, the senior POW command gave Anzaldúa a green light to infiltrate the Peace Committee.

Unlike Riate and Kavanaugh, José Anzaldúa was not convinced by the

North Vietnamese ploy to divide the POW population. "I didn't buy into it," recalls Anzaldúa; "being part of the Marine Corps and being in Vietnam my only concern was that we all take care of each other and follow the Code of Conduct."[62] Anzaldúa never joined the Peace Committee, but did gather intelligence on them. Instead, Anzaldúa openly confronted the group: "I stood at their door and told them you are in violation of the Code of Conduct by cooperating with the enemy. You are to cease and desist if not you are to be labeled and charged as traitors," claimed Anzaldúa. He continued,

> Next thing you know, The Cheese came in with six guards opened the door they grabbed my ass and dragged me out. Got beat by fourteen guards with bamboo sticks. Six hours on my knees. And got hung up on the wall. Then went into solitary confinement. I got beat an excess of sixteen hours with bamboo sticks and I was not going to let this affect who I actually am. I would never stoop to their low. Knowing the compassion and kindness that this country fosters within its society is one of the things that personally kept me going.[63]

Anzaldúa absorbed the painful consequences for refusing the Peace Committee, but being a tough Marine, he was willing to stand his ground, and by this point he had already survived a near-death experience that culminated in his capture. Giving in was not an option for Anzaldúa.

Corporal Anzaldúa's capture occurred several years after Riate's and Kavanaugh's. In January 1970, Anzaldúa, who was just short of finishing his tour, agreed to serve as a liaison to a South Vietnamese special unit in Duy Xuyen in Quang Nam Province. Anzaldúa served as an S-2 Scout (a utility man for the battalion) due to his fluency in Vietnamese, and was assigned a Kit Carson Scout (a "rehabilitated" Viet Cong) by the name of Nguyen Ngoc Anh.[64] On January 17, Anzaldúa encountered an overwhelming number of enemy forces, causing his South Vietnamese allies to retreat. The confrontation would result in his capture and with the execution of Anh. "Before I could hit the ground I got hit twice in my arm and foot. Firefight lasted hours. I ran out of ammo. Before I got captured, I went into a spider hole. SVA ran away. For about two seconds I thought about shooting the other way."[65]

With the wounds he had received it was almost impossible for Anzaldúa to continue fighting. After ditching his weapons in the depths of a rice paddy, Anzaldúa surrendered and was taken prisoner.

For the next three months, Anzaldúa was marched until he arrived at his first permanent jungle camp. Realizing the minimal attention experiences like his have garnered, Anzaldúa acknowledged that historians have overly focused on the "the plight of the pilots." He resumed,

> It would be so outlandish and so ... almost unreal for anyone within our society to understand it. In the South, the jungle camps under triple or quadruple canopy. Living like a caveman! It was like living like an animal. Worse than an animal! In that camp, there was twenty-six people. After two years only twelve people lived. Everybody else died as a result of their wounds or of starvation.[66]

The challenging nature of the jungle camp posed several obstacles for Anzaldúa and the rest of the POW populations. In addition to starvation and disease, the Viet Cong threatened Anzaldúa's life regularly. In highly contested areas it would have been inconvenient for the Viet Cong to hold captives. The presence of American captives would either reveal them as indeed being Viet Cong or at least slow them down, thus making Anzaldúa more fearful of the threats on his life.

Despite being threatened on an almost daily basis, Anzaldúa avoided execution, but he needed perseverance and a little luck to survive the jungle. Anzaldúa's situation overwhelmed the toughest of men as the harsh beatings and the diet took a toll. "Starvation! And when I say starvation. They are not gonna give you anymore than what will minimally keep you alive. They are not gonna give you their food. They are just not gonna give it to you!," recalled Anzaldúa. "The equivalent of the palm of your hand [is what you were fed]. [I kept alive by eating] snakes, bats, lizards, frogs, and stealing chickens and cats."[67]

Anzaldúa went into survival mode. His humble upbringing did not allow for pride or pettiness to hinder how he lived. Growing up in the agricultural community of Refugio, Texas, created a sense of ruggedness within

Anzaldúa.[68] Moreover, growing up Mexican American in Refugio trained Anzaldúa to overcome barriers caused by social and economic limitations. Hard physical labor was the way of life in racially conscious South Texas. Mexican Americans served as stoop laborers in a society that was racially structured. The Marine no longer dealt with discrimination, but with tropical diseases such as beriberi, amoebic dysentery, and malaria.

Anzaldúa's identity and the manliness instilled in his youth in rural Texas contributed to his survival. The situation was not easy by any means, as Anzaldúa remembered:

> It was so absent, the very fundamentals of nutrition to sustain life. This instinct to survive and one's ability to acknowledge that you'll do whatever needs to be done to achieve the end result which is to walk out of that mess alive. I had a good friend of mine, Sgt. Dennis Hammond die because he refused to eat rats, bats, and snakes. "I am not gonna live like an animal. I'd rather die" [he said]. I never consciously said I'm gonna live like an animal. I just said I'm not gonna die in this damn place.[69]

Anzaldúa did not shy away from doing what it took to survive in the jungle camps. His stoicism paid off, and he was eventually moved north across the 17th parallel in February 1972.

Living in the relatively "cushier" camps in the North proved to be a tremendous upgrade from life in the South for Anzaldúa. He had been housed at the deadly Kushner Camp, which had a mortality rate of nearly 50 percent. At Plantation Gardens, Anzaldúa experienced a sophisticated prison system similar to penitentiaries in the United States. Due to his trilingual abilities (he spoke English, Spanish, and Vietnamese), Anzaldúa proved to be a valuable asset for the communication system. In the North, Anzaldúa noticed guards and their associates of various nationalities. He saw Russians, Chinese, and Cubans aiding the North Vietnamese.[70] Only after the Peace Committee allegedly informed on Anzaldúa's language ability did the Vietnamese learn of his fluency in Vietnamese.

Another Mexican American prisoner moved systematically from South Vietnam to North Vietnam was Army Specialist E-4 Juan L. Jacquez. On

May 10, 1969, on his last night in-country, in the vicinity of Pleiku, Jacquez's sergeant suggested that since his tour was all but over it would be fitting for him to go on patrol one last time. The sergeant's questionable judgment would have drastic consequences. "As soon as it got dark, they only moved in the dark . . . we went out on patrol and ran right into them [the enemy]. It's just that there were so many of them and they were just sneaking up. We were right in the middle of it. Right dead center," recalled Jacquez about that particular night.[71] The incident was extremely vivid in his memory and he further explained:

> I still wonder what the hell happened. That night it was me, the Georgia guy and the Hawaiian guy. I was the ranking guy that night. I don't remember who had the radio. There was a company coming in a "V." I told them get ahold of the bunker. I don't know if they were asleep. I don't know what the hell happened. We never got through. The sons-a-bitches were right on top of us. It was a whole company of vc. I told them shut the radio off and lay flat on the ground. The antenna gave us away from our ditch. If I would have fired one shot, I wouldn't be here. When I told them shut the radio off and lay flat, not only did I save my life I saved those two guys' lives. It was too late they were on top of us. And we almost made it through except for that little antenna that sticks out on the radio. That little antenna is what gave us away. They must have known that place with their eyes closed, because I couldn't see nothing. I always wondered what happened that night. Whoever decided to take a nap and sleep that night instead of answering the radio I am pretty sure he didn't come home because they were a lot of damn troops that night.[72]

In the hope that the enemy would pass them, Jacquez ordered his companions to lie flat on the ground and keep quiet. As a result of his orders, all three men survived. If they had retaliated, death would have been all but certain. The Vietnamese quickly marched the group away from the site to avoid detection from other Americans who may have been aware of the whereabouts of their men. In an attempt to rescue the group, U.S. forces began bombing the surrounding countryside and to no avail continued the following day. "The next day B-52s, Air Force, started bombing the hell out of them. I figured my own people are gonna kill me. Bombs falling all over the place! They had one kid guarding me. They put me in a bunker. It's an experience I wouldn't change it for nothing," admitted Jacquez. He continued, "I went through it. Lucky enough I went through it. No regrets on any decision I made that night. Don't regret anything. Nothing! It happened it's over. I have no pity. I'm not pissed at the people. They didn't know any better anyway."[73] The near-death experience put the situation in perspective for Jacquez, as he was humbled and realized how fortunate he was to be alive.

Jacquez and his companions were transferred through a series of villages en route to what he believed was Cambodia. "We passed through some villages because I knew exactly where I was. I couldn't believe what they [Americans] called a friendly. I mean, people that I would see during the day and all of that. At night they were the enemy."[74] On the day he should have returned to "the world," Jacquez now hopelessly traveled the remote jungles of Southeast Asia as a POW. Looking at the villagers whom he had previously considered "friendlies" must have been heartbreaking, especially as he was now grudgingly extending his tour in Vietnam. "It took us about two days and we got to the Cambodian border. We got there; I was surprised to see fourteen guys in that little prison camp," recalled Jacquez about his travels.[75] The conditions were deplorable and would make most people cringe at the mere thought of having to spend a night in the jungle. Nevertheless, Jacquez stayed true to his smart-alecky nature as he sarcastically described his stay in Cambodia as having spent one year in bamboo cages with "room service, color TV; the whole works."[76] The amenities in the jungle were not quite as Jacquez mockingly described; yet forty years later, he can joke over his living conditions.

After almost a year, the Vietnamese began to prepare Jacquez and the rest of the group, which had dwindled to a total of twelve, for the march northward. In preparation, the group exercised to build up endurance for the sixty-day trek. "We walked two months from sunup to sundown, down the Ho Chi Minh Trail. They had it all *chingón* dude! At sunup they had us walk. At sundown we would hit a camp."[77] As he marched north, Jacquez encountered angry civilians who were eager to confront him and the group through physical hostilities. "I was beaten up by the spectators, by the civilians, they spit on you and kicked you," claimed Jacquez.[78]

After being cautiously and systematically moved to avoid detection, Jacquez and the group arrived at Farnsworth or D-1, a prison camp just southwest of Hanoi. In plain sight from the outside, Jacquez felt that it had the potential of being a decent prison, yet when placed in his first cell he was proved wrong. With black walls his cell was "pure darkness." The only light in the room entered from tiny holes in the ceiling. "I would stare at that little hole and just daydream. When I would least expect it, there was no hole it was dark. I would spend my whole day meditating," recollected Jacquez about a typical day at D-1.[79]

After D-1 shut down, Jacquez was relocated to Plantation Gardens, which proved to be a great contrast from D-1 and a vast improvement. The walls at Plantation Gardens were white and an abundance of light glimmered through the cells. However, Jacquez quickly found the loneliness of solitary confinement particularly troublesome. "Every time they open the damn door, you had to bow and all this fucking shit," described Jacquez over his expected behavior. "I didn't do it one time, I was pissed off. They threw my ass in solitary for several months."[80] Being held alone took an emotional and psychological toll on Jacquez and the rest of the POW population.

Another form of mental and psychological abuse came with interrogation sessions by the North Vietnamese and their allies, such as the Cubans and Russians. Jacquez attested to being interrogated frequently: "I have a feeling a lot of them [interrogators] were Cubans. I hardly spoke Spanish to them. The less they saw in me, the better. Cubans told me I did not know how to speak Spanish."[81] Despite the ridicule and criticism of his identity, Jacquez remained true to himself and to the Code of Conduct. "You get to the point sometimes that you are not afraid to die," asserted Jacquez. He continued, "A few times I thought I was going to get my head blown off. They put it [gun] on your forehead and cock it [*mimicking the action and the Vietnamese chatter*]. I wasn't afraid to die anymore. I was ready then. You get to that point. Nobody wants to die, but you accept it. You're ready."[82]

The grim experiences engendered in Jacquez a consciousness associated with the inevitability of death. "My main concern was that I would get back. I didn't want to die over there. I asked God to keep me alive, to keep me alive to get back to the States. I wanted to see my family at least one more time," confessed Jacquez.[83] The motivation to get back and see his family fueled Jacquez's quest for survival. "When we were young we were raised with very little. I was ready. I wasn't one of those guys that needed everything. I had already survived my teenage years of hell, so surviving over there was just part of it," reiterated Jacquez. "There was one guy who had nothing physically wrong. But he was weak mentally. He thought he wasn't coming [home]. He gave up and died."[84] Jacquez's humble beginnings and his will to survive, which had been reinforced from *colonia* life in New Mexico, kicked in and sustained him during these dire times.

In North Vietnam, Jacquez confirmed that interrogation and indoctrination sessions increased dramatically. Jacquez recalled the propaganda sessions: "'Here read that book. Did you read book? Page twenty-four paragraph three what does it say?' So you start guessing. 'You didn't read book! Read it again!' After a while you start going through all the high spots, about all their heroes and shit. How in the hell are you supposed to know?"[85] While Jacquez did not become indoctrinated, he did witness others such as Kavanaugh and Riate accept Communist ideologies.

Despite the indoctrination and interrogation sessions, the overall treatment improved significantly in North Vietnam in comparison to the brutality Jacquez faced in the jungles in Cambodia and South Vietnam. "Actually, the Hanoi Hilton was the best one [POW camp] I had ever been in. Just like a state prison here," recalled Jacquez.[86] It can be argued that treatment in the North appeared to improve for several reasons: First, living conditions in South Vietnam prison camps were plainly deplorable. Second, after the death of Ho Chi Minh in 1969, overall POW treatment improved. And third, the bombing campaign in late 1972 had an immense effect on the negotiation talks and brought vast improvement. As the war dwindled in December 1972, the North Vietnamese, in preparation for their departure, attempted to fatten POWs during their last three months of captivity, and consequently food services improved.

The American bombing campaign of Hanoi in 1972 also instilled a sense of hope and reassurance in Jacquez and the rest of the POW population. In late December 1972, during Operation Linebacker II, also known as "the Christmas Bombings," they began to believe the war to be almost over, as the bombing campaign surely would bring the North Vietnamese to the negotiation table. "That is the most beautiful sound I ever heard," remembered Jacquez about the bombings over North Vietnam. "When they would sound the sirens; you should see those Vietnamese scatter like ants all over the place. And we knew it was a matter of time that those bombs would start hitting. I was happy. I was very happy and at the same time very scared too."[87] Jacquez saw the personal threat the air strikes posed to American POWs, as they could have easily fallen victim to friendly fire. At the same time, the bombing campaign brought tremendous destruction to Hanoi and the North Vietnamese.

A fellow Mexican American prisoner of war, Specialist Five José M. Astorga, concurred with Jacquez about the joy and fear of the bombings and agreed the attacks in large part brought them home. "President Nixon brought us home," reflected Astorga.

> President Nixon started bombing them around the clock. Twenty-four hours a day. All around them, you would see the aircraft coming down at night. They hit the ground. Big ol' line of B-52s coming down. You could see their SAMs [surface-to-air missiles] from the prison camp we were in, taking off; they were hitting aircraft: B-52s. Day and night you would see pilots coming down, parachuting. They [the North Vietnamese] would be shooting at them as they came down. The B-52s would come down and crash and the whole night would look like daylight as they [the planes] were burning. Because of that we came home. When we were getting ready to come home during the Paris Peace talks, they started treating us better and feeding us better.[88]

Before the situation improved, however, Astorga looked death straight in the eye and did not blink.

While on his second tour in Vietnam, Astorga took part in the largest rescue mission in the history of the Air Force. On April 2, 1972, Astorga was called to replace a team member who was ill. "The guy who was supposed to fly with Pascali was sick," remembered Astorga. "So about five in the morning, Pascali came to my room, 'You want to go on a mission?' I said okay, since the other guy was sick." They went aboard a UH-1H helicopter towards Da Nang, where they picked up a Vietnamese general and a civilian. In the evening after finishing their mission, they received a call concerning a downed aircraft. Astorga and his team responded and searched for Bat 21, the call sign for the fallen Air Force lieutenant colonel Iceal Hambleton. Despite the story being featured in a Hollywood film, Astorga's role in the rescue has been overlooked in the historical narrative.

As the team approached the vicinity of the downed aircraft, they encountered enemy fire, and the helicopter Astorga traveled in was shot down north of Phu Bai in Quang Binh Province. Astorga, who was the helicopter door gunner, broke a leg as soon as the "jolly green" went down. "We were the first aircraft on the scene and we went down. And then, my whole crew as far as I know all perished right there. And I was captured," Astorga recalled with overwhelming emotion. "Oh Pascali was still alive! The aircraft was on top of his body. There was nothing I could do for him. There was a lot of enemy activity."[89] Astorga still carried the emotional toll of the death of his partner.

Although lucky in comparison to his companions who were dead and dying, Astorga sustained serious injuries. "My left leg was broken. Between the hip and kneecap. My kneecap was injured too. I injured my back. I crushed three disks in my spine. I was captured ten to twenty minutes later by the vc and I think North Vietnamese," recalled Astorga over the day of his capture.[90] With several severe injuries Astorga could not put up a fight and fell prisoner of war.

Surrounded by the enemy and unable to defend himself, Astorga feared for the worst. Initially, his captors gave orders to execute him, but after further deliberation, per Astorga's recollection, "they changed their minds. I don't know why."[91] This would not be the last time Astorga's life was threatened, as his captors frequently threatened to kill him as a means of psychologically abusing him.

Astorga recalled the uncomfortable feeling that remained so present in his mind: "I was mentally tortured. I was almost executed a couple of times.

Once, they put a rifle to my head. That was before I arrived to any prison camp. I told them go ahead. He started squeezing the trigger little by little. A captain yelled 'Wait!' After deliberation they said, 'we have decided to spare your life.' At that time, I really didn't care either way."[92] Exhausted and overwhelmed by his dire situation and having lost his entire crew, Astorga reached a point where he did not care whether he lived or died.

It took about thirty-days travel before Astorga reached his first permanent prison camp. Further complicating Astorga's transfer was his broken leg, which made travel much more difficult and painful. "When I was first captured on the second day, I was taken to some high mountains by the vc," recalled Astorga. "I was limping with one leg going down the mountain. I did that twice. I was in a bunker with a lot of fighting [going on around me] and I was left there. Planes bombing. I tried to escape. I had a real high fever. No food, no water."[93] As the Viet Cong transported Astorga through the jungles and across the DMZ, not only did the rugged elements pose a threat, but friendly fire did as well. At his first temporary camp, the Viet Cong set Astorga's leg, which allowed him more mobility.

Finally, on May 1, 1972, Astorga reached Plantation Gardens, his first permanent prison camp. At Plantation Gardens, Astorga was interrogated daily from May 1 to May 22.[94] Astorga faced intense indoctrination sessions. The sessions included exposure to reading material, films, and audio recordings of Communist propaganda.

The Vietnamese attempted to motivate Astorga to participate in the production of a propaganda film by offering medical treatment, which he badly needed, as an inducement for cooperation.

> I was kept in solitary [confinement] for a month. Because of my broken leg, they wanted me to make a film. And it depended on how I cooperated with them on how I would get treatment. "The film seemed like we are forcing you." So, they wanted to do another film . . . They wanted for us to admit that we were war criminals against the Vietnamese people and not POWs. "If we like it we will give you medical treatment." Then finally I was taken to a hospital. I stayed six months with a cast. Then transferred to the wounded room.[95]

Despite needing medical attention, Astorga attempted to remain true to the Code of Conduct. After frustrating the North Vietnamese with his less-than-convincing performance in front of the cameras, he was relieved of his acting duty and sent for medical care.

In preparation for repatriation, Astorga and the majority of POWs were moved to the Hanoi Hilton in late December 1972.[96] A couple of weeks earlier, on December 9, Air Force Lieutenant Hector M. Acosta, on his ninety-second mission with the 14th Tactical Reconnaissance Squadron, was shot down in Nghai Dan in Nghe An Province.[97] Aboard an RF4C "Phantom," which was shot down by a surface-to-air missile, Acosta received numerous injuries prior to a successful but painful ejection. Along with the burns to his elbows and knees, Acosta took some shrapnel to the chest and right arm.

As the enemy closed in on Acosta's location, two rescue attempts failed under heavy fire. With bullets flying all around him, Acosta was pinned down, and before being captured, he radioed his situation. The North Vietnamese closed in on Acosta, and the San Antonio native was surrounded with nowhere to go. Simultaneously, a bullet grazed the top of his head and he then felt a warm trickle of blood oozing out. "The thought was that someone bigger than Muhammad Ali, Cassius Clay hits me at the side of my head," recalled Acosta.[98] As he reluctantly touched his head, he was consoled by realizing that it was blood and not his brains. Bleeding, beat-up, and suffering from the injuries sustained, Acosta was taken captive. Yet, he remained composed, thinking of two things: that his wife would kill him if he indeed returned home one day and that he badly needed a cigarette.[99]

A North Vietnamese guard led Acosta to his first interrogation and with one blow of a banana knife sliced the hose off of Acosta's flight suit. "Shit, if the guy is worried about a G-suit hose, what the hell is he going to think about this Smith & Wesson .38 combat masterpiece I've got strapped on my hip?," Acosta thought to himself. "I pointed to the gun and I thought he was going to pull it off, but uh-uh. The knife goes up again and he chops the gun off my leg."[100] Despite being in a vulnerable position, Acosta was defiant. He went as far as reaching for a cigarette in his pocket and attempted to smoke it while his captors surrounded him with an arsenal of automatic weapons.[101] Many people, including civilians, have been shot for less drastic movements; Acosta, willing to push the situation to the limit, was beyond fortunate.

His captors did not know what to make of this short man with Asian features. At one point, they thought that he was Laotian. Out of fear of being executed on the spot, Acosta quickly convinced his captors that he was American and not Laotian. At his first interrogation, Acosta was asked, "You Lao? You Lao? [*points at skin*]." He responded, "'Holy shit, no! Yankee air pirate! I go Mexican!' He goes 'Mex, Mex-i-can? Mex-i-can!' I was different looking from most air pirates. Brown Yankees! The problem with being Laotian is that they kill those people [instantly]. They get it a lot worse."[102] His life was spared as his quest for survival began.

Acosta now began what he considered a race to reach Hanoi before the scheduled bombings planned for December 18 (the Christmas Bombings). Prior to being captured, Acosta had learned of Operation Linebacker II, the plan to bomb Hanoi that would begin just before Christmas. If he wanted to avoid possibly falling victim to friendly fire, he had to reach a POW camp before December 18. It was now about December 13 and Acosta was being transported to temporary locations that could easily have been targeted.[103] He wanted to make sure he reached a secure location that American bombers would recognize as a POW camp and not unleash their bombs indiscriminately.

Acosta's pitiful appearance aided his transportation process. After believing he was in grave condition, his captors called in a jeep and had Acosta transferred to the Zoo. "The neat thing about looking like hell is you can act like you are really damaged when you are not. Any time I could have run a mile," attested Acosta over his condition.[104] One of the guards even gave him a cold Vietnamese beer (though, given my experience in 2008, it is somewhat unbelievable that one could find cold beer in Vietnam). "Probably the best hour of captivity," recalled Acosta. "I think he respected me. I didn't treat him with arrogance. I was surprised at how most of them seemed not to act extremely hostile."[105] As the war wound down, treatment of POWs vastly improved, and Acosta's experience can attest to the enhancements.

Since he was a late arrival (three months before release), Acosta's experience is almost completely different, as most POWs would argue that he was there only to experience the "better days." From a civilian standpoint, Acosta's experience was not easy or joyous. He faced interrogations and indoctrination sessions, not to mention a near-death experience when his plane was shot down. As with the other Chicano POWs, the Vietnamese played upon the divisive history endured by Mexican Americans living in the United States. "We know that you Americans from Mexican descent have been treated very badly in your country and oppressed," remarked an interrogator to Acosta.[106] Acosta, who had the habit of grinning and smiling, much to the displeasure of the Vietnamese, smiled at them. He attempted to calm the situation by explaining, "You need to live in America to know what it's like to be an American. I am very happy and proud to be an American. I haven't experienced any great oppression. I am not here because I am an American who hates America."[107]

Aside from occasional beatings and pain from the injuries sustained at the time of capture, Acosta's experience was decent compared to the other Mexican American POWs. "We were treated reasonably honorably and reasonably well," reflected Acosta. One day while he was showering, a piece of shrapnel began to push out of his chest. Acosta sought medical treatment, and the doctor who saw him was surprised he was not dead! The doctor pulled a half-inch piece of metal out of Acosta's chest, cleaned it with alcohol, and awkwardly remarked to Acosta, "You are strange."[108]

At the Zoo and then at the Hanoi Hilton, Acosta noticed two distinct factions among the POW population: "The FOGs (freaking old guys) and FNGs (freaking new guys). No doubt about it. The FNGs never disrespected the old guys from what I experienced. They had structure. Underground structure. The FOGs deserve a lot of credit."[109] Being an airman, the structure imposed by the FOGs or SROs did not seem foreign to Acosta, as it would have to an infantryman coming up from South Vietnam.

The senior officers or FOGs dictated, or at least attempted to dictate, the behavior of the rest of the POWs. "At times you couldn't be resisting because senior guys were negotiating," uttered Acosta over the complex nature of following orders from the senior cadre.[110] Acosta attempted to be defiant by not shaving his mustache on his first shaving day. "You go by rank and share a safety razor. I have a lot of Indian in me so I don't grow much facial hair. I leave my mustache. Guard tells me to cut mustache. I respond, according to Air Force Regulation 35-10 this is a legal mustache," recollected Acosta.[111] After counseling with a senior POW, Acosta was ordered to shave his mustache. Acosta did not respond with frustration, but it could be understood why other POWs, especially ground troops, would be annoyed by such orders.

By the time Acosta was captured, the North Vietnamese had improved daily rations and treatment noticeably. Acosta concluded, "We ate in a way I think that was comparable to the population. They weren't feeding us bad food, they were feeding us like they fed themselves. Their average caloric intake was just much lower than Americans' typical [intake]."[112] Due to the difference in diets, POWs dropped significant weight and dealt with malnutrition.

Acosta credited his humble beginnings with shaping his character, which propelled him to survive the POW experience. "My dad, I think, taught me to have a high threshold. He could tolerate discomfort. He didn't like to make a big deal of things."[113] These elements, which had been ingrained in him at such a young age, allowed Acosta to thrive without any major reservations.

By the fall of 1972, nevertheless, the possibility of a homecoming was palpable for all POWs. The December bombings, many POWs believed, resulted in improved treatment and eventually brought the North Vietnamese to the negotiation table. Due to his fluency in Vietnamese, Joe Anzaldúa became one of the first to know about the Paris Peace Accords, and more importantly of their impending release in January 1973. Anzaldúa reminisced:

The peace talks were on again off again. They consolidated us at the Hanoi Hilton. One evening, I heard the guards talking in Vietnamese, "The Americans are going home." I didn't say nothing to nobody. The next morning I went straight to Colonel Ted Guy. I told him, I didn't want to tell him in front of nobody in case it were not true. I heard guards say that the peace agreement had been signed, that there would be a prisoner exchange and that we would all go home. He said, "Joe, I don't want to disappoint anyone here, there is no doubt in my mind you heard what you say you heard. I don't want to mention this to nobody because if it falls through it's going to demoralize them. We don't need to say anything to anybody."[114]

Anzaldúa recalled the moment as if it were yesterday as he was excited and hopeful, yet at the same time uncertain of the situation. "When I heard it, it went in the ear and went in the brain. It was so surreal that I said to myself, I can't tell anyone except Colonel Ted Guy," confessed Anzaldúa. After counseling with Colonel Guy, they decided not to tell anyone in case it did not happen. "Shit! Here we are again another five years," exclaimed Anzaldúa over their decision on not revealing the peace agreement to the entire POW population.[115] Three weeks later the first group went home.

The captivity portion of the prisoner-of-war experience ended with the repatriation of the men, but the experience that helped them cope with captivity started long before their capture. The qualities, skills, discipline, and characteristics that propelled Mexican American POWs to survive Vietnam had been ingrained in them in the rural communities, border towns, and *barrios* of the Southwest. The persistence and resolve developed by hard labor during their youth created a tolerance that allowed them to prevail in conflictive contexts. Yet, the same *macho* mentality that had enabled them to sustain high levels of tolerance for discomfort and that prompted them to persevere with limitations also hindered them from sharing their experiences and coping with their invisible wounds.

After their release, Mexican American prisoners of war now faced the challenge of rebounding from being broken down and reduced to such a low state of existence. The physical, mental, and emotional wounds needed healing. The POW experience had created challenges within each man. Now they had to restore their masculinity and reclaim their place at home. For Álvarez and three other Chicano POWs, divorce from their spouses could not be avoided. The greatest challenge in returning home, however, was adjusting to a changed society and to a different sense of self, as the many years of captivity had led to many changes within themselves.

CHAPTER 6

Homecoming
or Rude Awakening?

Soon after the signing of the Paris Peace Accords in January 1973, the United States prepared for Operation Homecoming. Five hundred and ninety-one American prisoners of war returned home from Vietnam during the two-month process. Previously, during the war, 129 POWs "escaped from, evaded, or were released by their captors," including 95 who were paroled early.[1] The first group left Vietnam on February 12, and the last group left on March 29. The POWs returned in order of capture, with the severely ill and injured moving ahead of the others. The excitement created a sense of euphoria inconceivable to some of the older POWs like Álvarez. After eight and a half years of captivity, Álvarez needed to see freedom in order to believe it. While Ciro Salas returned home in 1954, and Isaac Camacho returned in 1965 after a successful escape, the other eight Mexican American POWs returned during Operation Homecoming. The POWs received a hero's welcome upon arriving in the United States. Tickets to ball games, keys to the city, and even brand new cars awaited the ex-prisoners on arrival.

Naturally, not all former POWs responded similarly to their newfound freedom. Even disparities within the Mexican American contingency existed, as each former POW reacted differently to his captivity. While several men went on to live "normal" lives, others faced severe mental, physical, and emotional issues. Their lives took different directions: some men left the military and others made a career of it. The military served as a comfortable and familiar setting for former POWs. Furthermore, the military setting sheltered soldiers from a changed society and allowed them more breathing room in coping with their POW experience.

Upon their return, Vietnam veterans, including POWs, were deeply impacted by post-traumatic stress disorder (PTSD). Although the condition can be traced back to early history, the term PTSD was not coined until the mid-1970s and not officially recognized as a disorder until 1980 due to the high volume of Vietnam veterans who suffered from the condition. Returning World War I veterans coped with what simply became known as "shell shock." After World War II, the condition became known as "combat stress reaction" or "gross stress reaction." By the Vietnam War era, with a great deal of returning soldiers experiencing "depression caused by post-Vietnam adjustment problems," which became known as "post-Vietnam syndrome," the military began to make systematic inquiries.[2]

Bringing "post-Vietnam syndrome" to public attention was the death of Congressional Medal of Honor recipient Dwight Johnson. After returning to his native Detroit, Johnson learned that opportunities were slim for African American veterans like himself. After he received the Medal of Honor and the adulation that came with the honor, work prospects rose and the Army brought him on board as a recruiter. He had trouble adjusting to his new surroundings and sought treatment at a VA medical center, where he was treated and diagnosed with "depression caused by post-Vietnam adjustment problems." In March 1971, Dwight was allowed to leave the hospital on a three-day pass, never to be seen again. On April 30, 1971, in a failed armed robbery of a Detroit liquor store, a clerk gunned down Johnson.[3]

Dwight Johnson's death caused the Pentagon to search for answers to "what had gone wrong" with returning Vietnam veterans. While the country waited for the return of prisoners of war from Vietnam, the Veterans Administration (VA) worked on a counseling program for POWs and their wives. With tragedies such as Dwight Johnson's, the government considered providing therapy to all returning veterans, not just POWs, who they suspected would need the extra guidance.[4] With the mounting emotional, psychological, and mental problems suffered by returning veterans, the country became more aware of the condition that would become known as PTSD.

Aside from the problems posed by PTSD, Mexican American former POWs also dealt with the challenge of reintegrating into a changed society, issues of alcohol/substance abuse, depression, and marital strife, not to mention with the haunting memories of their Vietnam experience that loomed over them. The war and captivity may well have forced the men to question their status as men; and their wives divorcing them during or after their captivity did not ease the situation. Among the eight Mexican American POWs who returned during Operation Homecoming (Salas returned in 1954 and Camacho escaped in 1965), half eventually divorced. So, yet another set of challenges arose for former POWs: reclaiming their masculine roles in a changed society and a changing family structure.

During their husbands' captivity, POW wives in general became accustomed to life without their men. Edna J. Hunter, who produced "The Vietnam POW Veteran: Immediate and Long-Term Effects of Captivity," concluded that inside a year of release about 30 percent of Army, Navy, and Marine Corps POWs divorced their wives. In 1983, *U.S. News and World Report* reported that of the 420 POWs that were married upon release, 90 had divorced. Hunter's study did not include Air Force POWs, and reflected higher divorce rates among Army, Navy, and Marine POWs, but making up the bulk of the 90 divorces in the *U.S. News and World Report* were Air Force POWs, who composed the majority of prisoners. Hunter summarized the situation: "When the men returned, the wives expected much change and found little. The husbands, on the other hand, expected little change in their wives and families, and found much."[5]

While some POW wives had been empowered by their activities in the National League of American POW/MIA Families, others had been shaped by their participation in the antiwar movement, and others had participated in the women's liberation movement. Their involvement took women out of the traditional home setting and created an independence that many had not experienced during their married life. One wife commented that she had "become pretty aggressive" during her husband's imprisonment, and another wife remarked, "I'm not a honey anymore."[6] Upon their husbands' return, women were expected to "return to their role of a docile homebody whose highest achievement is a casserole," "to change back to a major's sweet wife," or to "revert to their passive 'yes, dear' roles."[7] By divorcing their husbands, these women, empowered by the women's liberation movement of the 1960s and 1970s, were relieving their men from their manly roles of providers, protectors, and lovers, which further emasculated them. The returning POWs now had to reassert their place as men in a changed society and through their actions reaffirm their manliness or *machismo*.

For one night, all the issues the POWs dealt with were set aside as they reconvened at the White House on May 24, 1973, for a bash sponsored by their commander-in-chief and now their champion, Richard M. Nixon. It would be the largest dinner party hosted by a U.S. president at the White House. John Wayne, Sammy Davis Jr., Bob Hope, Ricardo Montalban, Jimmy Stewart, Irving Berlin, and even a Playboy Playmate roamed the White House South Lawn socializing with the returning POWs. Bob Hope hosted the dinner party and joked, "This is what I like, a captive audience."[8] The festivities included an extravagant dinner followed by an evening of entertainment, and then culminated with a dance until two in the morning.[9] The highlight of the night was when celebrities joined President Nixon and Irving Berlin, the author of "God Bless America," for a spectacular rendition of the song in which the former POWs present also chimed.

In the eyes of most prisoners of war, with the exception of the members of the Peace Committee, there was not much wrong that President Nixon could do. Most prisoners were willing to overlook Nixon's transgressions and demonstrated their gratitude to the man they believed to be responsible for bringing them home. "At this point I can say two people brought me home," recalled Juan Jacquez. "One is God and the other one, I don't care what anybody says to me, my number one man is Ex-President Nixon. He is the one who brought me home."[10] Jacquez demonstrated fondness for the president's masculine ideals: "To me, President Nixon is the only one who had enough balls to do what it takes to end the war. He didn't need to go ask permission from Congress. He didn't need to have approval from his wife. He didn't have to go tell nobody what he was gonna do. That son-of-a-bitch just went ahead and he ended it when he bombed the hell out of North Vietnam."[11] Jacquez correlated Nixon's aggression with masculine values that he admired.

Everett Álvarez Jr. also expressed admiration for Nixon and thanked him, as most prisoners of war did, for bringing them home. Joe Anzaldúa agreed as well and also held President Nixon in high regard: "I am and will forever be eternally grateful to President Nixon for bringing me back. I know, I believe, why he did what he did and that was to bring us back and for that I am grateful. Absent that, I don't know what the hell I would have done. I don't know if I would have lived much longer. In the North, I probably could have [survived] because like I said, the formal prison system."[12] The majority of returning POWs admired Nixon's aggression during the late bombing campaigns in December 1972.

Those critical of the president argued that the return of the POWs and their celebration served merely as a diversion from the looming Watergate scandal. The party, as well as POW stories, soon filled newspaper headlines that previously had concentrated on the president's scandal. Ninety POWs declined President Nixon's invitation, amongst them Larry Kavanaugh, who had been critical of Nixon during captivity.[13] As most POWs celebrated, men like Kavanaugh, Alfonso Riate, and the remaining members of the Peace Committee had difficulty coming to terms with repatriation.

On June 27, 1973, Marine Sergeant Abel Larry Kavanaugh became the second returning POW to commit suicide (Captain Edward Alan Brudno was the first). Colonel Ted Guy had charged Kavanaugh and the seven other members of the alleged Peace Committee with collaborating with the enemy. Perhaps the pending charges disturbed the Marine and caused him to pull the trigger that ended his life. Kavanaugh's wife Sandra certainly believed that to be the case. "I blame Col. Guy and the Pentagon for his death," Mrs. Kavanaugh stated. "Without their insistence on pursuing these fictitious charges, my husband would be here today."[14] Anger consumed the young widow as she blamed the government for her husband's death.

Even though Colonel Ted Guy levied the charges against the Peace Committee and was blamed by Mrs. Kavanaugh for being responsible for Larry's death, he did so under manipulation. Guy described the pressure used to convince him of going public with the charges:

> My report was sent to Washington. I got a telephone call from the secretary—from the Air Force. I'm not going to mention the fellow's name. He had read my intelligence debriefing and he wanted me to make a statement to the press about it. He gave me the name of Fred Hoffman of the Associated Press in Washington and told me to call him. If Hoffman wouldn't listen to my story about the collaboration, I was to call Senator Barry Goldwater and tell him about it. This was on a Thursday. I thought about it and said to myself, "No, this is not the way to do it. I'll wait for justice to run its course." On Friday the officer phoned again, and once more on Sunday. The message was the same: "Call the AP." So I sat down and gave an interview which practically wiped Watergate off the front page of the *New York Times*. I thought I was doing it with the sanction of the Air Force. I thought they wanted me to go ahead and get it out in the open. After the story hit the *Washington Post* I got another call from the officer. He said, "Okay, you've done your job. Don't say anything else." By this time cameramen from CBS, NBC, and ABC were converging on my home in Tucson, Arizona. I called back and said, "My God, what do you mean don't say anything else? That's impossible."[15]

To the dismay of Guy and the Peace Committee, the story generated headlines throughout the nation. The Peace Committee members became guilty in the court of public opinion, while the press inundated Guy, forcing him into seclusion. On the other hand, benefiting from the breaking news was President Nixon, whose Watergate scandal took a back page to the POW controversy. Shortly, Kavanaugh's suicide would also overshadow the president's scandal.

The shock the POW and military communities exhibited in response to Kavanaugh's death paled in comparison to the blow endured by his family. At the time, the Kavanaughs had a five-year-old daughter, Cindy, and Sandra was two months pregnant with their first son, Larry Jr. Larry Kavanaugh Sr. spent just short of five years as a POW and, according to his wife, faced collaboration charges for demonstrating against the war.[16] After wasting away in a POW camp in Vietnam, it was clear to Kavanaugh that he intended to never set foot in a prison again.

Sandra expressed gratitude to the North Vietnamese for having kept her late husband alive. "He went to Vietnam and the North Vietnamese kept him alive for five years," she said, "then he came back to America and his own people killed him."[17] Perhaps Kavanaugh's inability to live up to the manly ideals of resistance provoked a deep depression, which caused his suicide. Or perhaps the mere fact that his manliness and integrity were being questioned provoked the young Marine to end his life. A fellow prisoner of war has come to believe that Kavanaugh's suicide stemmed from a guilty conscience. "He probably couldn't handle it. He only lasted three months then committed suicide. *Digo yo.* He was one of them that was getting special treatment and shit. He committed suicide. I'm pretty sure that is why. He couldn't handle it. *Digo yo.*"

The causes of Kavanaugh's suicide remain a mystery. His son, Larry Kavanaugh Jr., who was born five months after his father's death, suggests that perhaps severe PTSD from the deplorable conditions in the jungle camps along with the brutal treatment and torture could have driven the Marine to take his life. Upon returning from Vietnam, Larry became extremely paranoid and believed he was being followed. On numerous occasions the family home had been ransacked as if the perpetrators were searching for something. Even Sandra and young Cindy, along with family and friends, were spied on. The anxiety and emotional strain proved to be too much to handle for Kavanaugh.[18] The fears of facing possible prison time along with mental instability plagued Kavanaugh and more than likely drove him over the edge.

Other former POWs aware of the accusations against Kavanaugh suggested that either the accusations themselves or his remorseful conscience are what drove him over the edge. The accusations or the actions committed by Kavanaugh may have not corresponded with his manly ideals and, therefore, led him to take his life. Years after returning home, Everett Álvarez Jr.

believed that if he had furnished the Vietnamese with propaganda statements he would not have been able to come back and feel manly. In a conversation with his father, Álvarez stated, "Maybe I could have come home
earlier ... but I couldn't have looked you in the eye. I don't think I could have
lived with myself if I had voluntarily given them the propaganda statements they wanted ... I wouldn't have been a man. I wouldn't be here under
these circumstances."[19] In Álvarez's perspective his manliness or *machismo*
was preserved through his resistance. The counseling system aviators had
in practice in North Vietnam also aided him during challenging moments
of grief while in captivity.

The charges against the remaining ex-POWs were dropped a week after
Kavanaugh's suicide. Mrs. Kavanaugh believed that by dropping the charges
the Pentagon admitted fault for her husband's death. "The dismissal of
these charges make it clear that the government realizes its responsibility
for Larry's death," argued Mrs. Kavanaugh. "In bringing these charges, the
government murdered my husband and caused indescribable hardship in
the lives of the other POWs."[20] To his fellow Peace Committee members,
Kavanaugh is a hero as he sacrificed himself for their salvation.

Alfonso Riate was plagued by the death of his friend and also by his own
collaboration charges. Riate and the members of the alleged Peace Committee served as pallbearers at their dear friend's funeral service. Prior to the
dropping of the charges, Riate went as far as hiring the renowned criminal
defense attorney Leonard Weinglass. He left the Marine Corps soon after
his return and became active in advocating for the rights of veterans, and
criticized President Nixon for his role in the Watergate fiasco.[21] On July 4,
1974, Riate participated in a march in Washington asking for benefits for
veterans. Riate spoke to a crowd gathered at the Lincoln Memorial: "We are
here in Washington today to make it known that we are struggling for the
rights of veterans, for the rights of all Americans to return to their country.
Unconditional universal amnesty for all Americans!"[22]

As the years passed, Riate came to terms with his prisoner-of-war
experience. After working in an outreach program with disabled veterans,
Riate was able to understand himself better and could articulate his feelings about the war in a manner he previously could not. "I tell them I suffer

a stigma from the war. Most of them are sympathetic. They say I have done something few have ever done, that I resisted the war in prison. As the years go by, I feel I am being vindicated," stated Riate.[23]

Former Vietnam prisoners of war shunned Riate, Kavanaugh, and the remaining members of the Peace Committee. The POW community created an online database, POW Network. On the site can be found the names of all POWs and the missing in action (MIAS). Each name has a link to a biography of each of the men. Some entries are lengthy while others provide minimum information, such as name, date of incident, branch of military service, and whether they returned or not. In addition to the basic information, Riate's and Kavanaugh's entries state that each was a member of the Peace Committee. Limited information is known about Riate upon his return and up to his passing in November 1984. There are two versions or accounts of his death: one that he died in Los Angeles and the other that he died in the Philippines.[24] Neither version could be confirmed, as the memory of Riate has faded with the passing of time.

As readjustment to the changed society of the 1970s plagued Kavanaugh and Riate, it also challenged many of the other men. José Astorga, for example, could never fully reintegrate himself into society. The negativity that surrounded the war plagued Astorga. "The reaction here was that Vietnam was an unpopular war. People thought we killed women and children," stated Astorga.[25] This atmosphere would lead him to self-destructive behavior. About a month after being discharged from the Army, Astorga was involved in a hit-and-run, which was later reduced to a speeding violation and unsafe lane change. Astorga received one year of probation for the incident.[26] This would not be his only run-in with the law, as he later had a violent confrontation with police that concluded with his internment at Patton State Hospital for evaluation.[27] Astorga could not understand why or what he experienced, and neither did the military, but they had an idea.

Between Captain Brudno's suicide on June 3, and Kavanaugh's on June 27, 1973, the U.S. military ordered psychiatric evaluations of the returning POWs. All POWs were to be evaluated in June 1973, then again after three months, and once more after six months.[28] The military's concern over the mental well-being of former POWs continued over the years, and the men continued to be evaluated on a yearly basis at the Robert E. Mitchell Center for Prisoner of War Studies in Pensacola, Florida. Something obviously had gone wrong with these men and the government demanded answers.

Former POWs wanted to forget their experiences and began battling with PTSD in a variety of ways. To subsist with constant depression, paranoia, and PTSD, Astorga began what he describes as "self-medicating."[29] Substance abuse momentarily eased Astorga's mental anguish. Yet, an array of issues emerged. The abuse of alcohol especially created an abundance of problems for the former POW. He could not hold down a job. His first marriage ended in divorce as his wife could no longer deal with his condition. Eventually, Astorga received a 100 percent disability from the military.

Astorga was plagued with severe PTSD and paranoia. His life seemed trivial. At times, Astorga wondered if he would have been better off dying in Vietnam, or for that matter pondered why he did not die while his entire crew had perished.[30] Survivor's guilt overwhelmed him on a daily basis. With his mental state worsening, Astorga sought help from the VA Healthcare System and continued attending the yearly evaluations in Pensacola. Yet, he could not stop self-medicating, as this became the only way to suppress the PTSD that now plagued him with flashbacks and dreams.

Astorga attempted to reconstruct his life. In restoring his life, Astorga also, in a sense, worked on reestablishing his manhood. He remarried and has grown children. Despite her husband's reluctance to discuss his POW experience, his second wife, Norma, dedicated her time and effort to understanding and helping him. In the first decade of the twenty-first century, José finally began to open up about his experiences and started to attend weekly meetings at the VA in San Diego. He was able to lead a quiet life while keeping to himself.

One of the earlier returnees was Isaac Camacho, who successfully escaped and returned in 1965. Upon receiving a furlough to spend time with his family in El Paso, Camacho and his family were inundated by media outlets. Camacho received orders from Colonel McBrim (the Army official overseeing Camacho's stay in El Paso) to maintain a low profile. Following orders, Camacho and his cousin Pete crossed the border into Ciudad Juárez, Mexico, and did what many *fronterizos* would do, have a great time in a border town. For three days, Isaac and Pete enjoyed Mexican food, beer, and *mariachi* music.[31]

Shortly after crossing back into the United States through the checkpoint in Fabens, the Camachos were pulled over and escorted back to Isaac's home. A dismayed Colonel McBrim awaited and sternly asked, "Sergeant Camacho, where in the hell have you been?" Camacho countered, "México, Colonel. You told me to go hide somewhere and not tell anyone where I was. Why are you so upset?" The colonel responded, "Sergeant Camacho, the President of the United States, Lyndon Johnson was in Texas, and wanted to meet you."[32] President Johnson left a telephone number, and an elated Isaac called the president and conversed for about twenty minutes.

Camacho spent the next ten years in the Army and finally retired as a captain in 1975. He then spent twenty-two years working for the United States Postal Service. While he saw his friends go through rough patches, Camacho managed to rebound from the POW experience and led a successful career in and out of the military. "A lot of my Chicano buddies were down and out. They were really depressed. I guess what complicated matters more was that they couldn't find jobs. A lot of them who were married got divorced. They had marital problems and all that," affirmed Camacho.[33]

Camacho dealt with insomnia and depression. "You go through all that kind of hell. It's very hard to get rid of it. And the only way you can get used to it, not get rid of it, is by getting together and talking about it, like at the Vet centers. Those dreams always come back," explained Camacho.[34] He began taking medication for his condition until he grew tired of being dependent on it. "One day I don't know, it hit me. I can't continue taking pills my whole life. I have to give them up. And so I told myself, I'm not gonna take anymore drugs. I'm gonna cold turkey out of these drugs," recalled Camacho.[35] He began to think about new activities that would keep him engaged: "I'm gonna enroll in school. I'm gonna keep my mind occupied with something else. Then I picked up golf, fishing, and some of the things I wanted to do before and never got around to do."[36] Staying occupied with what have been traditionally considered manly outdoor activities proved to be therapeutic for Camacho, who had suffered long enough.

Juan Jacquez also found that keeping occupied was therapeutic in dealing with the lasting effects of the POW experience. Juan remained in the Army until 1978, when he retired after serving eleven and a half years. He remained active by working on and riding motorcycles for a hobby.[37] Despite leaving the military, the torments of the POW experience still impacted Juan. "Still dealing with PTSD and anger. I feel a lot of anger and I don't know at who or for what," admitted Jacquez. He continued, "I don't need a reason. That is why with you, I wasn't gonna do it [the interview]. My daughter talked me into it. People who know me don't know shit about me. They know I'm a POW and that is it. I just don't want to talk about it."[38] Following his repatriation, Jacquez, with the hopes of not dealing with or addressing the lasting POW effects, avoided talking about his experiences. Finally, after almost a year of debating my request, he decided to sit down and talk to me—and almost cancelled at the last minute.

Jacquez attempted to suppress his memory and simply tried to forget about Vietnam. "You won't believe this. I can't even remember, I used to call it the dirty dozen; when we were in the jungle there were twelve of us. I can't even name them, two or three. I spaced it all out. Blanked it out. I tried to forget it all," confessed Jacquez. "And every once in a while I try to remember. I remember the faces I just don't remember the damn names. I tried to forget it all. I made it a point to blank it out. To me I pretend that it never happened. Like a bad dream and that's the way I have lived with it. I talked to a psychiatrist. He predicted it would all blow up."[39] When recalling the name of the two men captured with him, Jacquez referred to them as "Georgia guy and the Hawaiian guy," as he has been successful at quashing an undesirable memory. Jacquez also sought soothing distractions to deal with effects of PTSD. "Tonight, I am going to a dinner. Tonight, I will have my beers. Come Friday I enjoy my beers and that is it. I have gone through this for thirty-five years."[40]

After his release in 1973, his life transformed as he went through a divorce and decided to start over. "When I left [for Vietnam], my wife was only sixteen. I was nineteen," recalled Jacquez. "At sixteen I knew she wasn't gonna be a true wife. Sixteen! Give me a break! I didn't expect it. So when

I came back I figured I'm just gonna start all over again. I got divorced. I started a new life when I got back. I kept custody of my son. Yea, she was history when I came back!"[41] About six months later, Jacquez married his second wife, Sylvia, and they had one daughter, Danelle.

Mrs. Jacquez was a devoted wife and an exceptional partner throughout the years. In 2009, Sylvia accompanied Juan to Washington when he visited the Vietnam War Memorial for the first time. "It's something he needs to do—go to the wall. I think that will help him," stated Sylvia prior to their trip.[42] After living with the former POW over a thirty-six-year period, Mrs. Jacquez has realized Juan needs to begin to deal better with his condition. Simple, everyday undertakings, such as watching a movie, became very stressful for Jacquez. "I get too personal with a damn movie. Even if it's a damn movie! Hello, how stupid can a movie be! Shh, *Rambo*! Hell no, it's not like that," roared Jacquez.[43]

Another jungle prisoner of war, José Jesús Anzaldúa also dealt with physical, mental, and emotional ailments following his repatriation. The Marine felt the effects of amoebic dysentery, intestinal parasites, and anemia.[44] However, like other former POWs, what affected Anzaldúa the most was PTSD and night terrors. "Night terrors are still there two or three times a week," admitted Anzaldúa. "Navy has helped me with the treatment. You could categorize all of us as somewhat unstable, maybe still; unstable to the point of being dangerous."[45] Anzaldúa's thirty-eight months in captivity (twenty-five of those months in jungle camps) took a toll on him, and his return and readjustment had its challenges.

Further complicating Anzaldúa's return was the changed society of the 1970s. The various movements of the 1960s and 1970s had transformed society to the point of making it unrecognizable to some of the men, including Anzaldúa. "We go into a topless joint," recalled Anzaldúa; "I didn't even know it was a 'titty' joint and I walked out. It was such a cultural shock to me. Eighteen when I left [for Vietnam]; didn't know nothing."[46] Anzaldúa's recollection is reminiscent of the behavior exhibited in *Taxi Driver* by returning Vietnam veteran Travis Bickle, who upon returning from combat had troubles readjusting to a changed society. After three years of captivity,

Anzaldúa felt as if he had returned to a totally different place. Jacquez, on the other hand, agreed with the openness of the 1970s and welcomed the miniskirts that young women wore at the time.[47]

During the Vietnam War era, the United States experienced a cultural and social revolution. By their active participation in demonstrating against social oppression, inequality, and the war in Vietnam, agents of change during the Chicano Movement played an integral role in bringing about these transformations. Also, fueling the social changes of the era were the disproportionate casualty rates among Mexican Americans in Vietnam, which created an awareness of their value to American society. For some returning veterans the changes were "like night and day."[48]

Anzaldúa was even more shocked by the social changes regarding race and ethnic relationships between the White and Mexican American communities in South Texas. During his ninety-day convalescence leave, Anzaldúa returned to Refugio to ponder his future and experienced the new social norm. "I always dated within our racial restrictions. My best friend Gary Heard, his youngest sister was the head cheerleader for Refugio County High School and I started to date her. Blonde hair, blue eyed, openly," confessed Anzaldúa. "Prior to that, there ain't no telling what would happen to you. Everything had changed, society had changed. In 1968, look at them, talk to them, smile with them, joke with them, come back five years later, dating them."[49] The changes that occurred in the 1970s, along with Anzaldúa's military service allowed for him to transcend preexisting social barriers.

Anzaldúa decided to remain in the Marine Corps, where he aspired to climb the ranks and surpass other obstacles. He had goals and planned to one day achieve the role of a major. "I was comfortable in it. I was successful in it. The surroundings I was in were conducive to providing me with help with any issues that arose. And they took care of me. It might have been different without the structure of the Marine Corps," stated Anzaldúa.[50] All appeared in good standing for Anzaldúa as the military setting provided the comfort level necessary for him to succeed.

Everything was going well until 1983, when Anzaldúa began to experience flashbacks and night terrors. "I was in Camp Lejeune. I was a major at the time. I started experiencing flashbacks where I would be sitting on my desk and all of a sudden I would have obtrusive thoughts where I would actually see myself in the jungle doing something I had previously experienced," acknowledged Anzaldúa. "And when it first happened, I went home and got drunk and then it kept happening more and more. They would last anywhere from a minute to five minutes. The last time they happened, I knew something was wrong."[51] Not knowing how to react to the flashbacks and night terrors, Anzaldúa began drinking to mask his ailment. "I was a willing participant in self-medication. Alcohol was helping," conceded Anzaldúa.[52]

In reality alcohol was doing Anzaldúa more harm than good. While drinking could settle him down, at times it also produced in Anzaldúa an aggressively violent behavior—so violent, in fact, that on one occasion Anzaldúa, with another Marine Corps friend, "cleaned house" at a bar. After a night of heavy drinking, Anzaldúa and his friend began a bar brawl that ended with the pair pummeling the other party. It was at this point that Anzaldúa realized, "Alcohol was not my friend."[53] Anzaldúa sought help for his condition and a life of sobriety.

Apart from the mentioned side effects, Anzaldúa lived a fairly "normal" life. He married in 1978. His wife remained aware of what he went through and was very supportive for over thirty years.[54] Anzaldúa continued in the Marine Corps for twenty-five years and retired as a major in 1992. He then led a relaxed retired life out in the countryside in North Carolina. In his free time, Anzaldúa enjoyed masculine hobbies such as riding his sports car and motorcycles. He lived by the motto "No guarantees for tomorrow, I live for every second. I live!"[55] In 2011, the Defense Language Institute Foreign Language Center inducted José Anzaldúa into their Hall of Fame. During his induction ceremony, Anzaldúa's Vietnamese language abilities were highlighted, and he was applauded for being able to provide intelligence during captivity that not many POWs could provide.

Returning to a military setting like Anzaldúa were the aviators who also made a career in the military. After spending six years as a prisoner of war, Captain José David Luna returned to the United States and remained in the military following his release. Shortly after his return, David and his wife, Pearl Saunders Luna, divorced.[56] The separation turned sour when disputes over David's pay arose. During his captivity, Luna wrote his wife, who was authorized to receive his pay, asking her to place as much of his money as possible in savings. Mrs. Luna followed her husband's wishes and had the money deposited in a Uniformed Services Savings Deposit Program (USSDP), a savings account.

Throughout Luna's captivity, Mrs. Luna only made four withdrawals, totaling $6,700.[57] During and after the divorce proceedings, the former POW filed a complaint regarding the funds Mrs. Luna withdrew. Luna argued that his money should have been protected under the Missing Persons Act and Air Force regulations. The court honored Air Force Form 246, which designated Mrs. Luna the sole beneficiary of David's pay. The claims court where Luna filed the complaint decided in favor of the United States and against the former POW.[58] If the failed marriage was not emasculating enough, his unsuccessful attempt to recover his hard-earned money sent him over the edge. After divorcing his first wife, Luna remarried and continued his career in the Air Force, where he retired as a lieutenant colonel in 1989. He then lived outside of Washington, DC, in Fort Washington, Maryland.

Hector Acosta, who spent slightly over three months in captivity, remained in the Air Force upon release and had few physical problems upon returning to the United States. Acosta spent time recovering from the injuries sustained during his shoot-down. He and his wife, Orphalinda, raised a family of three and lived in San Antonio, Texas. The Air Force provided a comfortable setting for Hector and he went up the ranks until he retired from active duty in 1998, also as a lieutenant colonel.[59] In the Air Force, Acosta spent time in California, New Mexico, Alabama, Texas, and abroad in Germany. While in New Mexico, Hector obtained a master's degree in experimental psychology from New Mexico State University.[60] After retiring, Acosta returned to New Mexico State University and pursued a doctoral degree in experimental psychology. In 2004, Acosta accomplished his objective and received his terminal degree.

Dr. Hector Acosta led a "normal" life following his brief captivity in Vietnam and did not encounter the issues experienced by some of the other POWs. Perhaps his short captivity explains his outcome. "I think a misconception is that POWs in any way are homogeneous," pointed out Acosta.[61] He believed that POWs faced various situations, and thus naturally they have reacted differently to their captivity. Some men, like Acosta, had no problems upon repatriation, while on the other hand, other men could never piece their lives together. Furthermore, there exists a degree of variance in the effects exhibited among POWs exposed to similar treatments, as it is human nature to react differently. Acosta's reaction was to stay busy by working and educating himself. Even after retirement, Acosta returned to work and was employed in the private sector by Northrop Grumman Information Technology.

The case of Everett Álvarez Jr. is similar, as he "bounced back" without any problems. In many ways Álvarez became the poster boy of the Vietnam War POWs, even before returning in 1973. As the longest-held POW in North Vietnam, the American public and soldiers alike became aware of Álvarez and his situation. After returning from Vietnam, Álvarez sought to make up for the eight and a half years of captivity. After all he had been through (his wife leaving him while in captivity), Álvarez deserved a fresh start at life. He remained in the Navy and by November 1973 was living with his new bride, Tammy, in Kingsville, Texas, where he took a refresher course in flying.[62] He remained in the Navy until 1980 and retired at the rank of commander.

Álvarez took advantage of his public status and soon found himself rubbing elbows with the nation's elite. He developed a close friendship with fellow Californians Ronald and Nancy Reagan. "She loved me [Nancy]. She would call and say, 'we have a party out East and want you to attend.' So I would catch the red-eye from California and go," recalled Álvarez.[63] In 1981, President Reagan appointed Álvarez deputy director of the Peace Corps, and a year later he was appointed deputy administrator of the VA.

Álvarez used his status to help fellow Vietnam veterans. Despite the recognition Álvarez received upon return, he admitted, "We didn't deserve all that recognition and notoriety. The kids did. Coming back with those legs missing, arms missing. Till this day, they are still suffering."[64] Álvarez worked extensively to help returning Vietnam veterans with the many issues they faced. He noticed that Vietnam veterans in particular "looked different," as he saw them having specific needs, especially the countless ones who suffered from PTSD. To serve those needs, Álvarez played a role in the rise of counseling centers throughout VA clinics and hospitals.[65] This treatment is reminiscent of the counseling sessions held by POWs in the Hanoi camps as they served as therapy in coping with the brutal and degrading interrogations.

Álvarez also kept busy by furthering his education. "My family has placed a high priority on higher education. You can't get in the game without the tickets," explained Álvarez.[66] The Álvarez family believed that Mexican Americans could overcome social barriers by attaining an education, which could be used as a "ticket" out of the *barrio* and into the Anglo-dominated society that had been previously barred to them. He went on to obtain a master's degree from the Naval Postgraduate School and a law degree from George Washington University. Aside from furthering his own education, Álvarez and his family were instrumental in establishing the Everett Álvarez, Jr., Scholarship Fund, which provides aid to Mexican American students attending institutions of higher education.[67] Through this nonprofit organization, the Álvarez family attempted to enrich the community by providing financial assistance to Mexican American youth attempting to obtain a college education.

The apparent social divisions experienced by the Mexican American community during the 1960s continued following the war. Clearly, Álvarez was unfazed by them as he personally transcended racial barriers. Despite not always emphasizing the racial barriers that existed, Álvarez did dedicate time to improving opportunities for Mexican Americans. Álvarez was able to understand the needs of young college students, but he could not relate to those involved in the Chicano Movement (including his sister).

Since he had been in Vietnam for over eight years, there were many things that occurred stateside that Álvarez missed out on, including the Chicano Movement. "They had all these Mexican flags and César Chávez flags [United Farm Worker Union flags]. What's all this! I love Mexican food you know. 'What are you gonna do for us.' Well, who are you? It was like cold water thrown on you. Who are you? Haven't I done enough?"[68] Álvarez could not comprehend the social atmosphere within the Chicano Movement and, quite frankly, he did not agree with it. He remained adamantly attached to his conservative beliefs that anyone can overcome poverty and prejudice and be successful. "This quote 'minority,' it's bullshit. You can work through discrimination," argued Álvarez. "People are bigots and biased. I ignored it. We ran into it. After a while you ignore it. I'm not going to stoop to their level. I was always just me. I was never ashamed of who I was. American of Mexican descent."[69] Many Chicanos would disagree with his approach, as activists during the time took a much more confrontational stance in combatting racism.

Álvarez could identify, however, with the struggles of the United Farm Workers Union (UFW). Having grown up in Salinas, California (the home front of the UFW), Álvarez worked in the fields and saw firsthand the struggles of the farmworker. "The farm movement I did [understand]," argued Álvarez. "César Chávez was different because of the economic condition of the farmworkers. It was entirely social-economics."[70] Álvarez's idea of being American stemmed from the fact that he worked and lived alongside Arkies, Okies, and *braceros* who struggled just like Mexican Americans did in Salinas. "Arkies and Okies stood up for me. We were all Americans. I grew up with Joe Kapp, who is Mexican American," recalled Álvarez.[71] For the retired commander, his Mexican American identity and his identity as an American are one and the same. Perhaps his political ties to the Reagans and his accomplishments allowed him to focus almost entirely (with a few exceptions) on his personal endeavors and not on the challenges the Mexican American community faced as a whole.

Álvarez continued his life as if nothing had ever derailed him. In 1990, he became the first and only Mexican American former POW to write his autobiography, *Chained Eagle*. After a warm reception, Álvarez followed it with a sequel, *Code of Conduct*, in 1991. He also established and ran Álvarez and Associates, a consulting firm in the Washington, DC, area.[72] He remained involved with the Republican Party and helped Senator John McCain in his campaign for the 2000 Republican presidential primary and in his bid for the presidency in 2008.

Despite their similar backgrounds and given what they experienced, Mexican American former POWs reacted differently to their captivity. Due to the different campaigns waged by the aviators and infantry, the soldiers' experiences differed. Aviators only saw a glimpse of the war as they dropped their bombs from a distance and returned to a more comfortable base. The infantry, on the other hand, spent significant time out in the field and saw firsthand the complexities and cruelties of war. These were two very different campaigns. Naturally, because of the infantry's close encounter with the enemy, PTSD effects plagued them at a higher rate than aviators and led to significant problems upon repatriation.[73]

It can also be argued that those former POWs who remained in a military setting also adjusted better than those who did not. The latter faced the rude awakening of civilian life where great contempt towards Vietnam veterans was commonplace. In many ways, remaining in the military allowed the former POWs to keep busy, while allowing for a smoother transition back into American society. The military environment eased tensions and sheltered those former POWs who remained in the military from the changing society of the 1970s that was not very accepting of the Vietnam War or the returning veterans. After years of captivity, those returning POWs who opted for a return to civilian life faced the grueling task of settling into a country that seemed unrecognizable. Thus, the post-captivity experience was not homogeneous, as the response and reintegration in society varied from man to man.

Conclusion

TODAY, THE AMERICAN PUBLIC HAS A DISTANT MEMORY OF THE VIETNAM War, especially since they have been in two wars since its conclusion, and the country remains embattled in the Middle East. However, in deep South Texas, the memory of the Vietnam War is vivid. April 9, 2011, was designated as LZ-RGV-Operation Welcome Home (Landing Zone-Rio Grande Valley). This celebration officially welcoming Vietnam War veterans was held in McAllen, Texas. Thirty-six years after the war, the community was hoping to bring closure to the features of the war that deeply impacted the Rio Grande Valley. Veterans were honored, politicians pumped hands, and the community turned out for music and festivities. Even a small replica of the Vietnam Veterans Memorial, "The Wall," was brought in. The black and white flags of POW/MIA were proudly waved in recognition of those individuals who were captives or never returned.

Over the years, Vietnam veterans and their supporters have embraced the POW/MIA symbol. Many came to see the return of American POWs as one of the few positives in the controversial and bitter war that resulted in American defeat. The POW/MIA symbol can be seen on bumper stickers, decals, flags, motorcycles, and mudguards on tractor-trailers. Former prisoners of war have obtained an exclusive status among Vietnam veterans. Perhaps their ability to overcome agonizing captivity has secured former POWs prominence among Vietnam veterans and the American public.

On May 23, 2013, the Nixon Presidential Library and Museum in Yorba Linda, California, also held a 40th Anniversary celebration commemorating the Prisoner of War dinner held at the White House in 1973. Only two hundred former POWs attended this time, and they were served the identical meal from forty years ago. Everett Álvarez attended the festivities and served on a panel discussing his POW experience. No other Mexican American former POW attended. However, earlier in March 2013, the Santa Fe Elk's Lodge hosted a party for Juan Jacquez to mark forty years since his return. Previously, Jacquez, like the majority of Mexican American former POWs, had become lost in obscurity and did not like to share his history.

American popular culture has embraced Vietnam War POWs slightly different than other veterans. They have been portrayed in some of America's more popular films and television shows, ranging from Sylvester Stallone's *Rambo: First Blood* to Robert De Niro in *The Deer Hunter* to Principal Seymour Skinner in *The Simpsons*. The prestige of being a Vietnam War POW has also attracted hundreds of "phonies" who have claimed to be former POWs in order to receive VA benefits or to simply boost their image. In 2009, the VA was awarding POW benefits to 966 alleged Vietnam POWs, yet the Department of Defense acknowledged that only 661 prisoners had returned alive from Vietnam.[1]

B. G. Burkett and Glenna Whitley in their study *Stolen Valor: How the Vietnam Generation was Robbed of Its Heroes and Its History* included a chapter looking at the droves of "phonies" who have been caught in a tangle of lies claiming to be Vietnam POWs. "In the hierarchy of Vietnam War victimhood, the POW is the ultimate hero/victim, a status that ranks above even a battle-scarred combat veteran," argued Burkett and Whitley.[2] The incredible status of Vietnam War POWs has attracted many men to desire the prominence held by POWs. Other "phonies" seek to reap the economic benefits that they have requested from the VA.

Today, Mexican American former POWs lead quiet lives and remain bonded to each other through the physical and mental anguish they experienced in Vietnam. Juan Jacquez, along with José Astorga, José Jesús Anzaldúa, José David Luna, Isaac Camacho, and Ciro Salas are retired. Everett Álvarez Jr. remains active in his consulting firm, while Hector Acosta has not been able to fully retire and has gone back to work. Former POWs are aware of those who served time with them, and their greatest insult is having "phonies" who falsely claim to have been POWs in Vietnam. "I have the book with all their names, all the POWs," commented Jacquez. "You have a lot of these people who say so-and-so was a POW. 'What's his name?' and I make it a point to remember the name. I go home and go through the book. Uh uh! If the name is not in that book, I don't care what, when, or where. You weren't a damn POW."[3] The prisoner-of-war community has remained close-knit and is aware of their fellow POWs.

The prisoner-of-war community has also connected on the Internet through their website, the POW Network. The group, however, continues to have its reservations in talking about the Peace Committee, and therefore much continues to be unknown about Abel Larry Kavanaugh and Alfonso Ray Riate. They are considered *personae non gratae*, and little to no information could be attained through the POW Network. More recently, Larry Kavanaugh Jr.'s wife, Heather, posted an online message requesting any information on her father-in-law. After speaking to Larry Jr., I can conclude that there is more to Kavanaugh's story than what is known. A longtime friend of Riate, Anthony Williams, also posted an online message requesting information on his fellow Marine Corps buddy. I disclosed that Riate had passed away in 1984, and Anthony could not believe the accusations made against his friend. Perhaps the POW community could never forgive the members of the alleged Peace Committee; still, unlike "the phonies," these men served under extraordinary circumstances and must be remembered as well.

Some prisoners of war, along with many Vietnam veterans today, continue to feel resentment toward people such as Jane Fonda and others who spoke against the war. In 2013, as Fonda's film *The Butler* debuted, Ike Boutwell, a Kentucky theater owner who trained pilots during the Vietnam War, boycotted the film in retaliation for Fonda's antiwar conduct. As the film neared release, conservatives also threated to boycott as Fonda was set to portray former first lady Nancy Reagan. Unfortunately, the country has not completely healed from the Vietnam War and the POW/MIA topic remains relevant today.

As a former POW, Walter Wilber once stated "that the whole [POW] story had yet to be heard," as "each person has to tell his own story."[4] Today, there remains significant history on Vietnam prisoners of war that has not been recorded. This work has added Mexican American perspectives to the history of Vietnam War POWs. It has gone beyond "the official story" and has provided an understanding of the Chicano POW while attempting to fill in various voids in Chicano and military history. The first returnees dictated "the official story" of Vietnam POWs in February 1973. These men were the senior ranking officers who had been held the longest in the North, and the voices of the junior officers and enlisted men were silenced. Many of the experiences included in this work have been recorded for the first time and bring attention to the identity of the former prisoners of war in regard to ethnicity, manliness, and social class.

The narrative of Mexican American prisoners of war also contributes to the field of Mexican American history as it sheds light on the Vietnam War, a topic forgotten and overlooked by most Chicano scholars. Through a social-historical lens, this study refrains from directly addressing the politics surrounding the conflict in Vietnam and focuses on the experiences of Mexican American prisoners of war before, during, and after their captivity. The oral histories of former Chicano POWs and others during the Vietnam War era bring to life the complexities among the Mexican American community and POWs alike who shared conflicting viewpoints over the war.

From a military history perspective, this study attempts to include Mexican Americans in the discussion of the American soldier. Given the immense contributions by Chicanos in Vietnam, it is vital to include them in the narrative. Military studies and historians have long overlooked the vast contributions of Mexican American veterans. Today, Mexican Americans, along with other Latinos, continue to demonstrate a strong dedication to the U.S. military tradition, making up almost 12 percent of active duty troops.[5]

This study has demonstrated that in spite of the complex ideologies that influenced them, issues of class, masculinity, and ethnic identity compelled Chicanos to serve in Southeast Asia and also helped them survive the brutal Vietnamese prisoner-of-war camps. The differences among Mexican American POWs are symbolic of the nuances within the Mexican American community during and since the Vietnam War. Today, while segments of the community embrace more progressive agendas such as comprehensive immigration reform and gun control, others who are more conservative support border control and take offense to any Second Amendment limitations, however rational they may be. Similarly, during the Vietnam War era, the war deeply divided the Mexican American community as the older generation supported the war effort while the young vocalized their disapproval.

As Mexican Americans continue to negotiate their identity and are also characterized by the media or the public in general, their tremendously rich patriotic history cannot be overlooked. The Mexican American community has paid a high price in America's defense and continues to make the ultimate sacrifice in preserving the nation's ideals and standing around the world. It is shameful that they are categorized as criminals, as illegal aliens, rapists, and as uneducated welfare leeches.

Military service remains high among Mexican Americans and Latinos today. In the Rio Grande Valley of South Texas, as in many Mexican American communities across the nation, the same factors that motivated Chicano Vietnam veterans to serve have encouraged them to serve today. Poverty, socioeconomic barriers, educational opportunities, *machismo*, and family military history continue to motivate Mexican Americans and other Latinos to enlist in the nation's armed forces. The Rio Grande Valley has lost over thirty-nine soldiers in the current conflicts in the Middle East.[6] While not many soldiers have fallen captive in the current wars, at least one soldier from Mission, Texas, was taken as a prisoner of war in 2003 during Operation Iraqi Freedom. Edgar Adan Hernández spent three weeks in captivity before being rescued by Marines.

The Vietnam War is long over, and the lessons learned from that conflict have been never-ending, as soldiers today do not face the tension and insolence the Vietnam veterans faced. Yet, the rise of White nationalism and its manifestations create an unwelcoming atmosphere to returning male, female, and transgender service members who have all sacrificed immensely. The antiwar rallies of today have made distinctions between the antiwar and anti-soldier movements of the Vietnam era. American society has seen a campaign that has welcomed today's veterans with open arms regardless of one's stance on the nation's conflicts. The lessons learned have come at a hefty price for Vietnam veterans, who either personally faced tense receptions and/or have had to distance themselves from their service in Vietnam. "The worst one I ever heard was 'baby killers,'" admitted Joe Anzaldúa as he unjustly dealt with ludicrous criticisms over his service in Vietnam.[7]

Former POWs have deep feelings of animosity about the time they lost in captivity. "Lost those years because of some idiot politician: not a waste but . . ." pondered Anzaldúa.[8] The group has reacted differently to their captivity, and several men still think about their experiences. "I still wonder what the hell happened," stated Jacquez, who could not believe how quickly he was overrun by enemy forces on that particular night.[9] Like most of his fellow POWs, he remained committed to the Fourth Allied Wing, as they called themselves, and combatted the enemy through resistance, passive-aggressive behavior, and otherwise frustrating their captors. Jacquez put it best: "If I come back, I will come back with pride or not at all."[10]

Differences have arisen as well in regard to each individual's return. For returnees who remained in the military, reintegration into society was easier than for those who left the service upon their release in 1973. Even though PTSD, flashbacks, and night terrors have plagued men from both groups, those who remained in the military have led more functional lives.

As some of these Mexican American men have attempted to incorporate themselves into their communities, their neighbors, although accepting, find them to be curiosities. In Anzaldúa's case, neighbors have asked him, "What are you Joe? 'I'm an American!' No seriously what are you?"[11] The question brought this work full circle, as most of the men in this group of former Vietnam prisoners of war have remained in the shadows. In mainstream America, the image painted of Mexican Americans has been a negative one that has ignored the rich history of military participation. This image has been perpetuated in the media, but has also been perpetuated by the lack of interest in promoting a deeper history of Mexican Americans. Historically, the image of Mexican Americans that has been propagated is that of laborer and blue-collar worker. Much remains to be told of the contributions of Mexican Americans. By including in the historical narrative the experiences of Mexican American veterans, in this case prisoners of war, we can attempt to bridge a gap that exists in the Mexican American community and that has also separated Chicanos from the American community.

Notes

Preface

1. In the summer of 2008, I visited Vietnam with the Texas Tech University Vietnam Delegation (study-abroad group) formed by professors, graduate students, and undergraduates. We spent thirty days in Southeast Asia, including Laos, Cambodia, Thailand, and Vietnam.

2. Although there was no formal declaration of war by the United States' government, the Gulf of Tonkin Resolution authorized President Lyndon Johnson military authority in Vietnam without Congress having to declare war. Vietnam is one of the numerous proxy wars during the Cold War between the United States and the Soviet Union. As in most Cold War conflicts, neither party engaged one another, but rather supported opposing governments, and in the case of Vietnam, engaged U.S. combat troops for what at the time was America's longest war. To simplify matters and following the definition of the military engagement, I will refer to Vietnam as a war. The terms conflict, war, engagement will be used interchangeably.

3. One of the most impressive expressions of the Vietnamese fondness for American culture was exhibited at the U.S. Embassy in Hanoi where we visited the American Center or Room. The center is a library or resource center open to the public, free of charge. It houses books, periodicals, and

videos along with computers available for personal use. It was humbling to see hundreds of Vietnamese in a line that wrapped around the outside of the embassy building, waiting to enter and educate themselves with the vast resources available to them.

4. Everett Álvarez Jr., interview by author, Silver Spring, MD, December 3, 2009.

5. "9-Year Captive: POW Held Longest in History of U.S.," February 12, 1973, Folder 05, Box 22, Douglas Pike Collection: Unit 03—POW/MIA Issues, The Vietnam Center and Archive, Texas Tech University. https://www.vietnam.ttu.edu/virtualarchive/items.php?item=2202205045.

6. National Liberation Front (NLF) and Viet Cong (VC) will be used interchangeably. The term Viet Cong refers to Vietnamese Communists, often called VC or Victor Charlie by Americans.

7. "Camacho, Issac 'Ike,'" POW Network, http://www.pownetwork.org/bios/c/c134.htm. The POW Network is an online network dedicated to POWs and MIAs. Billy Waugh, *Isaac Camacho: An American Hero* (Tampa: Digital Publishing of Florida, 2010), 12. The figures presented by Billy Waugh indicate that between two and three hundred VC overran the camp, while figures from the POW Network state that between four and five hundred VC attacked the camp.

8. "Red Holding 5 U.S. Airmen in Indochina," *Washington Post and Times Herald*, June 19, 1954, 1.

9. The terms Mexican American, Chicano, Mexican, Hispanic, *Raza*, and Latino will be used interchangeably. When noting political or national differences, the terms will be explained as pertaining to such descriptive allegiance in the text.

Introduction

1. Craig Howes, *Voices of the Vietnam POWs: Witnesses to Their Fight* (Oxford: Oxford University Press, 1993), 217.

2. Howes, *Voices of the Vietnam POWs*, 211.

3. Ibid., 4, 211. There are multiple accepted figures on the U.S. POW population in Vietnam ranging from 629 (military personnel only) to 766 (including civilians). The variation in these figures represents POWs who were captive for merely a few days, who are included on some lists but not on others. Former POW, Mike McGrath has recently offered new numbers: 737 POWs total, including 75 who died in captivity and 662 who returned home. Mike McGrath, e-mail correspondence with the author, July 26, 2017.

4. Ibid., 4.

5. Ibid., 211; Stuart I. Rochester and Frederick Kiley, *Honor Bound: American Prisoners of War in Southeast Asia, 1961-1973* (Annapolis, MD: Naval Institute Press, 1998), x. Kiley and Rochester have the count at 80 instead of 79. Additionally, they state that fewer than two dozen of the officers were not pilots.

6. Howes, *Voices of the Vietnam POWs*, 4.

7. Raúl Ruiz, "The POW," *La Raza: News & Political Thought of the Chicano Struggle*, April 1972, 30.

8. Howes, *Voices of the Vietnam POWs*, 4. According to Howes, 129 POWs "escaped from, evaded, or were released by their captors." Ninety-five were released early or paroled.

9. Ibid., 200.

10. Ibid., 200.

11. Ibid.

12. Ibid., 200-201. With a death rate of nearly 50 percent, the Kushner Camp in South Vietnam was easily considered the deadliest of all POW camps.

13. Ibid., 4.

14. José Manuel Astorga, interview by author, El Cajón, CA, May 9, 2009.

15. U.S. Department of Defense, *2014 Demographics: Profile of the Military Community* (Washington, DC: U.S. Department of Defense), iv.

Chapter 1. ChicaNamization

1. Charley Trujillo, *Soldados: Chicanos in Viet Nam* (San José: Chusma House Publications, 1990), vii; "Vietnam Warriors: A Statistical Profile," *Veterans of Foreign Wars* magazine, April 1997, 14. The term Chicanamization is akin to Vietnamization, the policy that was to hand the war over to the South Vietnamese and bring American troops home. The Chicano community during the war contended that draft boards heavily relied on Mexican Americans to fill their quotas as the middle class sought draft deferments.

2. Bob Drury and Tom Clavin, *Last Men Out: The True Story of America's Heroic Final Hours in Vietnam* (New York: Free Press, 2011), 247.

3. Rodolfo Acuña, *Occupied America: The Chicano's Struggle toward Liberation* (San Francisco: Canfield Press, 1972).

4. Stuart I. Rochester and Frederick Kiley, *Honor Bound: American Prisoners of War*

in Southeast Asia, 1961–1973 (Annapolis, MD: Naval Institute Press, 1998), 1-2.

5. Lea Ybarra, *Vietnam Veteranos: Chicanos Recall the War* (Austin: University of Texas Press, 2004), 4.

6. "The Declaration of Independence of the Democratic Republic of Vietnam," *Ho Chi Minh: Selected Works* (Hanoi: Foreign Languages Publishing House, 1960-1962), 3:17-21.

7. Ibid.

8. "Dien Bien Phu: Did the US Offer France an A-bomb?," *BBC* magazine, May 5, 2014, http://www.bbc.com/news.

9. Ibid.

10. John Prados, *Vietnam: The History of an Unwinnable War, 1945–1975* (Lawrence: University Press of Kansas, 2009), 50-54.

11. Ibid., 57.

12. David Halberstam, *The Making of a Quagmire: America and Vietnam during the Kennedy Era*, rev. ed. (New York: Rowman & Littlefield Publishers, Inc., 2008), 8.

13. Prados, *Vietnam*, 59.

14. Ibid., 77.

15. Ibid., 81; George C. Herring, *America's Longest War: The United States and Vietnam, 1950-1975* (New York: Wiley, 1979); 101-5; and Halberstam, *The Making of a Quagmire,* 188-200.

16. Ibid., 94.

17. George C. Herring, *America's Longest War: The United States and Vietnam, 1950-1975* (New York: Wiley, 1979); Neil Sheehan, *A Bright Shining Lie: John Paul Vann and America in Vietnam* (New York: Random House, 1988); and David Halberstam, *The Best and the Brightest* (New York: Random House, 1969).

18. Everett Álvarez Jr., interview by author, Silver Spring, MD, December 3, 2009.

19. Rosalío Muñoz, interview by author, East Los Angeles, CA, May 7, 2009.

20. Ibid.

21. *Ruben Salazar: Man in the Middle*, directed by Phillip Rodriguez, video (Arlington, VA: PBS, 2014).

22. Ernesto Vigil, conversation with the author, East Lansing, MI, June 30, 2016.

23. "The Murder of Ruben Salazar," *La Raza: News & Political Thought of the Chicano Struggle*, no. 3, special issue (1970): 36.

24. Rosalío Muñoz, interview by author, East Los Angeles, CA, May 7, 2009.

25. Ernesto Chávez, *"¡Mi Raza Primero!": Nationalism, Identity, and Insurgency in the Chicano Movement in Los Angeles, 1966–1978* (Los Angeles: University of California Press, 2002), 65. Quote from a Chicano Moratorium pamphlet.

26. *Raza* translates to race. However, Chicanos used the term and continue to use it in referring to themselves and other Chicanos. It is also a term of endearment. Chicanos who demonstrated pride in their heritage embraced the phrase *raza de bronce*, or bronze people, as they took ownership and pride in their complexion.

27. Chávez, *"¡Mi Raza Primero!"*, 62–65. Translates to "Hell No, We Won't Go," "To Hell with the Draft," and "Bring All Our Brothers Home…Alive!"

28. Ibid.

29. *Woodstock: 3 Days of Peace and Music, the Director's Cut!*, directed by Michael Wadleigh, (Burbank, CA: Warner Bros. Pictures, 1994); *Joan Baez at Woodstock*, video, August 16, 1969, Bethel, NY. Inferring that Reagan was gung-ho about the Vietnam War and eagerly sending Californians to war.

30. Julie Leininger Pycior, *LBJ and Mexican Americans: The Paradox of Power* (Austin: University of Texas Press, 1997), 194.

31. Grady Phelps, "Pena, Troupe Back from 17-Day Tour of Vietnam Bases," *Corpus Christi Caller*, January 20, 1968, 12C.

32. Ibid.

33. Ibid.

34. Pycior, *LBJ and Mexican Americans*, 192.

35. Ibid.

36. "Camacho Band Set through Wednesday in Hilton Lounge," *Los Angeles Times*, September 13, 1992, 200.

37. "After Korea, Bandsmen Say 'You Don't Play the Same When Scared,'" *Fresno Bee*, April 20, 1969, 4D.

38. Pycior, *LBJ and Mexican Americans*, 192.

39. Ibid.

40. Ralph Guzmán, "Why Our High Death Rate," *El Chicano*, November 10, 1969, 1.

41. In Mexican and Latino culture, *machismo* associates numerous "manly" behaviors that often have an impact and dictate how a boy/man should act. *Machismo* is a blend of manliness and toughness. Some of the behaviors are quite extreme and range from male chauvinism to the chivalrous *caballero* or gentleman. *Machismo* is a concept many young Chicanos grow up with

culturally and the men under study here were most definitely. Chapter 3 provides an in-depth look at the impact of *machismo* on the Mexican American Vietnam War veteran.

42. "Valley Casualties in Viet War Higher Than National Average," *Valley Evening Monitor* (McAllen, TX), March 24, 1968.

43. Guzmán, "Why Our High Death Rate," 1.

44. *Justice for My People: The Dr. Hector P. Garcia Story*, directed by Jeff Felt, video (Corpus Christi: KEDT-TV, Public Television, 2004).

45. Brenda L. Moore, *Serving Our Country: Japanese American Women in the Military during World War II* (New Brunswick, NJ: Rutgers University Press, 2003), xii.

46. Scott Sigmund Gartner and Gary M. Segura, "Race, Casualties, and Opinion in the Vietnam War," *Journal of Politics* 62, no. 1 (2000): 115–46.

47. *Chicano! The History of the Mexican American Civil Rights Movement: Quest for a Homeland*, directed by Héctor Galán, video (Los Angeles: NLCC Educational Media, 1996).

48. See Ernesto Vigil's *Crusade for Justice: Chicano Militancy and the Government's War on Dissent* (Madison: University of Wisconsin Press, 1999).

49. Eddie Morin, "First to Escape," *Vietnam* magazine, June 2000, 30–36, 32.

50. Galán, *Chicano!*

51. Quote of José Angel Gutiérrez in *Justice for My People*.

52. Michael J. Allen, *Until the Last Man Comes Home: POWs, MIAs, and the Unending Vietnam War* (Chapel Hill: University of North Carolina Press, 2009), 57.

53. Raúl Ruiz, "The POW," *La Raza: News & Political Thought of the Chicano Struggle*, April 1972, 30.

54. Ibid.

55. Ibid.

56. Allen, *Until the Last Man Comes Home*, 5.

57. Ibid., 14.

58. Interview with Delia Álvarez, *Reflecciónes: Chicano POW's*, video (Los Angeles: KABC-TV, 1972), Stanford University, Meyer Media Center ZVC 6126 pt. 3.

59. Lorena Oropeza, ¡Raza *Sí! ¡Guerra No!: Chicano Protest and Patriotism during the Viet Nam War Era* (Los Angeles: University of California Press, 2005), 4.

60. Everett Álvarez Jr., interview by author, Silver Spring, MD, December 3, 2009.

61. Interview with Delia Álvarez, *Reflecciónes: Chicano POW's*.

Chapter 2. The Formative Years

1. Everett Álvarez Jr., interview by author, Silver Spring, MD, December 3, 2009.

2. David Montejano, *Anglos and Mexicans in the Making of Texas, 1836–1986* (Austin: University of Texas Press, 1987), 162.

3. Ibid.; and Arnoldo De León, *Mexican Americans in Texas: A Brief History* (Wheeling, IL: Harlan Davidson, 1993), 110-12.

4. George J. Sánchez, *Becoming Mexican American: Ethnicity, Culture and Identity in Chicano Los Angeles, 1900–1945* (Oxford: Oxford University Press, 1993), 253.

5. Ibid.

6. Ibid., 265.

7. Ibid., 267.

8. De León, *Mexican Americans in Texas*, 112.

9. Ibid., 115.

10. Eddie Morín, "First to Escape," *Vietnam*, June 2000, 30.

11. Billy Waugh, *Isaac Camacho: An American Hero* (Tampa: Digital Publishing of Florida, 2010), 118.

12. Ibid., xxi-xxiv.

13. Everett Álvarez Jr. and Anthony S. Pitch, *Chained Eagle: The Heroic Story of the First American Shot Down over North Vietnam* (Washington, DC: Potomac Books, 1989), 80.

14. Ibid.

15. Everett Álvarez Jr., interview by author, Silver Spring, MD, December 3, 2009. *Braceros* were Mexican guest workers that were contracted to work in the United States from 1942 to 1965.

16. Ibid.

17. Ibid.

18. Ibid.

19. Ibid.

20. Ibid.

21. "Jose David Luna," Veteran Tributes, http://www.veterantributes.org/ TributeDetail.php? recordID=1815.

22. Larry Kavanaugh Jr., telephone conversation with author, July 23, 2013.

23. Ibid.

24. Ibid.

25. Juan L. Jacquez, interview by author, Santa Fe, NM, February 12, 2010.

26. Ibid.

27. Ibid.

28. Ibid.

29. Ibid.

30. Hector Acosta, interview by author, San Antonio, TX, February 6, 2010; and Acosta, email interview by author, August 8, 2011.

31. Hector Acosta, interview by author, San Antonio, TX, February 6, 2010.

32. Rodolfo Acuña, *Occupied America: A History of Chicanos*, 4th ed. (New York: Longman, 2000), 265.

33. José Manuel Astorga, interview by author, El Cajon, CA, May 9, 2009.

34. Ibid.

35. Sánchez, *Becoming Mexican American*, 253.

36. Anthony Williams, interview by author, Dallas, TX, February 17, 2011.

37. Zalin Grant, *Survivors: American POWs in Vietnam* (New York: Berkley Books, 1975), 264.

38. Albert Cuéllar, interview by author, Refugio, TX, December 21, 2012. Describing the segregated neighborhoods in Refugio: the African American, Mexican American, and Anglo communities.

39. Ibid.

40. Ibid.

41. Ibid.

42. José Jesús Anzaldúa Jr., interview by author, Coats, NC, June 2, 2009.

43. Albert "Smiley" Cuéllar, interview by author, Refugio, TX, December 21, 2012. *Y nada y nada y nada* translates to "and no word or response."

Chapter 3. The Manly Ideals of Machismo, Duty, and Patriotism

1. Juan L. Jacquez, interview by author, Santa Fe, NM, February 12, 2010.

2. *Héroes Hispanos*, directed by Robert Seoane, video (New York: History Channel, 1993).

3. With the end of the U.S.-Mexican War in 1848, a new ethnic group, Mexican Americans, was officially created. Mexicans living on the newly acquired and occupied territories in the (now) Southwestern United States as per the Treaty

of Guadalupe Hidalgo had the option of becoming citizens of the United States. Hence, Mexican Americans came into existence. There were people of Spanish and Mexican descent who served in the Texas Revolution in 1836 and in the U.S.-Mexican War, but the first war after the creation of a Mexican American ethnicity is the American Civil War.

4. Ray González, *Muy Macho: Latino Men Confront Their Manhood* (New York: Anchor Books, 1996), 37 and 58.

5. Ramón A. Gutiérrez, *When Jesus Came, the Corn Mothers Went Away: Marriage, Sexuality, and Power in New Mexico, 1500-1846* (Stanford, CA: Stanford University Press, 1991), 8 and 26.

6. Ibid., xix.

7. Américo Paredes, "The Problem of Identity in a Changing Culture: Popular Expressions of Culture Conflict along the Lower Río Grande Border," in *Folklore and Culture on the Texas-Mexican Border*, ed. Américo Paredes and Richard Bauman (Austin, TX: CMAS Books, 1993), 45.

8. Octavio Paz, *The Labyrinth of Solitude* (New York: Grove Books, 1985), 16.

9. Américo Paredes, "The United States, Mexico, and *Machismo*," *Journal of the Folklore Institute* (June 1971): 17-37.

10. Ibid., 19, 25-26.

11. Ibid., 18.

12. Ibid.

13. Norma E. Cantú, "*Muy Macho*: Traditional Practices in the Formation of Latino Masculinity in South Texas Border Culture," in *Manly Traditions: The Folk Roots of American Masculinities*, ed. Simon J. Bronner and Alan Dundes (Bloomington: Indiana University Press, 2005), 118.

14. Samuel Ramos, *Profile of Man and Culture in Mexico* (New York: McGraw-Hill, 1962), xiii.

15. E. Anthony Rotundo, *American Manhood: Transformations in Masculinity from the Revolution to the Modern Era* (New York: Basic Books, 1993), 233, 238, 247-48.

16. Gail Bederman, *Manliness and Civilization: A Cultural History of Gender and Race in the United States, 1880-1917* (Chicago: University of Chicago Press, 1995), 214.

17. Ibid., 170-71.

18. *Héroes Hispanos*, dir. Seoane.

19. Rotundo, *American Manhood*, 42.

20. Ibid., 43.

21. "Family, Duty to Country with Pride: WWII to Vietnam," *National Forumeer*, March/April 1995, 9. The *National Forumeer* was a newsletter/periodical published by the American G.I. Forum.

22. Kim Mattingly Kelliher, "Memorial Day Is Special for Mother, Her Family: Mom of 10 Who Joined Military Is Honored," *Arizona Daily Star*, May 28, 1991, 2B.

23. Mary M. Heidbrink, "De La Peña, 93, Fought in 3 Wars, Adored His Wife," *San Antonio Express-News*, September 20, 2012, 4B.

24. Ronald Takaki, *Double Victory: A Multicultural History of America in World War II* (New York: Little, Brown & Co., 2000), 98–99.

25. Frederick Aguirre, Linda Martinez, and Rogelio Rodriguez, *Undaunted Courage: Mexican American Patriots of World War II* (Orange, CA: Latino Advocates for Education Inc., 2005).

26. Natasha Zaretsky, *No Direction Home: The American Family and the Fear of National Decline, 1968–1980* (Chapel Hill: University of North Carolina Press, 2006), 5.

27. Ibid., 4–5.

28. Gutiérrez, *When Jesus Came*, 26; and Zaretsky, *No Direction Home*, 7.

29. "Reds Capture Group of U.S. Air Mechanics," *Valley Evening Monitor* (McAllen, TX), June 18, 1954, 1.

30. Mario T. García, *Mexican Americans: Leadership, Ideology, and Identity, 1930–1960* (New Haven, CT: Yale University Press, 1989), 18.

31. José Manuel Astorga, interview by author, El Cajon, CA, May 9, 2009.

32. Ibid.

33. Ibid.

34. Ibid.

35. José Jesús Anzaldúa Jr., interview by author, Coats, NC, June 2, 2009.

36. Ibid.

37. Ibid.

38. Department of Defense, "Counterintelligence Investigation Report on José Jesús Anzaldúa, Jr.," Pentagon, Washington, DC.

39. Anthony Williams, interview by author, Dallas, TX, February 17, 2011.

40. Juan L. Jacquez, interview by author, Santa Fe, NM, February 12, 2010. *Muy chingón* is Spanish for "tough guy."

41. Ibid.

42. Ibid.
43. Ibid.
44. Eddie Morín, "First to Escape," *Vietnam*, June 2000, 30.
45. Billy Waugh, *Isaac Camacho: An American Hero* (Tampa: Digital Publishing of Florida, 2010), xxi, xxiii.
46. Raúl Ruiz, "The POW," *La Raza: News & Political Thought of the Chicano Struggle*, April 1972, 30.
47. Everett Álvarez Jr., interview by author, Silver Spring, MD, December 3, 2009.
48. Leroy F. Aarons, "For Álvarez It Will Be a Different World: Former POW Must Ask: Where Do I Pick Up?," *Pacific Stars & Stripes*, March 14, 1973, 11.
49. Ibid.
50. Everett Álvarez Jr., interview by author, Silver Spring, MD, December 3, 2009.
51. Ibid.
52. Hector Acosta, interview by author, San Antonio, TX, February 6, 2010.
53. Ibid.
54. Ibid.
55. Interview with Mr. Floyd Luna, *Reflecciónes: Chicano POW's*, video (Los Angeles: KABC-TV, 1972), Stanford University, Meyer Media Center ZVC 6126 pt. 3.

Chapter 4. Resisting, Enduring, and Surviving Captivity, the Early Years, 1954–1967

1. Everett Álvarez Jr., interview by author, Silver Spring, MD, December 3, 2009.
2. Stuart I. Rochester and Frederick Kiley, *Honor Bound: American Prisoners of War in Southeast Asia, 1961–1973* (Annapolis, MD: Naval Institute Press, 1998), 25.
3. "L.A. Airman Taken by Reds in Indo-China," *Los Angeles Times*, June 20, 1954, part I, 16.
4. "5 Yanks Seized by Viet Minh Shipped South," *Chicago Daily Tribune*, June 21, 1954, part 1, 18.
5. "Captured L.A. Soldier, 4 Others on Way Home," *Los Angeles Times*, September 6, 1954, part I, 8.
6. Ibid.
7. Rochester and Kiley, *Honor Bound*, 26.
8. Ibid.
9. "5 U.S. Airmen Freed, Vietminh Reports," *New York Times*, September 1, 1954,

10; "U.S. Airmen Released by Red Captors," *Laredo Times*, September 5, 1954, 1; and "El Vietmin Liberto a 5 Norteamericanos: Estaban detenidos por los Rojos desde la Primera Pasada," *La Prensa de San Antonio*, September 2, 1954, 1.

10. Rochester and Kiley, *Honor Bound*, 27.

11. "Captured L.A. Soldier, 4 Others on Way Home".

12. Ibid.

13. "Reds Capture Group of U.S. Air Mechanics," *Valley Evening Monitor* (McAllen, TX), June 18, 1954, 1.

14. "Five Americans in Saigon after Release by Reds," *Los Angeles Times*, September 4, 1954, part I, 5.

15. Interview with Isaac Camacho, in Eddie Morín, "First to Escape," *Vietnam*, June 2000, 30–36, 32–33.

16. Ibid.

17. Office of International Information Programs, "Defense POW/MIA Office Analyst Testimony on 'Cuban Program,'" November 4, 1999, CubaNet, http://www.cubanet.org/htdocs/CNews/y99/nov99/05e13.htm.

18. John G. Hubbell, *P.O.W.: A Definitive History of the American Prisoner-of-War Experience in Vietnam, 1964–1973* (New York: Reader's Digest Press, 1976); Craig Howes, *Voices of the Vietnam POWs: Witnesses to Their Fight* (Oxford: Oxford University Press, 1993); and Rochester and Kiley, *Honor Bound*.

19. Howes, *Voices of the Vietnam POWs*, 4.

20. Interview with Isaac Camacho, *Hispanic Vietnam Veterans, the Mi Carrera (My Career) Program*, Rosemary Católicos, video (San Antonio: KLRN, 1990, c1989), Stanford University Location: Meyer Media Center ZVC 3392 no. 213. Local television program in San Antonio.

21. Operations Report-Lessons Learned, Report 4-66, "The Evasion and Escape of Sgt Camacho in Vietnam," Department of the Army, Office of the Adjunct General: Washington, DC, December 30, 1965 (Previously Classified Confidential), 1.

22. Billy Waugh, *Isaac Camacho: An American Hero* (Tampa: Digital Publishing of Florida, 2010), 16.

23. Ibid.

24. Ibid., 21–22.

25. Ibid., 22.

26. Ibid., 89.

27. Frank Anton, *Why Didn't You Get Me Out? A POW's Nightmare in Vietnam* (New York: St. Martin's Paperbacks, 1997), 57.

28. "Oral History Program (OHP) Report—Mr. Truoung Huynh Mao," *Isaac Camacho: An American Hero*, June 5, 2010, http://isaaccamachoamericanhero.com/documents/moa_interview.html. For a guide for Billy Waugh, *Isaac Camacho: An American Hero* (Tampa: Digital Publishing of Florida, 2010), see http://isaaccamachoamericanhero.com.

29. Waugh, *Isaac Camacho*, 78.

30. Interview with Isaac Camacho, in Morín, "First to Escape," 33.

31. Ibid.

32. Ibid.

33. George Smith, *P.O.W.: Two Years with the Vietcong* (Berkeley, CA: Ramparts Press, 1971), 45.

34. Ibid., 219.

35. Ibid., 141. "*Giai phong mien nam, chung quyet tien buoc. Diet de quoc my, pha tan be luc ban nuoc.*" Which translates into "All forward march, to liberate the South! Death to the Yankee invaders! Death to the clique of traitors!"

36. Ibid.

37. Ibid., 86.

38. Ibid., 153.

39. Waugh, *Isaac Camacho*, 138.

40. Ibid., 90.

41. Smith, *P.O.W.*, 202.

42. Ibid., 170. Prevaricator was one of the guards and Suave was one of the camp's head officers.

43. Ibid., 171.

44. Waugh, *Isaac Camacho*, 136.

45. Ibid., 118.

46. Ibid., 106.

47. Interview with Isaac Camacho, in *Hispanic Vietnam Veterans, the Mi Carrera (My Career) Program.*

48. Ibid.

49. Ibid.

50. Operations Report-Lessons Learned, Report 4-66, 18-19.

51. Interview with Isaac Camacho, in *Hispanic Vietnam Veterans, the Mi Carrera (My Career) Program.*

52. Operations Report-Lessons Learned, Report 4-66, 18-19.

53. Ibid.

54. Waugh, *Isaac Camacho,* 178.

55. Ibid., 178.

56. Operations Report-Lessons Learned, Report 4-66, 24.

57. Waugh, *Isaac Camacho,* 180.

58. Ibid., 182.

59. Ibid., 188.

60. Ibid., 191.

61. Ibid.

62. Interview with Isaac Camacho, in *Hispanic Vietnam Veterans, the Mi Carrera (My Career) Program.*

63. Ibid.

64. Waugh, *Isaac Camacho,* 197.

65. Ron Milam, *Not a Gentleman's War: An Inside View of Junior Officers in the Vietnam War* (Chapel Hill: University of North Carolina Press, 2009), 21-22.

66. Everett Álvarez Jr. in *Return with Honor,* dir. Freida Lee Mock and Terry Sanders, video (Washington, DC: PBS, 2001).

67. Everett Álvarez Jr. and Anthony S. Pitch, *Chained Eagle: The Heroic Story of the First American Shot Down over North Vietnam* (Washington, DC: Potomac Books, 1989), 26.

68. Álvarez in *Return with Honor,* dir. Mock and Sanders.

69. Álvarez and Pitch, *Chained Eagle,* 68.

70. Everett Álvarez in *Vietnam P.O.W.s: Stories of Survival,* dir. Brian Leonard, video (Washington, DC: Discovery Channel, 1998). Footage from his actual interrogation was used by the filmmakers.

71. Álvarez in *Return with Honor,* dir. Mock and Sanders.

72. Ibid.

73. Álvarez and Pitch, *Chained Eagle,* 80.

74. Ibid.

75. Everett Álvarez Jr., interview by author, Silver Spring, MD, December 3, 2009.

76. Álvarez and Pitch, *Chained Eagle*, 125.

77. Ibid., 250.

78. Ibid., 125.

79. Rochester and Kiley, *Honor Bound*, 405–6.

80. Ibid., 405.

81. Álvarez and Pitch, *Chained Eagle*, 184.

82. Everett Álvarez Jr., interview by author, Silver Spring, MD, December 3, 2009.

83. Álvarez in *Return with Honor*, dir. Mock and Sanders.

84. Ibid.

85. Álvarez and Pitch, *Chained Eagle*, 238.

86. Ibid., 229.

87. Ibid., 243.

88. Ibid., 231.

89. Defense Prisoner of War/Missing in Action (DPMO) file on José David Luna, Department of Defense, Pentagon, Washington, DC; Tom Wilson, "Day of the SAM," *Retired Officer* magazine, December 1993, 31–35.

90. "Capture of LT. CMDR. David Everson and CAPT. José D. Luna in Thai Nguyen," *Nhan Dan*, March 17, 1967, 3; "Steel Workers Capture American Pilot in Thai Nguyen Steel Region," *Quan-doi Nhan-dan*, March 15, 1967, 1 and 4.

91. Defense Prisoner of War/Missing in Action (DPMO) file on José David Luna, Department of Defense, Pentagon, Washington, DC: "Defense Information Report Evaluation," May 5, 1975 (Previously Classified Confidential).

92. Interview with Mr. Floyd Luna, *Reflecciónes: Chicano POW's*, video (Los Angeles: KABC-TV, 1972), Stanford University, Meyer Media Center ZVC 6126 pt. 3.

93. José David Luna, telephone conversation with author, April 6, 2009.

94. Rochester and Kiley, *Honor Bound*, 340.

95. James Bond Stockdale in *Return with Honor*, dir. Mock and Sanders. Stockdale was the highest-ranking Navy POW during the Vietnam War. He received the Congressional Medal of Honor after being released from captivity.

Chapter 5. Resisting, Enduring, and Surviving Captivity, the Latter Years, 1967–1973

1. Craig Howes, *Voices of the Vietnam POWs: Witnesses to Their Fight* (Oxford: Oxford University Press, 1993), 5.

2. Ibid. Rochester and Kiley have the figure slightly higher, at twenty-three American civilian prisoners, in addition to several other allied civilian prisoners. For more information, see Stuart I. Rochester and Frederick Kiley, *Honor Bound: American Prisoners of War in Southeast Asia, 1961–1973* (Annapolis, MD: Naval Institute Press, 1998), 449–54.

3. Rochester and Kiley, *Honor Bound*, 449–54.

4. "Statistical Information about Casualties of the Vietnam War," National Archives, https://www.archives.gov/research/military/vietnam-war/casualty-statistics.html.

5. This bill became PL 90-5 (S 665). "Public Laws, 90th Congress, 1st Session," CQ Almanac, http://library.cqpress.com/cqalmanac/document.php?id=cqal167-1311772#5.

6. Lewis L. Gould, preface to *1968: The Election That Changed America* (Chicago: Ivan R. Dee, 2010), vii–viii.

7. Defense Prisoner of War/Missing in Action (DPMO) file on Alfonzo Riate, Department of Defense, Pentagon, Washington, DC, "Investigation Report" dated June 10, 1967 (Previously Classified Secret).

8. Ibid.

9. Ibid.

10. "Hope for Christmas: Letter from a 'Dead' Marine," *Los Angeles Times*, December 24, 1971, part II, 1.

11. Rochester and Kiley, *Honor Bound*, 270.

12. Ibid.

13. Defense Prisoner of War/Missing in Action (DPMO) file on Alfonzo Riate, Department of Defense, Pentagon, Washington, DC, "Investigation Report" dated June 10, 1967 (Previously Classified Secret).

14. Ibid.

15. Ibid.

16. Howes, *Voices of the Vietnam POWs*, 22. Article 3 of the Code of Conduct.

17. Rochester and Kiley, *Honor Bound*, 461.

18. Ibid.

19. "U.S. Pilots in Vietnam: Preparing for the Day to Return to the U.S," *Nguoi cao tuio* (Vietnam), June 17, 2010.

20. Pham Tuyen, "Play Your Guitars American Friends!," recorded by Alfonzo Ray Riate, January 1, 1975, and translated by Hai Nguyen, Lubbock, TX.

21. Defense Prisoner of War/Missing in Action (DPMO) file on Abel Kavanaugh, Department of Defense, Pentagon, Washington, DC, "Investigation Report" dated May 17, 1968 (Previously Classified Confidential).

22. "Fellow Prisoner Tells How Kavanaugh Changed as POW," *Rocky Mountain News*, June 29, 1973, 5-6.

23. Ibid.

24. "Kavanaugh Victim of War, Laments Ex-POW Comrade," *Rocky Mountain News*, June 28, 1973, 12.

25. John G. Hubbell, *P.O.W.: A Definitive History of the American Prisoner-of-War Experience in Vietnam, 1964–1973* (New York: Reader's Digest Press, 1976), 532-33.

26. "Kavanaugh Victim of War, Laments Ex-POW Comrade," 12.

27. Rochester and Kiley, *Honor Bound*, 562; and Howes, *Voices of the Vietnam POWs*, 109.

28. Howes, *Voices of the Vietnam POWs*, 218.

29. Ibid.

30. Rochester and Kiley, *Honor Bound*, 575; and Howes, *Voices of the Vietnam POWs*, 217-18.

31. Howes, *Voices of the Vietnam POWs*, 200.

32. Ibid.

33. Ibid., 6.

34. Ibid., 218-19.

35. Ibid., 211.

36. Ibid., 34.

37. Ibid., 26.

38. Ibid., 107.

39. Ibid., 34.

40. Ibid., 211 and 217.

41. Ibid., 211.

42. Ibid., 39.

43. Ibid., 218.

44. Ibid., 109; and Zalin Grant, *Survivors: American POWs in Vietnam* (New York: Berkley Books, 1975), 265.

45. Hubbell, *P.O.W.*, 585.

46. Howes, *Voices of the Vietnam POWs*, 26.

47. Billy Waugh, *Isaac Camacho: An American Hero* (Tampa: Digital Publishing of Florida, 2010), 106; and Grant, *Survivors*, 272.

48. Howes, *Voices of the Vietnam POWs*, 200–201.

49. Ibid., 199–200.

50. Ibid., 107.

51. Juan Jacquez, interview by author, Santa Fe, NM, February 12, 2010.

52. José Jesús Anzaldúa Jr., interview by author, Coats, NC, June 2, 2009.

53. Grant, *Survivors*, 264 and 298.

54. Charley Trujillo in *Soldados: Chicanos in Viet Nam*, dir. Charley Trujillo and Sonya Rhee (San Jose: Chusma House Publications, 2003).

55. "Kavanaugh Victim of War, Laments Ex-POW Comrade," 12.

56. Ibid.

57. Anthony Williams, interview by author, Dallas, TX, February 17, 2011.

58. Howes, *Voices of the Vietnam POWs*, 108; and Hubbell, *P.O.W.*, 529.

59. Howes, *Voices of the Vietnam POWs*, 108.

60. José Jesús Anzaldúa Jr., interview by author, Coats, NC, June 2, 2009.

61. Howes, *Voices of the Vietnam POWs*, 219.

62. Ibid.

63. Ibid.

64. Ibid.; and Defense Prisoner of War/Missing in Action (DPMO) file on José Jesús Anzaldúa Jr., Department of Defense, Pentagon, Washington, DC, "Counterintelligence Investigation Report" dated February 27, 1970 (Previously Classified Confidential).

65. José Jesús Anzaldúa Jr., interview by author, Coats, NC, June 2, 2009.

66. Ibid.

67. Ibid.

68. Ibid.

69. Ibid.

70. Ibid.

71. Juan Jacquez in *Above and Beyond*, dir. Dale Sonnenberg (Santa Fe, NM: KNME, 1984).

72. Juan Jacquez, interview by author, Santa Fe, NM, February 12, 2010.

73. Ibid.

74. Ibid.

75. Ibid.

76. Juan Jacquez, interview by author, Santa Fe, NM, February 12, 2010.

77. Ibid. Jacquez refers to how systematically the Vietnamese planned the trek when stating, "They had it all *Chingón* dude."

78. Ibid.

79. Jacquez in *Above and Beyond*, dir. Sonnenberg.

80. Juan Jacquez, interview by author, Santa Fe, NM, February 12, 2010.

81. Ibid.

82. Ibid.

83. Jacquez in *Above and Beyond*, dir. Sonnenberg.

84. Juan Jacquez, interview by author, Santa Fe, NM, February 12, 2010.

85. Ibid.

86. Ibid.

87. Jacquez in *Above and Beyond*, dir. Sonnenberg.

88. José Manuel Astorga, interview by author, El Cajon, CA, May 9, 2009.

89. Defense Prisoner of War/Missing in Action (DPMO) file on José Manuel Astorga, Department of Defense, Pentagon, Washington, DC, "Defense Information Report Evaluation" dated June 6, 1972 (Previously Classified).

90. José Manuel Astorga, interview by author, El Cajon, CA, May 9, 2009.

91. Ibid.

92. Ibid.

93. Ibid.

94. Defense Prisoner of War/Missing in Action (DPMO) file on José Manuel Astorga, Department of Defense, Pentagon, Washington, DC, "Defense Information Report Evaluation" dated June 6, 1972 (Previously Classified).

95. José Manuel Astorga, interview by author, El Cajon, CA, May 9, 2009.

96. Ibid.

97. Defense Prisoner of War/Missing in Action (DPMO) file on Hector M. Acosta, Department of Defense, Pentagon, Washington, DC, "Circumstances of Loss Report" dated March 8, 1976 (Previously Classified).

98. Hector M. Acosta, interview by author, San Antonio, TX, February 6, 2010.

99. Ibid.

100. Ibid.; and Gil Domínguez, *They Answered the Call: Latinos in the Vietnam War* (Baltimore, MD: Publish America, 2004), 195.

101. Hector M. Acosta, interview by author, San Antonio, TX, February 6, 2010; Domínguez, *They Answered the Call*, 196.

102. Hector M. Acosta, interview by author, San Antonio, TX, February 6, 2010.

103. Domínguez, *They Answered the Call*, 196.

104. Hector M. Acosta, interview by author, San Antonio, TX, February 6, 2010.

105. Ibid.

106. Ibid.

107. Ibid.

108. Ibid.

109. Ibid. Acosta, being mild-mannered, did not use the traditional term used in FOG and FNG (fucking old guys and fucking new guys).

110. Ibid.

111. Ibid.

112. Ibid.

113. Ibid.

114. José Jesús Anzaldúa Jr., interview by author, Coats, NC, June 2, 2009.

115. Ibid.

Chapter 6. Homecoming or Rude Awakening?

1. Craig Howes, *Voices of the Vietnam POWs: Witnesses to Their Fight* (Oxford: Oxford University Press, 1993), 4.

2. William P. Nash and Dewleen G. Baker, "Competing and Complementary Models of Combat Stress Injury," in *Combat Stress Injury: Theory, Research, and Management*, ed. Charles R. Figley and William P. Nash (New York: Routledge, 2007), 38; and Wilbur J. Scott, *Vietnam Veterans since the War: The Politics of PTSD, Agent Orange, and the National Memorial* (Norman: University of Oklahoma Press, 2003), 29–43.

3. Ibid., 42.

4. Ibid., 38.

5. Edna J. Hunter, "The Vietnam POW Veteran: Immediate and Long-Term Effects of Captivity," in *Stress Disorder among Vietnam Veterans: Theory, Research, and Treatment,* ed. Charles R. Figley (New York: Brunner/Mazel Publishers, 1978), 194–95; and Howes, *Voices of the Vietnam POWs,* 11.

6. Natasha Zaretsky, *No Direction Home: The American Family and the Fear of National Decline, 1968–1980* (Chapel Hill: University of North Carolina Press, 2006), 49.

7. Ibid.

8. "POWs: Nixon Throws a Party," *Time* magazine, June 4, 1973, 32.

9. "White House Salute to POW's," Nixon Presidential Library and Museum, White House Communication Agency, File WHCA VTR# 6299, tape 1, May 24, 1973.

10. Juan Jacquez in *Above and Beyond,* dir. Dale Sonnenberg (Santa Fe, NM: KNME, 1984).

11. Juan Jacquez, interview by author, Santa Fe, NM, February 12, 2010.

12. José Jesús Anzaldúa Jr., interview by author, Coats, NC, June 2, 2009.

13. Larry Kavanaugh Jr., telephone conversation with author, July 23, 2013.

14. Suzanne Weiss, "Sergeant's Widow Blames Pentagon for His Death," *Rocky Mountain News,* June 29, 1973, 5.

15. Zalin Grant, *Survivors: American POWs in Vietnam* (New York: Berkley Books, 1975), 315–16.

16. "Here Is a Text of Statement by Widow of Kavanaugh," *Rocky Mountain News,* June 29, 1973, 87; Larry Kavanaugh Jr., telephone interview by author, October 27, 2010.

17. "Here Is a Text of Statement by Widow of Kavanaugh," 87.

18. Larry Kavanaugh Jr., telephone conversation with author, July 23, 2013.

19. Eric Brazil, "The Eagle Unchained: POW Finally Tells His Story of Survival," *San Francisco Examiner,* January 2, 1990, 1C and 4C.

20. Ibid.

21. Andreas Killen, *1973 Nervous Breakdown: Watergate, Warhol, and the Birth of Post-Sixties America* (New York: Bloomsbury, 2006), 89.

22. Bill Downs, Howard K. Smith, and Frank Tomlinson, "Washington, DC Celebration" (includes an interview with Alfonso Riate), ABC News, July 4,

1974, Vanderbilt Television News Archive, Vanderbilt University, Nashville, TN.

23. Peter Arnett, "POWs Who Opposed the War Find Battle Goes on at Home," *Washington Post*, August 29, 1978.

24. Anthony Williams, interview by author, Dallas, TX, February 17, 2011.

25. José Manuel Astorga, interview by author, El Cajon, CA, May 9, 2009.

26. "POW Placed on Probation," *The Monitor* (McAllen, TX), July 15, 1973, 12C.

27. José Manuel Astorga, interview by author, El Cajon, CA, May 9, 2009.

28. "Psychiatric Tests Set for 565 Ex-POWs," *Rocky Mountain News*, June 12, 1973, 32.

29. José Manuel Astorga, interview by author, El Cajon, CA, May 9, 2009.

30. Ibid.

31. Billy Waugh, *Isaac Camacho: An American Hero* (Tampa: Digital Publishing of Florida, 2010), 234.

32. Ibid.

33. Interview with Isaac Camacho, *Hispanic Vietnam Veterans, the Mi Carrera (My Career) Program*, Rosemary Católicos, video (San Antonio: KLRN, 1990, c1989), Stanford University Location: Meyer Media Center ZVC 3392 no.213. Local television program in San Antonio.

34. Ibid.

35. Ibid.

36. Ibid.

37. Juan Jacquez, interview by author, Santa Fe, NM, February 12, 2010.

38. Ibid.

39. Ibid.

40. Ibid.

41. Ibid.

42. Jessica Dyer, "An Emotional Journey: Ex-POW in Washington for Visit to Vietnam Memorial," *Santa Fe Journal*, November 1, 2009.

43. Juan Jacquez, interview by author, Santa Fe, NM, February 12, 2010.

44. José Jesús Anzaldúa Jr., interview by author, Coats, NC, June 2, 2009.

45. Ibid.

46. Ibid.

47. Juan Jacquez, interview by author, Santa Fe, NM, February 12, 2010.

48. José Jesús Anzaldúa Jr., interview by author, Coats, NC, June 2, 2009.

49. Ibid.

50. Ibid.

51. Ibid.

52. Ibid.

53. Ibid.

54. Ibid.

55. Ibid.

56. 810 F.2d 1105, *José David Luna, Appellant, v. The United States, Appellee*, Appeal No. 86-1275, United States Court of Appeals, Federal Circuit, January 14, 1987.

57. Ibid.

58. Ibid.

59. Hector M. Acosta, interview by author, San Antonio, TX, February 6, 2010.

60. Ibid.

61. Ibid.

62. Gloria Bigger, "POW Speaks of Experiences: Pilot Held in Captivity Longest," *Kingsville-Bishop Record News*, November 14, 2012, 1C.

63. Everett Álvarez Jr., interview by author, Silver Spring, MD, December 3, 2009.

64. Ibid.

65. Ibid.

66. Gloria Bigger, "POW Speaks of Experiences," 1C.

67. Ibid.

68. Everett Álvarez Jr., interview by author, Silver Spring, MD, December 3, 2009.

69. Ibid.

70. Ibid.

71. Ibid. Joe Kapp quarterbacked the Minnesota Vikings to Super Bowl IV, and in 1970, *Sports Illustrated* named him "the toughest Chicano" and placed his picture on the cover.

72. Ibid.

73. Nash and Baker, "Competing and Complementary Models of Combat Stress Injury," 38; and Joseph A. Boscarino, "The Morality Impact of Combat Stress 30 Years after Exposure: Implications for Prevention, Treatment, and Research," in *Combat Stress Injury: Theory, Research, and Management*, ed. Charles R. Figley and William P. Nash (New York: Routledge, 2007), 68.

Conclusion

1. "AP: POW Benefit Claimants Exceed Recorded POWs," *The Monitor* (McAllen, TX), April 12, 2009.

2. B. G. Burkett and Glenna Whitley, *Stolen Valor: How the Vietnam Generation Was Robbed of Its Heroes and Its History* (Dallas: Verity Press, 1998), 494.

3. Juan L. Jacquez, interview by author, Santa Fe, NM, February 12, 2010.

4. Ibid.

5. Erika L. Sánchez, "U.S. Military, A Growing Latino Army," *NBC Latino*, January 1, 2013. http://nbclatino.com/2013/01/01/u-s-military-a-growing-latino-army/.

6. Elizabeth Findell, "Valley Native Killed in Afghanistan," *The Monitor* (McAllen, TX), September 7, 2012, 1A and 7A.

7. José Jesús Anzaldúa Jr., interview by author, Coats, NC, June 2, 2009.

8. Ibid.

9. Juan L. Jacquez, interview by author, Santa Fe, NM, February 12, 2010.

10. Ibid.

11. José Jesús Anzaldúa Jr., interview by author, Coats, NC, June 2, 2009.

Bibliography

Primary Sources

Archival Material/Government Documents

Defense Prisoner of War/Missing in Action (DPMO) file on Hector M. Acosta, Department of Defense, Pentagon, Washington, DC. "Circumstances of Loss Report" dated March 8, 1976. (Previously Classified Confidential).

Defense Prisoner of War/Missing in Action (DPMO) file on José Jesús Anzaldúa Jr., Department of Defense, Pentagon, Washington, DC. "Counterintelligence Investigation Report" dated February 27, 1970. (Previously Classified Confidential).

Defense Prisoner of War/Missing in Action (DPMO) file on José Manuel Astorga, Department of Defense, Pentagon, Washington, DC. "Defense Information Report Evaluation" dated June 6, 1972. (Previously Classified Confidential).

Defense Prisoner of War/Missing in Action (DPMO) file on Abel Kavanaugh, Department of Defense, Pentagon, Washington, DC. "Investigation Report" dated May 17, 1968. (Previously Classified Confidential).

Defense Prisoner of War/Missing in Action (DPMO) file on José David Luna, Department of Defense, Pentagon, Washington, DC. "Defense Information Report Evaluation" dated May 5, 1975. (Previously Classified Confidential).

Defense Prisoner of War/Missing in Action (DPMO) file on Alfonzo Riate, Department of Defense, Pentagon, Washington, DC. "Investigation Report" dated June 10, 1967. (Previously Classified Secret).

Department of Defense. "Counterintelligence Reports." Washington DC: Pentagon Files.

José David Luna, Appellant, v. The United States, Appellee, 810 F.2d 1105, Appeal No. 86-1275, United States Court of Appeals, Federal Circuit, January 14, 1987.

Nixon Presidential Library and Museum. "White House Salute to POW's." White House Communication Agency, File WHCA VTR #6299, Tape 1, May 24, 1973.

Operations Report–Lessons Learned, Report 4-66. "The Evasion and Escape of Sgt Camacho in Vietnam." Department of the Army, Office of the Adjunct General, Washington, DC, December 30, 1965. (Previously Classified Confidential).

"Rescue of Bat 21," USAF National Museum, Dayton, OH, March 25, 2011.

Interviews

Acosta, Hector. Interview by author. San Antonio, TX, February 6, 2010.

Álvarez, Everett, Jr. Interview by author. Silver Spring, MD, December 3, 2009.

Anzaldúa, José Jesús, Jr. Interview by author. Coats, NC, June 2, 2009.

Astorga, José Manuel. Interview by author. El Cajon, CA, May 9, 2009.

Camacho, Isaac. Conversation with author. San Antonio, TX, March 4, 2010.

Cuéllar, Albert. Interview by author. Refugio, TX, December 21, 2012.

Jacquez, Juan L. Interview by author. Santa Fe, NM, February 12, 2010.

Kavanaugh, Larry, Jr. Interviews by author via telephone. October 27, 2010, and July 23, 2013.

Luna, José David. Conversation with author via telephone. April 6, 2009.

Williams, Anthony. Interview by author. Dallas, TX, February 17, 2011.

Recorded Material

Above and Beyond. Directed by Dale Sonnenberg. Santa Fe, NM: KNME, 1984. Interview with Juan Jacquez.

Chicano Veterans. Video. Los Angeles: KABC-TV, 1972. Stanford University, Meyer Media Center, ZVC 6126 pt. 4.

Chicano! History of the Mexican American Civil Rights Movement, vol. 1, *Quest for a Homeland.* Directed by Hector Galán. Video. Los Angeles: National Latino

Communications Center: Media, 1996.

Downs, Bill, Howard K. Smith, and Frank Tomlinson. "Washington, DC Celebration" (includes an interview with Alfonso Riate), ABC News, July 4, 1974. Vanderbilt Television News Archive, Vanderbilt University, Nashville, TN.

Héroes Hispanos. Directed by Robert Seoane. Video. New York: History Channel, 1993.

Hispanic Vietnam Veterans, the Mi Carrera (My Career) Program; Rosemary Católicos. San Antonio, TX: KLRN, 1990, c1989. Stanford University, Meyer Media Center, ZVC 3392 no. 213.

Justice for My People: The Dr. Hector P. Garcia Story. Directed by Jeff Felts. Video. Corpus Christi, TX: KEDT-TV, Public Television, 2004.

Pham Tuyen. "Play Your Guitars American Friends!" Recorded by Alfonzo Ray Riate and translated by Hai Nguyen, January 1, 1975, Lubbock, TX.

Reflecciónes: Chicano POW's. Video. Los Angeles: KABC-TV, 1972. Stanford University, Meyer Media Center, ZVC 6126 pt. 3.

Return with Honor. Directed by Freida Lee Mock and Terry Sanders. Washington, DC: PBS, 2001.

Ruben Salazar: Man in the Middle. Directed by Phillip Rodriguez. Video. Arlington, VA: PBS, 2014.

Soldados: Chicanos in Viet Nam. Directed by Charley Trujillo and Sonya Rhee. Video. San Jose: Chusma House Publications, 2003.

Vietnam P.O.W.s: Stories of Survival. Directed by Brian Leonard. Video. Washington, DC: Discovery Channel, 1998.

Woodstock: 3 Days of Peace and Music, the Director's Cut! Directed by Michael Wadleigh. Burbank, CA: Warner Bros. Pictures, 1994.

Secondary Sources

Aarons, Leroy F. "For Álvarez It Will Be a Different World; Former POW Must Ask: Where Do I Pick Up?" *Pacific Stars & Stripes,* March 14, 1973, 11.

Acuña, Rodolfo. *Occupied America: The Chicano's Struggle toward Liberation.* San Francisco: Canfield Press, 1972.

———. *Occupied America: A History of Chicanos.* 4th ed. New York: Longman, 2000.

Aguirre, Frederick, Linda Martinez, and Rogelio Rodriguez. *Undaunted Courage: Mexican American Patriots of World War II.* Orange, CA: Latino Advocates for Education Inc., 2005.

Allen, Michael J. *Until the Last Man Comes Home: POWs, MIAs, and the Unending*

Vietnam War. Chapel Hill: University of North Carolina Press, 2009.

Álvarez, Everett, Jr., and Anthony S. Pitch. *Chained Eagle: The Heroic Story of the First American Shot Down over North Vietnam.* Washington, DC: Potomac Books, 1989.

Álvarez, Everett, Jr., and Samuel Schreiner Jr. *Code of Conduct: An Inspirational Story of Self-Healing by the Famed Ex-POW and War Hero.* New York: Donald I. Fine, Inc., 1991.

Anton, Frank. *Why Didn't You Get Me Out? A POW's Nightmare in Vietnam.* New York: St. Martin's Paperbacks, 1997.

Appy, Christian. *Working-Class War: American Combat Soldiers and Vietnam.* Chapel Hill: University of North Carolina Press, 1993.

Bederman, Gail. *Manliness and Civilization: A Cultural History of Gender and Race in the United States, 1880–1917.* Chicago: University of Chicago Press, 1995.

Benavidez, Roy, with John R. Craig. *Medal of Honor: One Man's Journey from Poverty and Prejudice.* Washington, DC: Potomac Books, 1995.

Bigger, Gloria. "POW Speaks of Experiences: Pilot Held in Captivity Longest." *Kingsville-Bishop Record News,* November 14, 2012, 1C.

Boscarino, Joseph A. "The Morality Impact of Combat Stress 30 Years after Exposure: Implications for Prevention, Treatment, and Research." In *Combat Stress Injury: Theory, Research, and Management,* edited by Charles R. Figley and William P. Nash. New York: Routledge, 2007.

Brazil, Eric. "The Eagle Unchained: POW Finally Tells His Story of Survival." *San Francisco Examiner,* January 2, 1990, 1C and 4C.

Burkett, B. G., and Glenna Whitley. *Stolen Valor: How the Vietnam Generation Was Robbed of Its Heroes and Its History.* Dallas: Verity Press, 1998.

Camarillo, Albert. *Chicanos in a Changing Society.* Cambridge, MA: Harvard University Press, 1979.

Campos, Stephen Paul. *Charlie Doesn't Live Here Anymore.* Concord, NC: Comfort Publishing, 2009.

Cantú, Norma E. "*Muy Macho*: Traditional Practices in the Formation of Latino Masculinity in South Texas Border Culture." In *Manly Traditions: The Folk Roots of American Masculinities,* edited by Simon J. Bronner and Alan Dundes, 116–33. Bloomington: Indiana University Press, 2005.

Chávez, Ernesto. "¡*Mi Raza Primero!*": Nationalism, Identity, and Insurgency in the Chicano Movement in Los Angeles, 1966–1978.* Los Angeles: University of California Press, 2002.

De León, Arnoldo. *Mexican Americans in Texas: A Brief History.* Wheeling, IL: Harlan Davidson, 1993.

Denison, Ray. *American Son: The Odyssey of John Espinoza; From the Texas Cotton Fields to Vietnam and the Michigan Legislature.* Port Sanilac, MI: Denison Arts, 2006.

Domínguez, Gil. *They Answered the Call: Latinos in the Vietnam War.* Baltimore, MD: Publish America, 2004.

Drury, Bob, and Tom Clavin. *Last Men Out: The True Story of America's Heroic Final Hours in Vietnam.* New York: Free Press, 2011.

Dyer, Jessica. "An Emotional Journey: Ex-POW in Washington for Visit to Vietnam Memorial." *Journal Santa Fé,* November 1, 2009.

Findell, Elizabeth. "Valley Native Killed in Afghanistan." *The Monitor* (McAllen, TX), September 7, 2012, 1A and 7A.

Flores, John W. *When the River Dreams: The Life of Marine Sgt. Freddy Gonzalez.* Bloomington, IN: Author House, 2006.

Galán, Héctor. *Chicano! The History of the Mexican American Civil Rights Movement: Quest for a Homeland.* Los Angeles: NLCC Educational Media, 1996.

García, Manny. *An Accidental Soldier: Memoirs of a Mestizo in Vietnam.* Albuquerque: University of New Mexico Press, 2003.

García, Mario T. *Mexican American: Leadership, Ideology, and Identity, 1930–1960.* New Haven, CT: Yale University Press, 1989.

Gartner, Scott Sigmund, and Gary M. Segura. "Race, Casualties, and Opinion in the Vietnam War." *Journal of Politics* 62, no. 1 (2000): 115-46.

Goff, Stanley, and Robert Sanders. *Brothers: Black Soldiers in the Nam.* New York: Presidio Press, 1982.

González, Ray. *Muy Macho: Latino Men Confront Their Manhood.* New York: Anchor Books, 1996.

Gould, Lewis L. *1968: The Election That Changed America.* Chicago: Ivan R. Dee, 2010.

Grant, Zalin. *Survivors: American POWs in Vietnam.* New York: Berkley Books, 1975.

Gutiérrez, Ramón A. *When Jesus Came, the Corn Mothers Went Away: Marriage, Sexuality, and Power in New Mexico, 1500–1846.* Stanford, CA: Stanford University Press, 1991.

Guzmán, Ralph. "Why Our High Death Rate." *El Chicano,* November 10, 1969.

Halberstam, David. *The Best and the Brightest.* New York: Random House, 1969.

Herr, Michael. *Dispatches.* New York: Vintage International, 1977.

Herring, George C. *America's Longest War: The United States and Vietnam, 1950–1975*. New York: Wiley, 1979.

Ho Chi Minh. "The Declaration of Independence of the Democratic Republic of Vietnam." *Ho Chi Minh: Selected Works*. 3 vols. Hanoi: Foreign Languages Publishing House, 1960-1962.

Howes, Craig. *Voices of the Vietnam POWs: Witnesses to Their Fight*. Oxford: Oxford University Press, 1993.

Hubbell, John G. *P.O.W.: A Definitive History of the American Prisoner-of-War Experience in Vietnam, 1964–1973*. New York: Reader's Digest Press, 1976.

Hunter, Edna J. "The Vietnam POW Veteran: Immediate and Long-Term Effects of Captivity." In *Stress Disorder among Vietnam Veterans: Theory, Research, and Treatment*, edited by Charles R. Figley, 188-206. New York: Brunner/Mazel Publishers, 1978.

Killen, Andreas. *1973 Nervous Breakdown: Watergate, Warhol, and the Birth of Post-Sixties America*. New York: Bloomsbury, 2006.

Kindsvatter, Peter S. *American Soldiers: Ground Combat in the World Wars, Korea, and Vietnam*. Lawrence: University Press of Kansas, 2003.

Mariscal, George. *Aztlán and Vietnam*. Los Angeles: University of California Press, 1999.

Marroquín, Sol. *Part of the Team: Story of an American Hero*. Mission, TX: Rio Grande Publishers, 1979.

Mattingly Kelliher, Kim. "Memorial Day Is Special for Mother, Her Family: Mom of 10 Who Joined Military Is Honored." *Arizona Daily Star*, May 28, 1991, 2B.

Milam, Ron. *Not a Gentleman's War: An Inside View of Junior Officers in the Vietnam War*. Chapel Hill: University of North Carolina Press, 2009.

Montejano, David. *Anglos and Mexicans in the Making of Texas, 1836–1986*. Austin: University of Texas Press, 1987.

Moore, Brenda L. *Serving Our Country: Japanese American Women in the Military during World War II*. New Brunswick, NJ: Rutgers University Press, 2003.

Morín, Eddie. "First to Escape." *Vietnam*, June 2000, 30-36.

——. *Valor and Discord: Mexican Americans and the Vietnam War*. Los Angeles: Valiant Press, 2006.

Nash, William P., and Dewleen G. Baker. "Competing and Complementary Models of Combat Stress Injury." In *Combat Stress Injury: Theory, Research, and Management*, edited by Charles R. Figley and William P. Nash, 103-56. New York:

Routledge, 2007.

Ordóñez, Robert L. *When I Was a Boy: One Year in Vietnam.* Lubbock, TX: CIMA Publishing Co., 1997.

Oropeza, Lorena. ¡*Raza Sí! ¡Guerra No!: Chicano Protest and Patriotism during the Viet Nam War Era.* Los Angeles: University of California Press, 2005.

Paredes, Américo. "The Problem of Identity in a Changing Culture: Popular Expressions of Culture Conflict along the Lower Río Grande Border." In *Folklore and Culture on the Texas-Mexican Border,* edited by Américo Paredes and Richard Bauman, 19–48. Austin, TX: CMAS Books, 1993.

———. "The United States, Mexico, and *Machismo.*" *Journal of the Folklore Institute* (June 1971): 17–37.

———. *With His Pistol in His Hand.* Austin: University of Texas Press, 1958.

Paz, Octavio. *The Labyrinth of Solitude.* New York: Grove Books, 1985.

Phelps, Grady. "Pena, Troupe Back from 17-Day Tour of Vietnam Bases." *Corpus Christi Caller,* January 20, 1968.

Prados, John. *Vietnam: The History of an Unwinnable War, 1945–1975.* Lawrence: University Press of Kansas, 2009.

Pycior, Julie Leininger. *LBJ and Mexican Americans: The Paradox of Power.* Austin: University of Texas Press, 1997.

Ramírez, Juan. *A Patriot After All: The Story of a Chicano Vietnam Vet.* Albuquerque: University of New Mexico Press, 1999.

Ramos, Samuel. *Profile of Man and Culture in Mexico.* New York: McGraw-Hill, 1962.

Rochester, Stuart I., and Frederick Kiley. *Honor Bound: American Prisoners of War in Southeast Asia, 1961–1973.* Annapolis, MD: Naval Institute Press, 1998.

Rodríguez, Joe. *Oddsplayer.* Houston: Arte Público Press, 1989.

Rotundo, E. Anthony. *American Manhood: Transformations in Masculinity from the Revolution to the Modern Era.* New York: Basic Books, 1993.

Ruiz, Raúl. "The POW." *La Raza: News & Political Thought of the Chicano Struggle,* April 1972, 30–31.

Sánchez, George J. *Becoming Mexican American: Ethnicity, Culture and Identity in Chicano Los Angeles, 1900–1945.* Oxford: Oxford University Press, 1993.

Saragoza, Alex M. "Recent Chicano Historiography: An Interpretive Essay." *Aztlán* 19 (Spring 1988–90): 1–77.

Scott, Wilbur J. *Vietnam Veterans since the War: The Politics of PTSD, Agent Orange, and the National Memorial.* Norman: University of Oklahoma Press, 2003.

Sheehan, Neil. *A Bright Shining Lie: John Paul Vann and America in Vietnam.* New York: Random House, 1988.

Smith, George. *P.O.W.: Two Years with the Vietcong.* Berkeley, CA: Ramparts Press, 1971.

Takaki, Ronald. *Double Victory: A Multicultural History of America in World War II.* New York: Little, Brown & Co., 2000.

Terry, Wallace. *Bloods: Black Veterans of the Vietnam War; An Oral History.* New York: Ballantine Books, 1985.

Trujillo, Charley. *Dogs from Illusion.* San José, CA: Chusma House Publications, 1994.

———, ed. *Soldados: Chicanos in Viet Nam.* San José, CA: Chusma House Publications, 1990.

Waugh, Billy. *Isaac Camacho: An American Hero.* Tampa: Digital Publishing of Florida, 2010.

Weiss, Suzanne. "Sergeant's Widow Blames Pentagon for His Death." *Rocky Mountain News,* June 29, 1973, 5.

Whitcomb, Darrel D. *The Rescue of Bat 21.* New York: Dell Publishing, 1998.

Wilson, Tom. "Day of the SAM." *Retired Officer* magazine, December 1993, 34.

Ybarra, Lea. *Vietnam Veteranos: Chicanos Recall the War.* Austin: University of Texas Press, 2004.

Zaretsky, Natasha. *No Direction Home: The American Family and the Fear of National Decline, 1968-1980.* Chapel Hill: University of North Carolina Press, 2006.

Index